Nomads and Crusaders
A.D.
1000–1368

Nomads and Crusaders
—————— A.D. ——————
1000–1368

Archibald R. Lewis

INDIANA
UNIVERSITY
PRESS
Bloomington and Indianapolis

Library of Congress Cataloging-in-Publication Data

Lewis, Archibald Ross, 1914–
Nomads and Crusaders, A.D. 1000–1368.
Bibliography: p.
Includes index.
1. Civilization, Medieval.   2. Comparative
civilization.   3. Europe—Territorial expansion.
4. Middle Ages—History.   I. Title.
CB353.L48   1988   940.1   87-45588

ISBN 0-253-34787-4

Contents

MAPS

INTRODUCTION

Today in the late twentieth century we live in an age in which the dominant civilization has, for some time, been that of Western Europe. We are all familiar with the broad outlines of how this came about since the time of Columbus and Vasco da Gama, as Western European explorers, mariners, merchants, colonists, and conquerors spread their dominion and their ideas everywhere and in the process overwhelmed all other peoples and civilizations. Talented historians as diverse in their points of view as Arnold Toynbee and William McNeill have told this story eloquently indeed, just as a number of others, like Robert Lopez, concerned with Western Europe proper, have explained how the latter in medieval times came to develop those special features which made its later success possible.

Despite all this we are still faced with the basic problem as to why Western Europe was able to develop in such a way that her civilization could prevail, in modern times, over others which earlier had seemed to be just as vigorous and just as promising. To explain this, it is not enough to concentrate one's attention upon Western Europe and the wider world of the fifteenth and sixteenth centuries only or even to delve deeply into the earlier medieval bases of the accomplishments of Latin Christendom. One must instead try to grasp why those other great civilizations of medieval times—the Byzantine-Russian, the Islamic, the Indic, and the East Asian—failed to match the medieval performance of Western Europe, for their failures obviously explain in part the successes of the latter.

Fortunately for those who would engage in such an enterprise, recent scholarship has made available to us a store of new information and insight which is concerned with Byzantium and Russia, the Islamic world, East Asia, and even India and Southeast Asia. Thanks to this we now have a clearer view of these civilizations during their medieval phase. This makes it possible for us to pursue a comparative history of them which promises us a better understanding than ever before, for our comparisons can be much more meaningful.

The pages which follow are dedicated to just such an enterprise as the author strives to compare Western European society in the broadest sense with sister civilizations of the Old World during the High Middle Ages from the year 1000 to 1368 in the belief that such comparisons will tell us something of value and help to explain both the success of the former and the failure of the latter in subsequent centuries. In doing so, the careful reader will note that the author has placed a heavy emphasis upon geographical, demographic, economic, technological, military, naval, and maritime factors, although political, religious, and cultural elements have by no means been entirely overlooked. He has done so in the belief that the former factors were the decisive ones in the story he is telling.

The reader will also soon be aware of the fact that when the author is dealing with Western Europe in particular during these centuries a very conscious attempt has been made to consider the positive accomplishments which every area of Western Europe has made to its development in medieval times. Thus one will find stressed here the role played by the Catalans and Provençals in the Mediterranean, which supplemented that of the better-known Italians, and of the Portuguese, the Castilians, the British, the Scandinavians, the Netherlanders, the French, the Germans, and the Slavs of northern and Atlantic Europe as well. Only when the accomplishments of all the peoples of medieval Western Europe are included can a true picture of its development emerge.

Finally, the author hopes that he has been able to write in a way which reflects little or no racial or cultural bias. He is well aware that even today the dominance of Western Europe throughout the world is by no means total and that the other great civilizations of medieval times still exist under the veneer of a modern Western European culture they have only partly accepted. Indeed, it seems quite possible to this observer that the next century may well emphasize the power and leadership of East Asia rather than that of Europe and the Americas, for the Japanese, Koreans, and Chinese all show signs that they are building cultures which may be better suited than our own to cope with a variety of modern problems. The historian is neither a prophet nor a seer, but if his craft teaches him anything it is that there can be no assurance that the Western European civilization which now seems so dominant in the world is more than a temporary phenomenon. Civilizations are and have been many, but man is one, so it may well be that our worldwide Western civilization at this very moment is in the process of giving place to another or others which are better adapted to the future needs of mankind.

Even if this proves to be the case, however, there is still a value to be found in explaining how, during the late Middle Ages, Western Europeans laid the bases for worldwide dominance in modern times, while at the same time those living in other civilizations failed to achieve as much. It is to this end that this volume is dedicated in the knowledge that it can only open up this subject to the talented historians who in the future will no doubt develop it more adequately.

Finally, since a project as ambitious as this has taken years of research and travel in all the areas of the Old World mentioned in these pages, the author must thank those who have aided him in special ways. Most important are those institutions at which he has taught—the University of South Carolina, the University of Texas at Austin, and the University of Massachusetts—

along with the American Council of Learned Societies, the Ford Foundation, and the United States government through Fulbright grants for study in both Belgium and Egypt, all of which have generously supported his researches. Second, he is indebted to a score of libraries and museums overseas as well as the University of Arizona Library, the Widener Library of Harvard University, the University of Massachusetts Library, Princeton University Library, the University of Texas Library, and the Libraries of Mystic Seaport and the Peabody Museum of Salem for use of their important collections.

Last of all he must thank those who have read these pages and made valuable suggestions. They are his colleagues at the University of Massachusetts, Frederick Drake and George Kirk; William McNeill of the University of Chicago; Richard Sullivan of Michigan State University; and Lynn White, Jr., of the University of California, Los Angeles. The errors found here are his own, but without their help they would be much more numerous. He also wishes to thank Doris Holden of Amherst and Nikki Matz of Tucson for their help in final drafts and his wife Elizabeth Lewis for long years of patience and understanding while he labored.

For Del and Allyson
who would have approved of this volume

The Matrix of Old World
Civilizations

East Asia and Greater India

EAST ASIA

In the year 1000 five great civilizations existed in the world of Africa and Eurasia: the East Asian, the Indic, the Islamic, the Byzantine-Russian, and the Western European. The first four of these had been considered the important ones by the Arab merchant and writer Suleiman more than a century earlier. By the year 1000 each had had a long history of development which gave them a distinct and different character.

East Asia consisted of a Chinese heartland which in 980 had just been reunited by a new dynasty called the Sung. Around this were clustered a number of smaller independent states which shared China's general culture. They were Annam in northern Vietnam, the Thai principality of Nan-Chao in what is now the Chinese province of Yunnan, the realm of Hsi Hsia centered in Kansu controlled by nomadic Tanguts, the Kitan kingdom of Liao which included most of Inner Mongolia and Manchuria and some of North China south of the Great Wall, the new united Korean kingdom of Koryō, and a Heian empire which controlled the Japanese islands. Three other regions might conceivably also be considered as part of this East Asian civilized complex but for various reasons, as will be noted, have been excluded from it. They are Tibet, Mongolia proper, and eastern Turkestan, which, although they tended to be much affected by various facets of East Asian civilization, had cultures which were sufficiently different from those mentioned earlier that their relationship to them was essentially ambiguous.

Geography was a major factor which shaped this East Asian civilization. It was cut off from the rest of the advanced civilized world by a number of great mountain ranges to its west, as well as by a series of high desiccated plateaus and deserts which dominated the terrain of Mongolia and Turkestan. These formed barriers between it and the Indic and Islamic worlds to the west and south. While it was possible to reach Burma over difficult mountain passes leading there from the upper Yangtze valley, the most practicable routes to the west were by way of Kansu, Inner Mongolia, and eastern Turkestan and then on to Khorasan and southern Russia. These were the famous silk roads which for centuries had served as the gateways to the East Asian world. In addition to such land connections, however, there also existed another route to the civilized worlds of Eurasia—by sea along the coasts of Annam and Champa, around or across the Malay Peninsula, to the Indian Ocean. By the year 1000, as we will note, this route had become as important as the older land routes to the north and west of it.

This relative isolation of the East Asian world had a climatic basis as well. Despite the tropical or subtropical weather which prevailed in Annam and parts of southern China and Formosa, on the whole the peoples of East Asia enjoyed a temperate climate, although it varied from the extremes found in Inner Mongolia, Manchuria, northern Korea, and Hokkaido to the more moderate weather which prevailed elsewhere. On the other hand, its rainfall pattern varied considerably. Most of East Asia enjoyed an abundant rainfall, but from the Yellow River on north the annual precipitation thinned out so that the land gradually changed, first to a steppe and then to a desert. In this geographical belt, by using irrigation, the Chinese had settled as a farming population right up to the Great Wall. Beyond this barrier, in Inner Mongolia, Jehol, and Manchuria, tillage was little practiced and a non-Chinese nomadic population of herdsmen and hunters prevailed. Furthermore, a combination of severe winters and limited rainfall toward the northeast played an important role in determining the food crops which could be grown. In Annam and all of China south of the Huai River, and in Japan and Korea as well, rice was the main food crop. North of the Huai up to the Great Wall the agricultural population had to rely upon wheat and millet. Thus we can divide East Asia into three zones—one of rice, one of wheat and millet, and one featuring both a pastoral and a forest, hunting economy. The decisive line, however, was along the Great Wall in China and the Yalu River in Korea, which separated the settled farming folk of East Asia from the nomadic or forest tribal societies which lay beyond.

The isolation of East Asia from the rest of the civilized world, alluded to above, was, however, not of serious consequence to its development because its Chinese heartland in particular possessed ample resources of all sorts necessary to sustain the high culture of its people. Its industrious peasantry produced abundant crops in great river valleys and coastal plains from both irrigated and nonirrigated fields, while rivers, lakes, and coastal waters teamed with edible fish and seafood. If its farmers raised few horses, cattle, sheep, and goats, preferring to leave this form of husbandry to their nomadic neighbors, they did produce large numbers of pigs which provided them with a needed protein element in their diet. And at this time China and East Asia in general still had ample forest resources, except in the northeast toward Mongolia, to meet the needs of its population as well as every necessary mineral except perhaps silver. Equally important is the fact that this civilization was blessed, as the other great civilizations of the time were not, with a remarkable system of internal communication via river, lake, canal, coastal, and oceanic waterways which made it possible to move its agricultural surpluses and natural commodities cheaply and easily to points where they were needed. This self-sufficiency and ease of internal communication had continued over a period of centuries and is one of the special features which distinguished East Asia from its neighbors and which, as we will note, was responsible for a number of the peculiarities found in its governments, its economy, and its culture.

A further basis of East Asian civilization was essentially cultural. By the end of the first millennium the Annamese, the Thais of Nan-Chao, the Tanguts of Hsi Hsia, the Kitans of Liao, the Koreans, and the Japanese all shared a common culture with the Chinese of the Sung empire. For instance, despite significant differences in their spoken tongues, they all used written scripts based upon Chinese characters. They also shared a set of Mahayana Buddhist, Taoist, and Confucian ideals which helped to mold their political ideas and institutions. And they all had patterned their governmental systems in various ways after that which had prevailed earlier in Tang China. This was true even though most of these smaller states, such as Annam, Hsi Hsia, Liao, and Japan, no longer recognized the Chinese emperor, or Son of Heaven, as a superior ruler to whom they had to pay tribute as a sign of inferiority. In short, all these peoples and kingdoms lay within the general framework of a common East Asian civilization, which was essentially Chinese in character.

The partial exceptions to this rule—the Tibetans of Tibet proper and the inhabitants of Outer Mongolia and eastern Turkestan—deserve some attention. As early as the seventh century, the Tibetans had managed to organize a state which was influenced both culturally and politically by the nearby Tang empire of China. But it had two special peculiarities. The Buddhism which it practiced had developed special localized tantric and lamaistic elements which made it essentially different from anything found elsewhere in East Asia. And, second, its writing was based upon an Indian sanskrit alphabetized system which was equally unique. So even though the Tibetan Tangut kingdom of Hsi Hsia must be considered essentially Chinese or East Asian in its culture, the same cannot be said about Tibet proper.

It is equally important for us to note the differences which prevailed in eastern Turkestan, Outer Mongolia, and parts of Manchuria. These regions had been periodically subject to strong Chinese–East Asian influences, es-

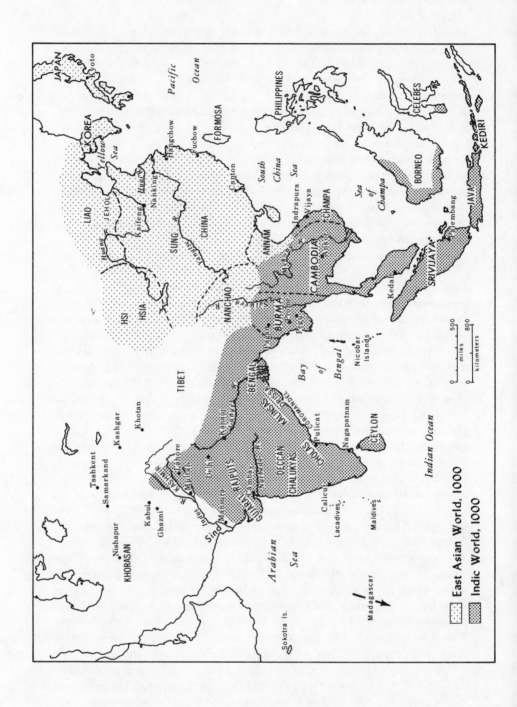

East Asian World, 1000

Indic World, 1000

pecially in early Tang times when the Chinese had allied themselves with the nomadic Uighurs of the region and conquered Turkestan, and dominated as well the Mongolian steppes. But this had not really made either the nomadic tribesmen of the area or the settled population of the oases Chinese in culture. For instance, in the oases during the late tenth century, Manichaeanism and Nestorianism from western Asia and forms of Buddhism which had died out in China still flourished. So did a new Islamic faith which had been introduced from the west and had spread until it had become the dominant religion of the nomadic Karakhanid Turkish confederacy of Turkestan. Among the Turkish and Mongol tribesmen to the east and in Manchuria as well, the prevailing religious ideas of the period were either Nestorian Christian or primitive, animistic ones which were interpreted by a native group of shamans. Thus one does not find in any of this region that particular blend of neo-Confucianism and Buddhism which prevailed in Sung China and many neighboring states.

Not only was religion different in this part of Asia but so was writing. The written script of Mongolia, Turkestan, and parts of Manchuria was totally unlike that of the rest of East Asia. It was an alphabetized one which had been originally derived from an early Syriac system of writing. It and much of the art, architecture, and culture found in the oases cities or among the tribesmen of these central Asian steppes seem closer to that of an Asia which was now under Islamic control than that which paid tribute to Chinese civilization. We can sum up our conclusions then as follows: eastern Turkestan, Outer Mongolia, and much of Manchuria formed a peculiar region in which a special central Asian culture which had survived from earlier times and a new Islamic element mingled with facets of East Asian civilization to form a blend which belonged to neither world or, in another sense, to both of them at the same time. And since this was just the region in which a Mongol empire was later to arise and then spread out to the east and west, this fact is of real importance to the historian.

Turning to the matter of demography during this period, the historian runs into serious problems despite the availability of relatively good Chinese records concerning population. Probably the best estimate that can be made of the number of people who lived in the Sung empire is about 74,000,000, or roughly the same as that found in later Tang times just before the Sungs took over China. Authorities have estimated that at this time the Liao realm had a population of about 4,000,000 of whom 2,500,000 were Chinese and the rest nomadic Kitan tribesmen or non-Chinese dominated by their Kitan rulers. Annam's population and that of Nan-Chao and Hsi Hsia could not have been very large and the same is true of tenth-century Korea and Japan. So it would not be unreasonable to estimate the entire population of East Asia during this period as being in the neighborhood of 85,000,000 or at most 90,000,000, of which almost four-fifths lived in Sung China. As for the nearby area of Tibet, eastern Turkestan, Mongolia, and Manchuria, estimates of its population vary, but it probably did not exceed 10,000,000 even if one includes in this number the non-Chinese peoples of Hsi Hsia and Liao. Probably 5,000,000 would be closer to the truth. Thus the ratio of the nomadic or nonsettled population to the settled ones in East Asia and its borderlands was probably about one to eight in the year 1000, and its overall population distribution was relatively dense compared with that found in other parts of the civilized world.

The Sung realm, which formed the geographical, economic, demographic, and cultural heartland of East Asian civilization in the year 1000, was already quite different from the China of late Tang times two hundred years earlier, for a number of changes had taken place there since the late eighth century which had altered its culture and its government. First of all, there had been a gradual shift of China's center of gravity toward the south and southeast, since now it was in the Yangtze valley and along the southern coasts that considerable economic expansion was taking place. Here in this rice-growing area agriculture had become increasingly productive, population was expanding rapidly, and both internal and external commerce had become more active than ever before. As this happened new mints were established in this part of China, and its urban centers attracted large numbers of merchants and settlers who swelled its population. This urban and commercial revolution demanded a larger money supply, so we now find an increased supply of copper coins (called *cash*) minted by the government. This money supply began to be supplemented from the ninth century on by the widespread use of credit by both private merchants and the government itself.

Such important changes in agriculture, commerce, and finance could not take place without affecting China's government itself and its ruling classes as well. First, by late Tang times these changes helped bring about the destruction of the older military aristocracy which had long ruled the Chinese and replaced it under the Sungs with a new gentry. This gentry formed a class of men who, although they often lived in the countryside on their estates, were closely tied to the money economy which prevailed in the towns and cities and were now recruited for office by a well-organized examination system. As a new gentry class or group of officials, they looked to the Chinese past and were inspired by a set of neo-Confucian ideals which dominated the Chinese intellectual scene and which caused them to run the centralized Sung empire in a different way than earlier regimes like the Tangs had done.

One change brought about by this new civilian bureaucratic, neo-Confucian government was in its capital. It now came to be located at Kaifeng, a growing industrial center at the head of the Grand Canal which linked the Yellow River system with the Yangtze. This capital had the advantage from the start of being closer to the new centers of Chinese civilization than the earlier capitals to the northeast. At the same time we find that the traditional corvées levied upon the peasant population, which forced them to supply foodstuffs to the capital, were abolished as taxation of the peasantry became more rational. Government itself could now become more thoroughly centralized than before and both its domestic commerce and its foreign trade much better organized.

If the Sung empire was better organized, richer, and more businesslike than its predecessors, it soon became apparent that it had a serious weakness from a military point of view. It allowed the older militia system, which relied on peasant levies to defend the empire, to disappear and its place to be taken by armies that were mercenary in character and which were recruited either from lower elements in Chinese society itself or from warlike foreigners. Armies so recruited could not hope to be very successful in battle, since they were not defending their own homes—which explains the Sungs' inability to reassert the same Chinese dominion over Annam and Nan-Chao which their predecessors had. It accounts, too, for the serious difficulties they had from the start in defending themselves against the Kitans of Liao or the Tanguts of Hsi Hsia to the north. Indeed, not only were they forced by 1004 to abandon all attempts to recover from the Kitans the sixteen Chinese-inhabited prefectures south of the Great Wall which were part of the latter's empire, but a little later in 1044 were forced to pay large subsidies in silk and silver to Hsi Hsia to preserve their borders with them. Part of their difficulties in this regard seem to have resulted from a lack of trained cavalry forces which could maneuver effectively in the northern Chinese plains against nomadic Tangut and Kitan contingents who specialized in mounted warfare. This was so even though the Sungs imported large numbers of horses for cavalry use, fortified their cities, and made use of both mines and rockets armed with gunpowder to defend themselves against their aggressive northern opponents. In the year 1000, despite their superior organization of a highly civilized, centralized, and prosperous empire, they were on the defensive along their northern borders and were destined to remain so.

Each of the other states which clustered around China at this time had a somewhat different character from the empire of the Sungs. We know least about Annam and Nan-Chao. Annam, whose inhabitants were Viets related to the southern Chinese, had thrown off the Chinese yoke in 939 to become independent and remained stubbornly outside the Sung orbit. By the year 1000 its people, who enjoyed an essentially Chinese culture that stressed Confucian, Taoist, and Mahayana Buddhist elements, were ruled by a native Dinh dynasty. Annam's administration system was modeled upon that of China, and its people were already advancing south at the expense of their Champa Indic neighbors and displaying a military prowess that made them formidable opponents. Thai Nan-Chao was also essentially Chinese in its culture and governmental system and, like Annam, had organized itself into a warrior state. Its inhabitants were also beginning to move south toward Burma, Laos, and Cambodia, which beckoned to Thai warriors as new homes and sources of booty. Since their eyes were firmly fixed upon expansion to the south, neither of these states represented any military threat to the Sungs.

If Annam and Nan-Chao represented essentially peaceful neighbors for the Chinese, so too did Korea and Japan, both of which were separated from the Sung realm by the waters of the Yellow and East China seas. Korea had been united into a single kingdom in the early tenth century by a new Koryō dynasty which had made Kaesong its capital. It recognized the Sung emperor as its superior, though it was also forced to do the same as regards the ruler of the nearby Liao realm. It had organized its government on the Chinese Tang model of earlier times and as a result clung to a Buddhism that had already been replaced by neo-Confucianism in the China of the Sungs. This Buddhism dominated both its cultural and its economic life from great monasteries established in the Korean peninsula as well as in China proper. During this same period the Koreans were an extremely active maritime people and tended to dominate the sea traffic between the Chinese mainland and Korea proper and a more distant Japan. But already below the surface a new, more aristocratic governmental system of powerful clan families was beginning to appear at Kaesong. It based its authority upon landed estates and was destined to destroy the influence of its merchant class and dominate the less-privileged commoners and peasants of the countryside as well.

Heian Japan represented still another pattern of development. By the year 1000 its centralized imperial government had changed considerably from what it had been during the preceding Nara period when imperial centralization had begun, and its emperors for more than a century had ceased to recognize the overlordship of the Chinese Son of Heaven. As this came about, its governmental institutions, copied slavishly from those of the Tangs, changed considerably as a new kind of private *shoen* estate system replaced state-owned land in the countryside. At Kyōtō, now the capital, the imperial house had lost much authority to a family of court aristocrats, the Fujiwara, although it clung to some control under a new *insei* system in which ex-emperors tended to dominate the central government. Even more important in the provinces and especially around the Kantō plain to the northeast, we now find real authority exercised by bands of mounted warriors known as *bushi* who dominated the countryside through a network of protofeudal family alliances. As this came about, Japan, unlike Sung China or Korea, remained backward, economically speaking. It still lacked both a money economy or a native coinage and participated only very peripherally in the commercial growth that characterized the rest of East Asia during this period. Nevertheless, certain rudimentary commercial centers like Sakai had already begun to appear, and some great Buddhist shrines were beginning to play an economic role in the development of trade and commerce on a local level. The Japanese, though backward, were on the threshold of a new era that was to characterize their economy during the next few centuries.

If one can characterize Annam, Nan-Chao, Korea, and Japan as essentially peripheral to the Chinese heartland of East Asian civilization, quite the contrary is the case with Hsi Hsia and the Liao realms—both of which were powerful enough to force the Sungs to pay them tribute and both of which developed societies and institutions important to the future of all of East Asia. The Hsi Hsia kingdom was composed of an essentially Chinese population which lived in both its countryside and its fortified urban centers and was controlled by a ruling minority of warlike Tangut nomadic tribesmen. Hsi Hsia was prosperous because the principal terrestrial trade routes from the west to China passed through its kingdom. Its government, from the little we know of it, seems to have been modeled on that of the Tangs and Sungs, although there is evidence that, as in Korea, Buddhism was so strong there that it was almost the state religion. Its armed forces, like those of nearby Liao, were composed of heavily armored, mounted archers, who could rely for protection upon a number of strongly fortified cities. This military organization, which was the basis of Tangut control of the population, was to continue to be formidable until the Mongols took over the realm two centuries later.

The Kitan kingdom of Liao was economically much less important than that of Hsi Hsia. On the other hand, it was unusually important from a political and military point of view and as an anticipation of the later empires of the Mongols and Manchus. It was divided into five provinces, each with its own administrative center, while its capital was located in Jehol just north of the Great Wall. Its population consisted of three distinct elements: a large Chinese element which lived south of the Great Wall near where modern Peking was to arise; a Kitan tribal confederacy which was the dominant group in Liao; and large numbers of non-Kitan, non-Chinese tribesmen, most of whom lived in Manchuria. The Kitans and others in the ruling tribal confederacy formed about a fifth of the population; the Chinese, three-fifths; the rest, one-fifth.

The Liao government in some ways was modeled upon that of nearby Sung China in that as early as 988 it seems to have established an examination system to determine the eligibility of its Chinese inhabitants for office. Here, too, Buddhism, which had ceased to be important in China, was so powerful that it was practically the state religion, despite some elements of Confucianism which were also to be found amongst its Chinese population. But the Kitan tribal system also played an important role in its government. Its rulers continued to preserve their own tribal language, written in an alphabetical system copied from the central Asian Uighurs and existing side by side with a script using Chinese written characters. They also maintained a set of tribal laws and customs for their Kitans which were much like the later *yasa* code of the Mongols.

The Kitans seem to have relied principally upon their own warrior tribesmen as the backbone of their military forces. These were organized into a central *ordo* or bodyguard of the ruler amounting to several thousand elite troops and eighteen other ordos who were recruited from both Kitan and non-Kitan tribesmen. This force of about 50,000 mounted cavalrymen rode into battle armed with bows and swords and was trained to maneuver with precision on the plains of North China and the nearby steppes of Mongolia. Within each ordo cavalrymen were organized into groups of five or ten men and then combined into larger groups, as was the case with the later Mongols. The military power of this elite cavalry was supplemented in the Liao kingdom by using large numbers of Chinese as infantry and by well-fortified cities organized much like those of the Sung Chinese and in Hsi Hsia.

What the Kitans had created by the year 1000, as had the Hsi Hsia Tanguts, was a military state, partly nomadic in character and partly Chinese, which was strong enough to overawe both the Sung empire and Korea and at the same time to dominate large numbers of nomadic tribesmen who lived north of the Great Wall. It had great military and political strength despite a certain backwardness one can discern in its economic and cultural life. Most important of all, it was the prototype of the later Chin, Mongol, and Manchu systems of imperial administration that were to be so much a part of subsequent Chinese history.

In one sense, the economic life of East Asia by the year 1000 was, as earlier, dominated by its Chinese heartland in many traditional ways. For instance, since China was economically self-sufficient in almost all respects, its people still made use of a copper coinage which had no value in markets beyond East Asia itself. Its Sung emperors, like their predecessors, still made use of a "tribute" system in their economic dealings with neighboring peoples in which trade with the outside world was based on concepts of political supremacy of a rather unique sort. Nevertheless, as its society became more commercial and urbanized and made an increasing use of money from late Tang times on, its trade relationships began to change with both neighboring East Asian areas and the civilized world beyond.

Some of the external commerce reaching China proper continued as in the past to follow the older silk routes which passed through Kansu on their way to and from the land of Uighurs in eastern Turkestan and beyond. Recently discovered records from Turfan and from the Buddhist monastery of Tunhuang reveal that this trade remained very active despite the troubled political conditions which prevailed. They show us that towns and markets continued to grow in importance throughout Hsi Hsia during this period despite strict governmental supervision and that there were a large number of active guilds of Chinese merchants called *hongs*. Most of the merchants who reached this part of China, however, seem to have been of foreign origin, mainly from eastern and western Turkestan—especially from Khotan or Samarkand. Some, came from Korea, too, for we find both a Korean monastery and a Korean merchant settlement here, which reflects the importance these enterprising people placed on tapping Chinese trade during these years. The chief imports seem to have been horses, hides, and other natural products which were exchanged for silk or Chinese manufactured wares.

Important as this well-established overland trade was from late Tang times on, it was probably less important than that which was now reaching China by way of various maritime routes. In northern China the principal merchants involved in commerce with Korea and Japan during the ninth and tenth centuries seem to have been Koreans whose monasteries were found everywhere and whose traders were particularly active in Shantung and near the mouth of the Huai River, according to Ennin's *Diary*, which describes this trade, and later contemporary records as well.

Even more important than this northern maritime commerce was that which reached southern Chinese coasts from Southeast Asia and the Indian Ocean. Initially, this traffic seems to have been dominated by Persian and Arab merchants who, according to Arab authorities, sailed to Canton and other Chinese ports in large numbers from the Persian Gulf, although a few, including some Mediterranean Rhadanite Jews, came from the Red Sea. These traders seem to have carried tropical products and cotton goods to South China where they exchanged them for silks, porcelains, and other Chinese manufactured wares which were in much demand in the Indic and Islamic worlds. At Canton several thousand of these merchants were in residence when serious riots against foreigners broke out in 878 or 879 and resulted in the death of a number of them. Not all foreign merchants who reached South China during these years, however, were Arab or Persian, for we know that traders from Champa also trafficked there as well as some from other parts of Southeast Asia.

Though probably the high-water mark of Moslem sea traffic to China was reached during the late ninth century just prior to the massacres of foreigners, trade continued with Canton and other Chinese cities throughout the tenth century. By this time, however, these Moslem merchants were overtaken in importance by traders from Annam, Champa, Cambodia, and Indonesia who arrived in increasing numbers judging from the trade treaties of the time. But even more important, we can now begin to see the rise of a new native Chinese maritime tradition among the merchants of Canton, Fukien, and the lower Yangtze valley which were now part of a united Sung Chinese empire.

The rather sudden appearance of a Chinese interest in external maritime commerce, in contrast to earlier passivity in this regard, seems to have been the result of a number of factors. In the first place, it was the result of a shift of Chinese civilization toward the south, to which we have already alluded. This made the Yangtze valley and the South China coasts increasingly important from an economic and commercial point of view. Since these areas faced the sea, it was natural for their maritime commerce to increase in importance. Second, this maritime commerce was also a reflection of a new emphasis by the Sung governmental service which was recruited from a new commercial-minded gentry and was much more responsive to the merchant class than had been the case in the earlier era of the Tangs. And last of all, it seems to have been in part the result of a number of technological changes in the way that Chinese ships were being built, especially as regards hull and mast construction, which made these junks much better able to navigate the difficult waters off the China coast or in the South China Sea. It is uncertain just how these changes came about, whether they were the result of indigenous changes within Chinese society, or came about as a result of contacts with the superior seamanship and maritime technology of the peoples of Southeast Asia, or were a combination of both of these. But whatever its cause by the year 1000 we can discern that an important and vital native Chinese maritime tradition had appeared based upon better ships and more advanced techniques of navigation which, as Needham has shown, was to characterize the next few centuries during Sung and Yuan times. This maritime tradition was to forge important links between East Asian civilization and that of its neighbors and modify in no small measure the relative isolation which had so long characterized the economic, political, and cultural life of its peoples.

GREATER INDIA

The second great civilization of this period was that of the Indic world, which, as we have noted, was now somewhat more closely linked with that of East Asia via Yunnan passes and maritime routes. This civilization was located in a tropical area which stretched east of Africa, encompassing India, Ceylon, Burma, Southeast Asia, and Indonesia. It also formed a world which had a very different geographical, economic, cultural, and historical character from the Islamic world to the west or the East Asian complex to the northeast. It is also one which we are only now beginning to understand in all its ramifications.

The Indic world was defined by several distinct features. In the first place, it was cut off from its civilized neighbors by a series of high mountain ranges to the north which stretched all the way from Afghanistan and Persia to

southern China. These ranges were pierced by only three gateways practicable for travelers—one in the west and two in the east. The western
gateway, the most important one, lay east and southeast of Persia and Afghanistan and consisted of a number of passes which connected these regions
with the upper Indus valley plain. This was the classic invasion route into
India which all invaders of this subcontinent had followed from the time of
the Aryans and Alexander the Great to that of the Arabs of the eighth century.
This route, however, was not completely satisfactory as an entry into the
heart of the civilized Indian world, since once invaders had established
themselves in the upper Indus valley, they still found their way barred on
one side by the formidable deserts of Rajistan, the Rann of Kutch, and the
foothills of the Deccan plateau, and on the other by the mountains of Kashmir
and the Himalayas, if they wished to advance into the Ganges valley or move
into central and southern India.

The two other gateways to this advanced Indic civilization were, however,
even less inviting. They consisted of a series of difficult passes which led
from Yunnan and the upper Yangtze valley to Burma and Thailand or a
narrow coastal plain between mountains and the sea which led south from
Annam to the Mekong Delta and Cambodia. Neither of these routes had
termini which were close to the heartland of Indic civilization.

Though relatively isolated by land from nearby Islamic and East Asian
civilizations, the world of Greater India was much more open to them by
sea—especially to the Moslem world along the western shores of the Indian
Ocean. Indeed, a glance at a map makes it clear that those regions in which
a distinctive Indic civilization had taken root—in India proper and in Southeast Asia—could themselves only have been formed by maritime connections
of a continuing sort, in contrast to the East Asian world whose heartland
had always been and still was essentially land-based. Fortunately, however,
down to the year 1000 no effective *foreign* naval power existed in the seas
linking the peoples who shared a common Indic culture, so they could continue to develop independently and relatively undisturbed—a situation
which lasted until the arrival of Portuguese fleets in the sixteenth century.

We are only now becoming aware that Indian civilization prior to A.D.
1000 was, in its broadest extent, based upon sea routes and sea connections,
for our information concerning this civilization has been both fragmentary
and incomplete. But it is now clear that, from the first century on, or perhaps
even earlier, a significant seaborne commerce and series of maritime routes
linked continental India—especially its Coromandel and Orissa coasts—with
Burma, the Southeast Asian mainland, and the islands of Indonesia. At an
equally early date, Indic mariners were also active in the waters of the
western Indian Ocean, where pirate fleets from Kutch and Gujerat prevented any Islamic advance beyond Sind and menaced Arab and Persian
merchants sailing from the Persian Gulf to the Malabar Coast, Ceylon, and

South China. During certain periods such pirates even seem to have established themselves on the island of Socotra at the entrance of the Red Sea
where they interfered with Arab shipping, while a number of other Indic-
speaking people, probably originating from Java or Sumatra, still lived along
the shores of East Africa and Madagascar in the tenth century where their
presence was noted by a number of Arab geographers and writers. Indic
civilization in the broadest sense, then, had been dependent for centuries
upon the sea and upon a generally peaceful use of maritime routes which
had allowed it to spread its distinctive civilization as far west as Madagascar
and East Africa and as far east as the Vietnam coast and the Spice Islands
of Indonesia.

Climate was a second feature uniting the world of Greater India. All of
its peoples lived in tropical or subtropical areas with abundant rainfall. The
only exception was a portion of northern India east of the lower and middle
Indus where scant precipitation produced a desert climate. It is important,
however, to note that the rainfall pattern which prevailed in most of the
Indic world was and is seasonal in character. The winter months, though
very hot, tend to be dry, while during the summer months, between May
and October, extremely heavy monsoon rains fall. Irrigation, then, was almost everywhere a necessity to space out monsoon precipitation so that crops
could be cultivated throughout a longer growing season. The main irrigation
systems were those built in river valleys like those of the Indus and Ganges
of North India or smaller ones in South India or along the Irrawaddy, the
Salween, the Chaupaya, and the Mekong river systems of Burma and Southeast Asia, as well as along a number of smaller streams in Malaya, Sumatra,
and Java. In certain parts of continental India and Ceylon, however, river
irrigation was less important than wells which tapped groundwater close to
the surface or dams in the hills which formed reservoirs whose water could
be released during the dry season.

In a large part of the Indic world these irrigation works proved ideal in
growing rice, which served as the main food crop of its population and which
was cultivated with the help of various varieties of water buffalo. In much
of northern and central India, however, rice was never grown, and, especially
in the Punjab and Kashmir, wheat and barley were the main food grains.
Buffalo, though found, were less important than various strains of Brahman
cattle, which served as draft animals and supplied the milk forming part of
the peasant diet. In other parts of southern India millet and various kinds
of pulse replaced wheat, barley, and rice as the staple crops. In addition to
food crops, cotton was regularly cultivated, especially in irrigated lands
of northern India, as was sugar cane. Equally important were a number of
dyestuffs, some grown as crops and others the result of the exploitation of
jungle products of various sorts. To these should be added spices like pepper
and other condiments, most of which came from southern India or Indonesian

islands to the east. The exchange of such natural commodities within the world of Greater India and beyond was the principal basis of its maritime commerce.

United by a relatively peaceful isolation from nearby civilizations, a tropical climate and rainfall pattern, and an agriculture dependent on irrigation, the Indic world had its own distinct civilization. India proper was the original home of this civilization, and from this subcontinent it had gradually spread eastward over a number of centuries until it had been adopted by the other peoples of Southeast Asia who combined it in various ways with their own traditions during the early Middle Ages.

Indic civilization, generally speaking, seems to have had two major aspects. One of these was the despotic power of its rulers. By the late tenth century such rulers, who often claimed divine origins and attributes, governed their relatively small quarreling kingdoms by organizing a fighting class of warriors who kept the peasant population in awe of them. They also used their authority to see that the vital irrigation systems were kept in good repair. By the end of the first millennium most of them also had firm control over the merchants and artisans who settled in the growing towns and cities of the Indic world.

There was, however, a second, even more important facet of Indic civilization: the temple and the priestly class associated with it. Temples, mainly Hindu, were found everywhere from Champa, Cambodia, and Java in the east to the great temple complexes of India proper in the west. They were controlled by a priestly class who, in India, were generally known as Brahmans. These priests played a role hardly less important than that of the kings or of the warrior class. Temples and priests helped maintain control over the peasantry by providing them with numerous gods whom they worshipped and many other vital services. For example, they were indispensable in the organization of agricultural and village life, as well as providing rulers, merchants, and artisans with centers in which their basic activities could be carried out.

But religion did much more in Greater India than provide these great temple complexes, for it was the cement which held society itself together. By the year 800, if not earlier, the Hindu faith was ubiquitous in the Indic world, although pockets of Jains and Buddhists persisted in parts of continental India and in even larger numbers in Ceylon, eastern Java, and Burma. This Hinduism stressed a worship of Siva and Vishnu while including in its pantheon a host of lesser divinities and even some Buddhist elements. This arrangement appealed on one level to the intellectual priestly and ruling classes who were heirs to the Upanishads, those early philosophical formulations of Hinduism, and on still another level to the animistic peasantry. It not only provided a theocratic justification for the power of rulers but was increasingly tending to justify a division of Indic society into four classes—

a priestly class, a warrior class, a class of merchants and artisans, and a class of peasant cultivators. By the end of the tenth century such classes, especially in India proper, were being organized or even subdivided into something akin to the later castes. Religion also provided intricate laws, like the Hindu *Laws of Manu*, which attempted to regulate every aspect of life. In short, the Indic world was one in which a common set of religious beliefs and practices tended to dictate both its class structures and the habits of all segments of its population in a way which differed substantially from that found anywhere else in the civilized world of Eurasia and Africa.

A discussion of Indic demography is problematic. Estimates of population are very risky for the scholar to attempt for a civilization with an oral tradition of learning and few written records. Recently, however, Professor Josiah Russell has supplied us with some figures for Indian population in medieval times which seem plausible. He estimates that the population of India proper during the seventh century was somewhere between 30,000,000 and 50,000,000. We have no reason to believe that it had increased significantly by the end of the tenth century. Judging from what we know of the limited areas occupied by the nonjungle population of Ceylon, Burma, Cambodia, Champa, and Indonesia, not one of which could have been much larger than 1,000,000 at this time, we can arrive at a figure of some 10,000,000 additional people living in the rest of the Indic world. Thus it seems reasonable to conclude that by the year 1000 Greater India had a population of somewhere between 40,000,000 and 60,000,000 or about one-half that found in East Asia.

An examination of the political and economic status of the various areas and peoples which formed this Indic civilization around the year 1000 shows that it had no central heartland comparable to Sung China in the East Asian civilization. Instead, it seems to have been formed from four generally distinct regions into which we can divide both its principalities and its peoples— two in India proper and two in Greater India overseas.

In continental India the first area which demands our attention was one stretching from the mountain chains of the north to the Nerbala River and the beginnings of the Deccan plateau in the south. It owed its overall unity to a number of factors. In the first place, it was inhabited by peoples whose languages were all of Indo-European origin and which in modern times were to develop into Hindi. Second, except in Bengal where rice formed the staple crop, wheat and barley were its basic foodstuffs. And in the third place it had at certain times a measure of political unity, particularly that imposed upon it by the empire of Harsha in the seventh century or the Gujara-Pratharas of the late ninth. Though this region faced Arab Moslems who had established themselves in force in Sind along the lower Indus as early as the eighth century, probably to assure themselves of ports at the mouth of the Indus where they could stop on their way to the Malabar coast and beyond, it seemed to have little to fear from the Islamic world. This was because until the late tenth century Hindu rajas still controlled the passes which led from the upper Indus to Afghanistan and eastern Persia while Gujerat sea power limited the Moslem threat from the sea along Indian Ocean shores.

By the end of the tenth century, however, all vestiges of any previous overall political unity within northern India disappeared as a series of small warring principalities arose immediately south of the Himalayas. Though two of these realms—that of the Chanellas and that of the Paranas—were in the process of attempting to assert some control over the rest, neither was yet able to do so. Their failure turned out to be an ominous one for Indic civilization, because at this very moment a new threat to it was arising in nearby Afghanistan. This was the appearance of a new and aggressive Moslem border state centering in Gazna and controlled by a Turkish family who owed allegiance to the Saminid rulers of Khorasan. The ruler of this border region, who was named Subuktuqun, in 988 gathered an army of Turkish ghazi warriors, advanced to the east, and defeated the forces of Jaipul, the Hindu raja who controlled the passes into northern India. When he died in 997, his son Mahmud succeeded him in Gazna. The latter had to face a confederacy of North Indian Hindu princes led by Jaipul's successor who advanced against him in an attempt to recover these strategic passes. In the battle that ensued in 998, the Hindus were disastrously defeated and Mahmud was able to advance unopposed into the Punjab which he occupied as far east as Lahore. By the year 1000 then, for the first time in centuries, the gateway which led into northern India was lost to a powerful and militaristic Islamic ruler with results which were to be incalculable for the future of Indic civilization as a whole.

A second area of the Indic world was formed by that part of India which lay south of the Vinya range and included the island of Ceylon as well. This region had never been part of the earlier northern Indian empires of Harsha or the Gujara-Pratharas but, like Ceylon, had always had its own native lines of kings. Although it shared with northern India a common Hinduism and general culture, it was inhabited by peoples who were almost all non-Aryan and Dravidian in race and who spoke languages which were also non-Aryan in character. Furthermore, here the main food crops were millet and rice rather than the wheat and barley of the north.

South India had never managed to achieve any overall political unity in historic times, and Ceylon always possessed its own rulers. By the late tenth century, however, the smaller principalities of the region had come to be dominated by two large kingdoms. These were the kingdom of the Chalukyas to the northeast, which centered in the general area of modern Bombay and which the Arab merchant Suleiman had considered the most important of all Indian realms, and a rising empire of the Cholas located along the Coromandel Coast in the general areas of modern Madras. There were also a number of other small principalities at this time in South India whose boundaries were essentially unstable ones. The most important were the Panya realm at the very tip of the Indian peninsula, Vengi and Orissa which lay between the lower Ganges and the Chola empire, and Ceylon which, although it was Buddhist, shared a common Indic civilization with its South Indian neighbors. Of all these states that of the Cholas was the most important and was already expanding to form an empire in southern India and overseas as well.

Overseas, in the eastern part of Greater India, we can also discern two rather distinct regions into which we can group its principalities and its peoples. The first was a mainland area which stretched from Burma eastward to the South China Sea. The second was essentially an island region which included the Malay Peninsula and most of modern Indonesia.

In Burma by the sixth century two Indianized kingdoms had appeared, one at Prome along the lower reaches of the Irrawaddy River, the other a Mon principality located in the lower Salween valley. Then during the ninth century large numbers of warrior tribesmen moved south from the Thai kingdom of Nan-Chao in Yunnan and conquered the small state located at Prome and Pegu as well and forced the Mons on the Salween to pay them tribute. By the early eleventh century they had begun to form a powerful Burmese state at Pagan around the middle reaches of the Irrawaddy with a mixed civilization that increasingly emphasized the Indic character of its culture.

To the east of Burma lay a second powerful mainland kingdom, that of the Khmers, which we call Cambodia and which the Chinese knew as Chen-lā. This state was the heir to a still earlier kingdom of Funan which seems to have been located in the same general region. By the late tenth century Cambodian monarchs had come to control a large expanse of territory east of the Mon principality and north of the Kra Malayan isthmus which included the entire river basins of the Chaupaya and lower Mekong rivers, whose waters they controlled through an elaborate system of reservoirs and irrigation works. And finally to the east of this Khmer kingdom we find the last powerful Hinduized mainland state, that of Champa, which was located along the coast of central Vietnam just north of the Mekong Delta. Champa was hostile to both Cambodia which lay to the west and Annam to the north and may have owed much of its power and cohesion to the active maritime commerce that passed its shores on the way to and from Sung China and in which its own merchants actively participated.

A fourth and last distinctive Indic region included Malaya and the island realm of the East Indies. It was controlled by two states. Smaller and less important was the Buddhist realm of the Sailendas. It seems to have appeared during the eighth century and by the tenth controlled eastern Java and exercised some authority over the Spice Islands to the east as well. Its great rival was the more powerful kingdom of Srivajaya. This state, with its capital at Palembang in Sumatra, extended its hegemony over western Java, Sumatra, and the Malay Peninsula and thus straddled the major maritime trade routes linking the Indian Ocean with the South China Sea. No merchants could pass through the Sunda Strait, or the Straits of Malacca, or cross the Isthmus of Kra without paying tribute to its rulers. It seems to have first appeared sometime during the seventh or eighth century and by the tenth was at the height of its power, judging from the many embassies it sent to Sung China and the accounts of Moslem geographers and travelers who wrote of it. Like Champa it owed its power and prosperity to the importance of the maritime commerce of this part of the Indic world.

Even though our knowledge of the economic conditions that prevailed in much of this Indic world remains fragmentary, a few general comments are possible. Every part of Greater India, except when the monsoon rains failed to arrive on schedule, produced sufficient foodstuffs locally to meet the basic needs of its population, and some even had a surplus available for export. On the other hand, the Indic world was somewhat less fortunate in mineral wealth. It had abundant gold supplies, much of which came from two regions, the Deccan in South India and Sumatra. It also had important deposits of iron in Orissa, northeast central India, and the Deccan and abundant tin in Malaya and Sumatra. But it lacked silver—all of which had to be imported from the Islamic world—or copper which reached it either from the Red Sea area or from northern Thailand or China. It was, on the other hand, the world's leading source of precious gems during these years: India and Borneo produced diamonds; rubies and sapphires came from Burma, Ceylon, and the Khmer realm; and emeralds were to be found in India proper. Though important pearl fisheries were to be found in the Persian Gulf, pearls of equally high quality were brought up from the shallow waters which lay between Ceylon and southern India.

Still another important resource available to this Indic world was timber, especially two varieties of wood which were important for shipbuilding— teak and coconut palm. Teak, which grew profusely along the Malabar and Coromandel coasts as well as in Ceylon, Burma, and much of Southeast Asia and Indonesia, provided shipbuilders with a wood which was relatively impervious to sea worms and, therefore, ideal for ship construction. The coconut palm, which grew everywhere in tropical waters from the Laccadive and Maldive islands off the Malabar Coast to the furthest reaches of Indonesia, also provided a cheap and easily worked material for ship construction and masts, while its coconut fiber could be woven into ropes and rigging. As we will note, the Moslem world just across the sea from India lacked these important shipbuilding resources.

The Indic world also produced a variety of dyestuffs, spices, and aromatic and resinous forest products which were in great demand throughout Greater India and in nearby civilized areas. Pepper, perhaps the most important of the spices, came from both the Malabar Coast and Sumatra, the latter being the more important production center, while to the east of Java lay islands like the Moluccas which were the source of cloves and nutmeg. These spices and a number of others which came from southern India and the East Indies were not only in great demand in foreign markets but were also needed within the Indic world itself to preserve food before the age of refrigeration. From these same regions and especially from Borneo came the sandalwood, the camphor, and the aromatic resins and lacquers which were particularly highly prized in China and which supplemented similar wares that Moslem merchants exported from South Arabia and the general area of the Red Sea.

To such natural products of fields, forests, and mines whose exchange over long distances helped to stimulate the internal commerce of Greater India, we need to add industrial wares. These consisted mainly of an infinite variety of cotton textiles produced in both northern and southern India from the abundant supplies of cotton grown on irrigated land, and considerable iron-ware and weapons, a good deal of which was produced in Orissa and the nearby Deccan plateau. Much of this production was shipped east in exchange for the gold and tin of Sumatra and Malaya and a variety of spices and other forest products, for India proper was the Indic world's industrial center, and eastern areas which lay across the Bay of Bengal remained essentially agrarian.

Consequently, by the tenth century or even earlier, one can discern the following general pattern of economic life for Indic civilization as a whole. In India proper, and especially in the plains of the Indus and Ganges rivers, an extensive commerce had developed over both river and land routes. Much of this commerce reached southern India by land, but more of it tended to follow coastal maritime routes, either those from Gujerat to Ceylon along the west coast or from Coromandel shores north to the Ganges delta, to Burma and beyond. There was also an important exchange of wares from India proper with those from Greater India overseas—an exchange which involved merchants not only from the Coromandel Coast but from the west coast as well.

The Indic civilization also carried its trade to the world beyond. Some of this trade was terrestrial and reached India via the Khyber Pass leading to Persia and Moslem central Asia. Along this route merchants brought Moslem silver, metal wares, and other industrial goods to India in exchange for a variety of cottons, gems, and other commodities. Still other merchants used more easterly passes to bring into India Chinese silks and manufactured wares which they traded for cottons, gems, and luxury products.

The land routes, however, were much less important to Indic trade than the maritime routes to western Asian and the Far East. Commerce with the

Red Sea, South Arabia, and the Persian Gulf was of such ancient origin that we find traces of it in Sumerian times. It continued to grow in volume and is described later on by Greek writers like Ptolemy and Cosmas Indicopleustes and a whole series of ninth- and tenth-century Moslem geographers. It seems to have been based upon an exchange of timber, spices, gems, gold, cotton textiles, bar iron, and swords—all of which originated in the Indic world—for silver, copper, copperware, aromatic resins, ivory, and horses shipped east from Islamic shores and East Africa. On the other side of Greater India, maritime trade to China was somewhat different: gems, spices, aromatic resin, gold dust, and tropical products were shipped north from the East Indies to southern Chinese ports in exchange for silks, porcelains, copper, and a variety of Chinese industrial wares. Some Chinese silks and porcelains were shipped from Indonesia directly to the Moslem world during the eighth, ninth, and tenth centuries, just as some Moslem frankincense and myrrh from the Red Sea reached East Asia by sea.

By the year 1000 the commercial traffic within continental India and beyond had created a prosperous class of merchants and artisans, which explains why Chinese visitors as early as the seventh century could comment favorably upon the urban civilization which they found in Harsha's northern Indian empire. Such accounts and the numerous gold and silver Indian coins from this period found in hoards throughout the subcontinent also make it clear that a money economy existed almost everywhere. According to inscriptions found in central India which date from the tenth century, some of India's merchants and artisans were already organized into guilds, some of which were specifically for lending money. The medieval Indian dramas written at this time also stress an active commercial life as do the Hindu *Laws of Manu*, which contain a number of provisions concerning both debts and debtors. That southern India shared in this active commercial life is shown by inscriptions found there which also mention merchant guilds, often in conjunction with great temple complexes. We know less about the economic development of overseas regions of Greater India, but it is significant that Champa merchants were found in ninth-century China, and many others were active at Canton and other Chinese ports during the last decades of the tenth. Obviously, by the end of the first millennium much of the Indic world had developed an urban commercial civilization of its own.

There is one aspect of the urban life found in this part of the world, however, which is puzzling and which differs considerably from that found in nearby advanced civilizations. Many Indic cities were relatively small in size and unstable in the way in which they developed. From Champa and Java in the east to India proper in the west, we regularly find a number of urban centers arising as a result of serving as capitals for Indic rulers or for their connection with great temple complexes. Such urban centers also seemed to attract, for a period, large numbers of artisans and merchants and to support both an active urban life and a money economy. Then again and again they declined almost as rapidly as they had arisen, leaving deserted ruins which were soon overtaken by the jungle. A number of examples of such a pattern spring to mind, such as Ankor Vat or Ceylonese capitals or a host of ruined cities found in India proper.

This instability of the individual Indic city was a very old phenomenon indeed and continued after the year 1000 with a few exceptions: Delhi, Ajmer, and Palembang, for instance. One reason for this instability may be that many Indic cities had little connection with village life, which usually existed apart from and separate from urbanization. Instead, cities tended to be the creation of rulers or to grow out of the presence of great temple complexes. As long as rulers remained powerful or temples were growing in influence, they attracted merchants and artisans to their cities. When a ruling house lost power, however, or new, more vital religious centers arose, merchants and artisans moved away from older religious or political centers to the new ones and the older ones fell into ruin. Thus we can regard the typical Indic city as essentially parasitical or nonfunctional in many cases, despite the active economic and commercial life found within its walls. It resembles much more the cities of the ancient Near East prior to the time of the Phoenicians, Arameans, or Greeks or the great temple complexes of pre-Columbian Mexico, Yucatan, and Peru than it does the active cities of tenth-century China or the Islamic world. And in the long run this instability of its cities was to make it difficult for Indic civilization to compete successfully with its civilized neighbors whose urban life was more organically and solidly built upon commerce and a close relationship with nearby peasant populations.

The scanty evidence available to us indicates that by the end of the tenth century four areas of this Indian world had developed considerable maritime strength. They were Gujerat, the Chola area of the Coromandel Coast, Srivajaya, and Champa. Two of these, Gujerat and Champa, were contiguous with the active maritime regions of the Persian Gulf and of South China, respectively. The other two dominated major legs along trade routes of an international character within the Indic world itself. While none of these regions seems to have possessed any organized naval fleets prior to the year 1000, all of them had significant maritime establishments which came close to being effective naval forces. For instance, pirates of Kutch could at times act as the terror of the western Indian Ocean and range as far west as Socotra. The Cholas after the year 1000 were able to organize a maritime empire. The rulers of Srivajaya were powerful enough to force merchants to pay them tribute in order to pass through the straits they controlled. And the inhabitants of Champa by the eleventh century possessed fleets they were able to use against their Annamese rivals. Despite this naval potential, however, we must conclude that generally peaceful conditions prevailed along

Indic maritime routes in contrast to those found in the Mediterranean world where fleets were found everywhere and pirates were ever-present. For between the seventh and tenth centuries Arab and Persian merchant shipping could sail relatively undisturbed through the heart of the Indic world and merchants from Western Asia could establish themselves as traders in the cities of the China coast—a situation, however, which began to change significantly soon after the year 1000, as we will see.

We know little directly about the ships which were used by Indic seafaring peoples except that they made use of boats called *katias* in Gujerat which were sturdier and better built than the traditional Arab *dhows* or *baggalas*, and that Indonesians sailed the seas in distinctive craft using a fore and aft rig which have been depicted for us on the walls of the Javan temple of Borobadur. It seems also clear that the possession of seagoing outrigger canoes made it possible for Malay peoples to sail west and settle in Madagascar.

But it is probable that the ships used by the Arabs in the Red Sea, southern Arabia, and Persian Gulf were actually of Indic origin and can give us a clear picture of how Indic ships were designed. Such craft, generically named *dhows*, were usually of small or medium size at this time, built of teak or coconut palm wood, with masts and rigging also made from the palm. They differed from either Mediterranean ships or the junks found along East Asian shores in being built without iron nails. Instead their timbers were tied or sewn together with ropes of coconut fiber, and the interstices between the planks caulked with a thick grease made of whale or shark oil.

Such ships, still sailing these waters at the time of Marco Polo, took advantage of the regular monsoon winds which blew across the Indian Ocean on a seasonal basis. These winds were both regular and steady, so that craft built in Indic fashion were seaworthy enough to sail with some degree of safety as far as the coast of Champa from the Persian Gulf and Red Sea ports with stops along the Malabar Coast, Ceylon, and in Srivajaya. Such a voyage took from two to four months, allowing some time to stop at ports to trade. The return journey using other monsoon winds was almost as fast. Thus a round trip to and from China took about a year and a half, with the only really dangerous part of the voyage being the leg from Champa to China and back, for here there were dangerous reefs and terrible typhoons, called *rhuks* by the Arabs, which could easily wreck ships built for the less dangerous seas found in the Indian Ocean.

We know less than we would like to about the methods of navigation in use during this period. But it seems clear that down to the year 1000 they were relatively simple, using sun and stars and the prevailing winds of the monsoons. We have no proof that Indic mariners yet possessed a compass or that their charts were of an elaborate sort, if they existed at all. In short, we have no evidence that Indic shipping techniques were as advanced as those used in East Asian, Mediterranean, or Atlantic waters, or that they needed to be.

Prior to the year 1000 Arab and Persian shipping was quite active in Indic waters. Until the middle of the sixth century merchants from both the Red Sea and the Persian Gulf sailed no further than the Malabar Coast and Ceylon, where they picked up spices, silks, and other eastern wares to bring back to western markets. For obscure reasons, perhaps including the lack of any organized Indic naval strength, by the seventh century Persian merchants began to sail further east, with Arab seamen soon following, all the way to Chinese ports. By the ninth century they appear to have been dominant in this trade, although they never completely excluded Indic merchants from it. Probably the high-water mark of this commerce was reached in the mid-ninth century when hundreds of such merchants and Rhadanite Jews from the Red Sea as well settled in Chinese ports like Canton.

Antiforeign sentiment in late Tang China, which resulted in a great massacre of Moslem merchants in Canton in 879, probably dislocated the Chinese side of this trade, as did Zeng slave revolts and Qaramathian incursions in the Persian Gulf area. At any rate, by the tenth century, although some Moslem merchants still sailed to China, most went no further east than Kedah and Srivajaya, which became the termini of their trade with China. Then by the eleventh century few went further than Malabar shores as a completely new situation developed along Indic and East Asian maritime routes which we will examine in later chapters.

The World of
Islamic Civilization

The third great civilization with which we are dealing, the Islamic, was in some ways the most remarkable of all. It had appeared by the mid-eighth century as a result of some ten decades of conquest by Moslem tribes whose original home was the Arabian Peninsula and by the late tenth had coalesced into a vast expanse of territory which enjoyed a common civilization. Its uniqueness was due, however, not only to the distinctness of its culture but also to the fact that it alone of all the civilizations of this period had direct contacts with all the others and with black Africa as well. It was, in other words, the great intermediary civilization of medieval times.

A number of factors contributed to the unity of the Islamic world. The first was geographical. All of it lay in a zone dominated by deserts which stretched along its southern rim from the Sahara and Nubian deserts of North Africa and the deserts of the Arabian Peninsula to the arid wastes of Persia and Sind. To the north a similar stretch of arid steppes and deserts was to be found from the lower reaches of the Volga to the desiccated plateaus of eastern Turkestan. Even Islamic Spain was to some extent separated from Christian Spain by the semiarid *meseta* of the Iberian Peninsula. Where desert wastes did not exist to serve as boundaries, their place was taken by salt water—the Atlantic Ocean and the Mediterranean and Caspian seas on one side, the Indian Ocean on the other. Thus one can almost characterize the Islamic world as one where a series of coastal plains, high plateaus, and oases—the latter often including whole river valleys like the Nile, the Tigris-Euphrates, and the Oxus-Jaxartes—were surrounded by the desert and the

sea. Where neither desert nor sea existed as a boundary between the Moslems and their neighbors, mountains tended to perform the same function
at this time. These were the Tien Shan and the Pamirs between Moslem
Turkestan and the world of the Uighurs and eastern Turks, the Hindu Kush
and Afghan mountains between Persia and northern India, and the Taurus
and Caucasus which separated Byzantium and Khazaria from Islamic Syria,
Mesopotamia, and western Persia. Even in Spain, where Christians had
breached the ramparts of the Pyrenees and Cantabrian mountains by the
year 800, a series of other mountain chains ran through the center of the
Iberian Peninsula which barred easy access to Al-Andālūs.

If one basis of unity was geographical, a second was religious. The Moslem
world's dominant faith was Islam, even though by the late tenth century
Moslems were divided into heretical Shias who were found in Fatimid domains, the Yemen, northern Syria, and Persia, and orthodox Sunni who
formed the majority of the population elsewhere. Side by side with this
dominant Islamic faith which the majority professed, however, there were
a number of others tolerated by Moslems. These included Christianity,
which was particularly strong in parts of Spain, Egypt, Syria, Lebanon,
Armenia, and in central Asia; Judaism in Spain, the Maghreb, Egypt, the
Yemen, and Iraq; and Zoroastrianism which still lingered on in a number
of centers in Persia. Though none of those who professed these faiths was
allowed to bear arms and they had to pay taxes not levied upon Moslems,
they were not only tolerated but allowed to govern many aspects of their
lives undisturbed. Nevertheless, by the tenth century mass conversion to
Islam had begun to diminish the number of non-Moslems—a conversion
which owed its success in no small measure to the fact that it brought with
it lower taxation and access to important economic, political, and cultural
privileges reserved for the Islamic majority.

Conversion to Islam, meant much more than an acceptance of the Koran
and of Mohammed as the chosen prophet of God. It meant becoming subject
to the provisions of an Islamic legal system which governed most facets of
their family, social, and economic life. This law, known as the *Sharia*, had
developed very slowly and by the year 1000 had come to be based upon a
combination formed by the Koran and traditions known as *hadiths* which
were interpreted by four great schools of jurists known as *ulema*. These
ulema did not form an organized priesthood in the Christian or Indic sense,
but instead were learned religious men, closely linked with the merchant
or administrative elite in Moslem cities and who even on occasion acted as
merchants themselves. Not only did some of them sit as judges in the religious courts but they also administered trusts or property known as *waqf*
which pious Moslems had established for a variety of charitable purposes.
Moslems were expected not only to subordinate their lives to the Sharia as
interpreted by the ulema, but also to follow certain regular customs of a

religious nature, the most important being ablutions and public prayer five times a day, fasting during the month of Ramadan, the regular giving of alms, and a pilgrimage to the Holy Places of Mecca and Medina once in one's lifetime. In short, for those who had accepted its precepts, Islam formed a totalitarian religion which ordered most aspects of life within the Islamic world.

If this religious social pattern of daily life tended to link the Moslem world together, so too did a culture which was based upon written and spoken Arabic. By the year 1000 the heart of the Islamic world between Tunisia and the Iranian highlands was inhabited by a population using Arabic, which had largely replaced earlier Semitic tongues and Coptic Egyptian. West of Tunis there did exist a considerable population who spoke Berber dialects, and inhabitants of the Iberian Peninsula used a Romance-based language, just as in the Iranian world Persian was the common speech of the people except along the borders of Turkestan where Turkish dialects prevailed. But even in non-Arabic-speaking areas, especially those to the west, an increasingly large number of people were switching to Arabic, which was of course the commercial language and the language of the Koran and that in which most scholarly writings tended to be composed. Its only rival was Persian which in the east was still used in cultivated poetry and other secular writing but even it already contained a number of words of Arabic origin. By the end of the first millennium, then, Arabic in both spoken and written form had become a *lingua franca* which served to unite the peoples who formed Islamic civilization, just as Latin and Greek did in the Christian West and Chinese in East Asian areas.

Also contributing to Islamic unity were certain socioeconomic elements of which the Moslem city was probably the most important of all. The Islamic city flourished everywhere from Bokhara and Sind in the east to Fez, Cordoba, and Saragossa in the west, and had certain features that tended to distinguish it from urban centers found elsewhere. By the tenth century it tended to be without fortifications and lacked any essential governmental autonomy, while being organized around three general elements—a mosque or series of mosques, the *souq* or market area, and a governmental or administrative center. The classes who formed its elite consisted of the ulema, to whom we can add non-Moslem Christian prelates and priests and Jewish rabbis, a class of merchants and artisans, and a class of bureaucrats. Some of this elite, like the ulema, could belong to more than one class and serve at the same time as merchants and bureaucrats as well as learned judges.

In Islamic cities no true merchant guilds seem to have appeared by the tenth century despite the fact that in eastern provinces certain occupational groups within the artisan class were organized into religious confraternities and that there was a tendency for governmental authorities to group merchants and workers alike under heads or leaders who could be held respon-

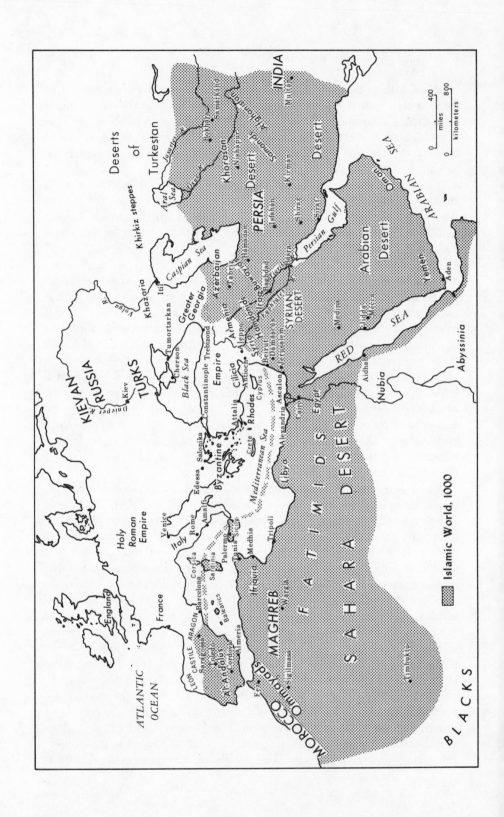

Islamic World, 1000

sible for their activities. With no real guilds available, the Moslem world relied for business upon an individualistic capitalism in which the dominant type of association was the partnership which took various forms. It could be a legally binding link between merchants, or between trader and artisan. Or it might even represent a valid contract across religious lines to unite the business interests of Moslem and non-Moslem in an association for gain of a temporary or continuing nature.

What is important for us to recognize, however, is that by the tenth century the Moslem city, like that of Sung China and unlike that of Greater India, had become organic rather than artificial in character. And it was everywhere performing a double role, serving as a market center and source of goods for the general region in which it was located and at the same time being linked by maritime and terrestrial routes to the great internal markets of the Islamic world and those which lay beyond its borders.

Class divisions also played a vital and important institutional and social role within the Islamic world. A class of important landlords, whom we can regard as gentry like those found in China, owned much of the fertile land in the coastal plains, the irrigated river valleys, and the oases. By the tenth century some of these landowners, and especially those of Khorasan, Al-Andālūs, and Tunis, were a rural class of country aristocrats. Most, however, were city folk who dominated an inert, servile peasantry through their control of estates on which they cultivated a variety of products. Except near Islamic frontiers these landowners were not a warrior class. Instead they were capitalistic landlords often closely linked to the governing, administrative class or the merchants of the towns through marriage and business arrangements. They also were largely responsible for what historians have called the Islamic green revolution, that acclimatization of new and valuable plants and those technical advances in agriculture which marked this period in Moslem history and had largely been completed by the end of the tenth century.

A second class of importance was a nonurban, tribally organized peasantry who inhabited the mountains and upland plateaus. Such peasants were to be found everywhere from the Sierra Nevada of Al-Andālūs or the Atlas Mountains of the Maghreb to the mountains of the Yemen, the uplands of Syria, the hills of Kurdistan, and the mountain valleys of Persia and Afghanistan in the east. Those who lived in such environments had little connection with either the towns or the estates which were located in oases or fertile river valleys. Though they practiced a husbandry in their high valleys which involved some irrigation, they were often semipastoral or dependent for their livelihood upon forest products which were plentiful near their mountain villages. In these upland areas they tended to be relatively free from the attention of governmental authorities seeking to tax them and were not subject to a money economy which dominated the lives of servile fellaheen like those of Egypt, Iraq, or Khorasan. Their hills and mountains had the further advantage of keeping them from being overrun by the more truly nomadic tribes who roamed nearby steppes and deserts. They formed a vigorous, independent population upon whom the more civilized Islamic world of town and fertile lowland could rely for hardy soldiers or men to populate its cities—even though the Islam which they practiced was a simple one mixed with all manner of primitive and superstitious vestiges.

Nomadic tribesmen formed a third broad socioeconomic group which populated the arid steppes and deserts. These nomads ranged over vast distances with their flocks and herds, following the scanty grass supply on a seasonal basis. In southern desert areas which stretched from the Sahara to Baluchistan they spoke Berber dialects or Arabic, while northern tribes who ranged the deserts and steppes of Turkestan, South Russia, and Persia tended to speak Turkish dialects. Most nomads lived on the sheep and goats they herded and used horses and camels as their beasts of burden or for riding. These latter varied according to the area. In Arabia and in the Nubian and Saharan deserts, the single-humped dromedary and the barb of North Africa and the Arab steeds of Syria and Arabia were to be found. In more northern arid regions and in Iran we find the two-humped Bactrian camel and the small, hardy central Asian pony, both of which were better adapted to the colder climate found there. Though such nomads depended mainly upon the animals they herded for their livelihood, they were also, upon occasion, hunters and active traders along the caravan trails which linked the various parts of the Islamic world or served as routes leading to nearby civilizations.

These nomads were grouped into tribes which were often hostile to one another but could upon occasion produce an able leader or a religious reformer who could organize them into huge confederacies, like that which made possible Islam's initial expansion out of Arabia during the seventh century. They were formidable warriors trained to the saddle and honed to a razor edge by the constant tribal feuds in which they engaged. Though all of them were nominally Islamic by the tenth century, their religion, somewhat like that of the mountain peoples, tended to be a superficial one which contained many animistic practices and beliefs and which bore little resemblance to that which prevailed in towns or among the more settled population of the Moslem world.

One of the principal problems which Islamic civilization had had to face up to the year 1000 and which was to continue thereafter was how to control these nomadic tribesmen. When controlled by governmental authorities they not only ceased to be a menace to the sedentary or urban population but made possible a profitable use of caravan routes leading to the wealth of nearby Byzantine-Russian, Indian, and East Asian peoples, as well as to the gold of the sub-Saharan African world. When united and organized as a hostile force, they not only made destructive raids upon towns and fertile agricultural areas alike but also interrupted trade along caravan routes and pilgrim traffic to Mecca and Medina upon which the prosperity of the Islamic world depended. At times such a military potential even allowed them to threaten the world of settled mountain villagers or plateau dwellers scattered throughout Dar-es-Islam.

Between the mid-eighth and late tenth centuries Moslem rulers in general had been able to control the nomads except for limited periods of time in the Maghreb and in Moslem Turkestan. But by the end of the first millennium in the Arabian Peninsula, however, the delicate balance between nomadic tribesmen and their more civilized and sedentary neighbors had begun to unravel. After the late ninth century, control over these nomads ceased to be effective. They organized themselves into a confederacy which seems to have been inspired by the radical religious Shia propaganda of the Qarmathians of Bahrain. So organized, these tribes raided both Syria and Iraq, made pilgrimage routes unsafe, and even plundered the Holy Places of Hejaz. Though they were partly curbed and contained by Fatimid diplomacy, they remained an ominous threat and one whose conduct was to be copied in the next century in other parts of the Islamic world with results which were to severely strain the fabric of its civilization.

In addition to the common social features mentioned above, the entire Islamic world had a governmental system which had many similar characteristics, whether one refers to the great caliphates into which parts of it had been forcibly divided by the late tenth century or the independent principalities which flourished elsewhere. In general, Islamic rulers, powerful and less powerful alike, had few religious functions except to appoint Moslem *cadis* who interpreted the Sharia or to choose Christian prelates or Jewish rabbis who played a similar role in regard to tolerated religious groups. They did, it is true, preside over Friday prayers in the main mosque located in their capital cities and often bore religious titles and were regarded as overall protectors of Islam within the areas they ruled. But once they had appointed cadis, it was the latter who had the main judicial authority, not the rulers themselves, except for administrative matters such as control of markets where appointed officials who were called *mūhtasibs* represented them in a special way.

Other aspects of government were much more under the control of the Islamic secular ruler. The latter, whatever his title, by now presided over a bureaucratic complex organized into a number of departments headed by a civilian official who generally bore the title of *wazir* or *vizir*. The most important duties of this bureaucracy were levying taxes and controlling revenues which came largely from taxes upon *djimmis* or tolerated non-Moslems, from a land tax, from various imposts on commerce, and sometimes from monopolies set up and maintained by the government itself. By the tenth century most of these taxes were collected in the form of money, though some levied in kind had survived from an earlier age. One of the most interesting features of the bureaucracies now used by Islamic rulers was the large numbers of Christians and Jews employed by them, often in the highest positions of responsibility. Their bureaucratic skills and experience helped to make Islamic government one of the most efficient in the civilized world of the time.

Another important role played by all Islamic governments was a military one and this deserves special attention. By the end of the tenth century we need to distinguish two general geographical zones within Dar-es-Islam— in each of which military and naval forces were organized quite differently. One zone lay along Islamic frontiers. The other represented interior regions where most Moslems lived.

Along external frontiers a special Moslem military organization had appeared by the ninth century as boundaries became relatively stable. It was composed of marcher warriors known as *ghazis* on land or pirates on the sea who manned a frontier defense zone studded with fortifications including, at times, fortified cities. All Moslems living in such a zone (and this included townsmen, merchants, landowners, and hill tribesmen) could expect to be called out on a regular basis to take part in offensive or defensive military operations as the occasion warranted. Included in such groups was a strong religious element attracted to frontier war zones by the Moslem tradition of the *jihad* or holy war. Such a zone existed along the Ebro and Duero lines which separated Al-Andālūs from the Spanish Christian kingdoms to the north or in the mountains and hills which lay between the Byzantine Empire and Khazaria and the settled Moslem population of Syria, Iraq, and western Iran. We find a third such zone also along the frontiers which separated Moslem Turkestan and Khorasan from Turkic tribal areas to the east and from northern India. They had their counterparts in the Mediterranean, where from the ninth century on a series of naval frontiers had appeared which were based upon Tortosa, the Balearics, Fraxinetum, Monte Garigliano, Sicily, and Bari in the west and Crete, Cilicia, and Cyprus in the east. No such zones existed along Indian Ocean shores because here the Moslem world faced no opponents who possessed organized navies.

By the late tenth century the Islamic world experienced serious difficulties along some frontier military zones, especially those facing the Byzantine Empire. Here a revived Byzantine military and naval establishment began by overrunning outposts like Monte Garigliano and Bari in southern Italy and advancing in force across the Taurus Mountains. This process accelerated during the tenth century as Byzantine fleets and armies regained Crete, Cyprus, and Cilicia and advanced deep into Armenia and northern Syria, leaving Islamic border defenses in a very sorry state. In the western Mediterranean, however, Moslem border defenses proved more able to resist pressures and here, despite the fall of Fraxinetum, Sicily, the Balearics, and

Tortosa remained in Moslem hands, and Christians were pushed back along the Duero and Ebro lines by Umayyad Spanish rulers. Finally, changes began to take place along the ghazi borders of Moslem Turkestan, which we will examine later. On the whole, however, it seems fair to state that until the end of the tenth century, except as regards Byzantium, Islamic civilization was able to maintain its military strength along its borders which protected its heartland from serious attack.

In the second or internal zone quite a different military situation had come to prevail. Here military power was organized into permanent naval establishments and military forces. Rulers like the Fatimids and their western viceroys or the Umayyads of Spain possessed well-organized war fleets, built in special dockyards, maintained in naval bases, and manned by professional sailors and naval officers. These same monarchs also kept contingents of professional troops in their capitals to maintain authority and to protect them from their enemies. Such troops were no longer composed of levies raised from among the settled or civilized Moslem population. Instead they were formed from well-trained slave and mercenary forces: for the most part Turkish *mameluks* in Egypt, Iraq, and the east with some Armenian, Berber, Negro, and Iranian hill folk mixed in; while in the Maghreb and Spain the most dependable forces were Berbers, Christian Spanish mercenaries, and European slaves bought from Italian or Jewish merchants. Such troops were extremely competent professional warriors, but they had no links with the rich unarmed Moslem elites of town and countryside. A divorce had taken place, except along frontiers, between the warrior class and the cultivated governing, religious, and business element, and this separation was to have serious consequences for Islamic civilization in the future.

By this time the Moslem world formed the largest expanse of territory yet to appear in which goods could flow relatively freely over vast distances. A flourishing local trade linked towns and nearby fertile lands using land routes or local river and sea transport. But, a much more important factor in the Islamic economy was the international commerce and pilgrim traffic to the Holy Places, which traveled vast distances over land and sea routes. The merchants and pilgrims who took part in this traffic faced long journeys through pirate-infested waters or along routes threatened by predatory local authorities and tribesmen. For profit and protection they formed huge caravans or groupings of ships in convoy when they traveled. Such convoys and caravans tended to become seasonal affairs, moving merchants, travelers, and their goods in a regular rhythm influenced by the winds and weather conditions along certain recognized routes.

Two main routes linked the center of the Moslem world with its western provinces. One was a sea route from Alexandria to Tunisian ports and Sicily and then on to Spanish shores, either by way of the coast of the Maghreb or by way of Sardinia and the Balearics. It then proceeded through the Straits of Gibraltar to Atlantic Morocco or to Seville and Lisbon. Within Andalusia traffic followed inland routes to Saragossa by way of Cordoba and Toledo or directly up the Ebro from Tortosa. A generally parallel route went by land from Cairo to southern Tunis and on to Sigilmasa in southern Morocco by way of Wargla. Wargla and Sigilmasa were also the termini of caravan trails that crossed the Sahara to Bornu and Kanem near Lake Chad or to Ghana and the bend of the Niger which was the source of much of the gold greatly prized by the Moslem world.

On the other side of Egypt, traffic either went by sea to Syrian ports or followed caravan routes to Jerusalem, Damascus, and Aleppo where they joined those leading to Mosul and Baghdad. Or merchants and pilgrims could proceed up the Nile and then cross the Nubian Desert to Red Sea emporiums like Aidhab where they could find ships and sail across to Jidda or down the Red Sea to Aden and then on to the coasts of India and Ceylon. From Aden they could also travel down East African shores to the land of the Zeng.

A second great complex of routes originated in Baghdad where a number of caravan routes had their termini. One of these led north to Trebizond by way of Hamadan and Tabriz. Still another went from Hamadan across northern Persia, either all the way to Bokhara and Samarkand or branched off to reach northern India by way of Afghanistan. Still a third went southeast from Baghdad to Shiraz and Kirman. Equally important were maritime routes reaching Baghdad. Deep-water ports in the Persian Gulf located at Siraf and the island of Kish were connected by small boats with Basra and lower Iraq. At Siraf and Kish larger vessels were to be found which traveled by sea to Sind and India's western shores and Ceylon along coastal routes or with monsoon winds sailed directly to Malabar and beyond or to East Africa. From the Turkestan termini of the great Iraqi trade, a number of routes fanned out, also. Several went northwest to Itil on the lower Volga and to the land of the Bulgars. Others went to China by way of Mongolia and the kingdom of Hsi Hsia.

By the late tenth century the more vital and prosperous of these two great route complexes was centered in Egypt, in contrast to the eighth and ninth centuries when the Baghdad-Turkestan complex was the more active.

Merchants who lived in the Islamic world during this period sailed all the way to China, as we have noted, or traveled in large numbers to black Africa, either by sea along the Somali coast or by following caravan trails which crossed the Sahara. But they were less active in traveling in other directions beyond Dar-es-Islam. For instance, by now few of them went beyond Itil and the land of the Bulgars and most trading with Byzantium only went as far as Cyprus, Antioch, Cilicia, and Trebizond. The same is true of Islamic traders in the west where few went north of Sicily or Naples or traded beyond Tortosa, Saragossa, Toledo, or Lisbon, for reasons which will be discussed later. Granted these limitations, the range and extent of the great international commercial traffic which merchants of the Islamic world carried on successfully by the end of the first millennium is staggering indeed.

One of the factors which facilitated Moslem international trade was an abundant supply of money in the form of gold *dinars* and silver *dirhems* which were to be found everywhere. Moslem coins were first issued about 700, and initially the dinar was only used in the central area, while the dirhem circulated as the main currency in Spain and in former Sassanian territory. During the late ninth and tenth centuries, however, the *dinar* spread throughout both eastern and western regions, in no small measure because of new large supplies of gold from the Sudan, until it became the prevailing medium of exchange in Umayyad Spain, Iraq, and western Persia. Though dinars also became more abundant in Khorasan and Turkestan at this time, they never completely replaced the silver dirhem as the prevailing currency in general use. Thus the entire Islamic world now operated with a bimetallist monetary system which facilitated commerce, with the dinar serving as the most important coin in international commerce.

Still another financial element linked the various parts of Dar-es-Islam and gave it a common economic life: the widespread development of credit by its merchants, its financiers, and even its governments. Such credit in various forms helped to develop industry and mining and made possible the introduction of advanced techniques in agriculture, since it obviated the need to transfer large amounts of cash in every business transaction. Particularly important was the development of universally accepted bills of exchange and checks which could take the place of cash and were issued by both Jewish and non-Jewish bankers and merchants in centers like Cairo, Basra, and Baghdad whose businessmen maintained a network of trading connections from Iraq, the Yemen, and Cairo in the east to the Maghreb, Sicily, and Spain in the west.

A regular exchange of primary raw materials and industrial wares throughout Islamic territory formed another economic link in Islamic unity. Northern Syria, Egypt, the Maghreb, and Sicily regularly exported surpluses of wheat to distant markets, just as Tunisia, Spain, and Syria did with their olive oil. Despite Koranic prohibitions against wine, it was exported from Syria, southern Persia, and Al-Andalūs, as was the sugar produced in Spain, Sicily, Syria, Persia, and Egypt, and rice grown in a number of places and especially near the Caspian and in Al-Andalūs. To these foodstuffs one should add dried fruits from the west, dates from newly acclimatized palm trees, and animals like the barbs of North Africa, the Arab steeds of Syria, the great horses of Iran, and the ponies of Turkestan which were prized in many sections of this world of Islam. There was even an export market for tuna caught off Moroccan and Spanish Atlantic coasts and in Tunisian waters.

Other natural products which formed the staple trade items of this period were wool and hides from the Maghreb, salt—especially that traded to the Sudan—pearls from the Persian Gulf, and coral found in Mediterranean and Red Sea waters, and a variety of metals such as copper, silver, lead, mercury, and iron. Important traffic also took place in alum, in dyestuffs such as saffron or woad, and in a number of perfumes.

Also reaching a wide export market were textiles, each area producing its own specialty, such as the silks woven in Persia, Khorasan, Syria, Al-Andālūs, and Sicily, the cottons from northern Iraq, Persia, and Khorasan, and the linens and brocades made in Egypt. Metal wares of various sorts and art objects also played a role in this fantastically varied and abundant trade.

Despite the variety of products which originated within the Islamic world and which were traded by the merchants who frequented its great maritime routes and caravan trails, there were still some which were in short supply and had to be imported from outside areas. Perhaps the most important of these was timber. Adequate wood for shipbuilding and other purposes was to be found only in Spain, along western Maghrebi coasts, and in Sicily. Elsewhere it was very scarce, especially after the loss of timber-rich areas of Crete and Cilicia to Byzantium. This meant that to the east of Tunis adequate supplies of wood could be found only along the Syrian coast, or in the mountains of Armenia or northern Persia. Though some wood could be sent east from Maghrebi shores, most of it had to be imported in Italian bottoms from the Adriatic or from western Italian shores, or from Byzantium, when the latter's authorities allowed it to be shipped from her islands, or from Anatolian forests. In addition, teak and coconut palm and naval stores left India for the Red Sea and the Persian Gulf.

Almost as important was a lack of iron, for this metal was only to be found in Islamic western provinces and in Armenian uplands. It was imported in the form of iron bars, swords, and other weapons from Western Europe via Italian ports like Venice and by way of Russian rivers. A particularly fine grade of iron and steel produced in continental India also found its way to the Islamic world. Other necessary imports were furs, honey, and wax from the Baltic and northern Russia, spices and gems from the Indic world, and gold mainly from the Sudan, but also from the Deccan. East Africa too was a source of gold as well as a prized variety of elephant ivory.

Finally, we need to add one rather specialized deficiency—slaves. By the tenth century a few slaves were still being imported from East Africa to serve as labor in the plantations of Iraq and southern Persia. But most were needed for other purposes such as domestic service, for the harems of the rich and powerful, or as soldiers serving in the armies of Islamic rulers. One important source of such slaves was the Zeng coast of East Africa, but many blacks also arrived in the Islamic world by way of the Nile or across the Sahara to the Mediterranean. Europe was still another source of slaves, especially its Slavic regions, whence they were shipped to the Moslem world by Jewish merchants of Verdun, by Venetian, Amalfian, and Rūs traders who traveled to Turkestan and Khorasan. Perhaps the most important group of slaves, however, were the Turks who were particularly prized as mameluks. They were sent from Turkestan all over the eastern and central provinces of Islam. Certainly the extent of this internal and external slave traffic can hardly be overestimated during the course of the tenth century.

One might well raise the question as to whether the extensive imports mentioned above resulted in an adverse balance of trade for the Islamic world despite the fact that most of them were exchanged for products which this civilization itself produced. It is difficult to give any definitive answer to such a question. We can, however, attempt some generalities. Trade with the world of black Africa, where gold, slaves, and ivory were exchanged for salt and a variety of trinkets and trade goods, was undoubtedly a favorable one for Islamic merchants. It would appear that commerce with the Indic world was generally in balance at this time. There is more doubt, however, when one examines trade carried on with Western Europe or with the Byzantine-Russian complex. Though trade with Western Europe was slight, being mainly carried on with a few Italian ports or with Spain, these probably sold more in the form of slaves, timber, and iron than they bought and thus a slightly unfavorable balance of trade for Islam resulted. The same thing seems to be true of the carefully controlled trade which was carried on with Byzantium, judging from the fact that this empire steadily increased its gold supplies during these years. But it was trade with Russia and the Baltic areas that really seems to have produced the most unfavorable balance of trade, considering the hoards of Moslem dirhems from this period which have been discovered there. Overall, however, it would seem that until the year 1000 the Islamic world's trade with the outside world was sufficiently in balance so that it was able to procure all the wares and goods of various sorts which were in short supply within the borders of its civilization and still maintain a remarkable level of economic activity.

No subject is more important and in the case of the Islamic world more hazardous for speculation than the matter of its population. This is because exact figures are all but impossible to establish and because most scholars who have attempted to estimate the size of Moslem cities have been misled by the figures given by writers and geographers of the period, most of whom exaggerate the population of the areas they treat. Second, we have no reliable figures concerning any part of the settled peasant population of the Islamic world except Egypt. And, finally, there is no reliable basis for estimating the size of the tribes in the mountainous regions or in the steppes and deserts of Islamic areas.

In the light of all this, perhaps the best way we can proceed is as follows. Since by the end of the tenth century the Islamic world had reached the optimum level in using its varied resources, we would probably be safe to consider that its hill and desert tribesmen were no more numerous than they were in relatively recent times, and so we can use modern figures for them. To this we should add the relatively good figures we possess for Egypt's rural population and apply them to other farming areas like Iraq and Spanish river valleys and coastal plains. Then we can try to use more realistic figures when we estimate the size of Islamic urban centers.

There is a general agreement among everyone that the largest Islamic city of the tenth century was Baghdad. A conservative estimate of its size would run between 200,000 and 300,000, perhaps a bit more if its suburbs are included. Cairo, Josiah Russell estimates, had a population of between 60,000 and 90,000. Bokhara, according to Richard Frye, may have had 100,000 inhabitants, but was probably smaller than that. Cordoba during these years was probably the largest western Moslem urban center and may have had between 50,000 and 100,000 people living inside its town area. Other towns in Al-Andālūs and the Maghreb probably did not exceed 30,000 to 50,000 inhabitants. The Moslem world then had one metropolis—Baghdad; a number of important cities whose population ranged between 50,000 and 100,000; a host of cities in the 30,000 to 50,000 class; plus a number of smaller ones as well. The population of Egypt numbered about 2,500,000 in the late tenth century, which gives us some clues as to the population density of Iraq, the coastal regions of Tunisia and Morocco, and the Oxus-Jaxartes region.

Taking all of this together and interpolating modern figures for the population of upland and desert areas, we can arrive at an overall total for the Islamic world of 50,000,000 to 80,000,000 people with 60,000,000 probably representing the best estimate and one which is only slightly higher than our estimate for the Indic world. Breaking that down still further, we can probably say that Islamic regions west of Libya had a population of about 15,000,000, and Egypt, Syria, Libya, and the Arabian Peninsula the same. Iraq, western Persia, and the Persian Gulf region may have also had some 15,000,000 inhabitants and so, too, did eastern Persia, Afghanistan, Sind, Khorasan, and Moslem Turkestan. These figures, of course, include all nomadic and seminomadic tribal peoples along with town dwellers and settled farmers. It is doubtful that the population of the Islamic world could have increased substantially during the period covered by this work, since it could not develop any new resources to support a larger population.

Having considered at length the Islamic world in the light of those factors which gave it a certain overall unity, let us now examine it in more detail, with special reference to its political structure and maritime organization on a regional basis. We should begin by emphasizing that, despite its overall unity, by the tenth century one can divide the Islamic world into three relatively distinct general areas. The first of these was a western region which extended from Libya to the Atlantic and lay south of Christian Spain and Italy and north of the Sudan. This area had long been separated politically from the rest of the Moslem world, since as early as 800 it was controlled by a number of independent local dynasties, the Umayyads of Iberia and the Idrissids, Rostemids, and Aghlabids of North Africa. By the end of the tenth century it was under the dominion of two great states, the Umayyad caliphate of Cordoba and the Fatimids of Cairo who ruled their western provinces using viceroys of whom the Zirids of Mehdia were the most important.

The power of Umayyad Spain had increased during the reign of Abd-ar-Rahman III, who had proclaimed himself caliph early in the tenth century. By the year 1000 it was ruled by a warlord called Almansor. The latter not only had firm control over Al-Andālūs and its Moslem Marcher lords but had used an army of slave and mercenary troops to force the Christian states of northern Spain to accept his overlordship after a series of campaigns which saw Barcelona captured in 985 and Santiago da Compostela sacked in 992. His fleets kept the Balearics in the Umayyad orbit and provided a defense against Viking incursions along Atlantic shores, the last of which had occurred in 995.

Almansor also controlled much of Morocco, thanks to alliances with the smaller princes of this region and with Berber Zenata tribesmen of the interior, and this dominion extended south to include Sigilmasa which was the main terminus of caravan routes leading to the gold of the Sudan. The great enemies of the Umayyads were the Fatimids, who still controlled the rest of the Maghreb and Sicily in the year 1000 and whose claims to the caliphate made this rivalry even more intense.

Western Fatimid lands were ruled by the Zirids who were of sedentary Sanhaja Berber origin and who had taken over Mehdia, the old Fatimid capital, when the latter moved to Cairo. As Fatimid viceroys, they ruled Tripoli and Tunis directly and supervised the Kalbite emirs of Sicily and another Sanhaja Berber family called the Hammadids who were supreme in what today is Algeria. Since both Ziridites and Hammadids were Sanhaja Berbers, they were the hereditary enemies of Zenata tribesmen who lived in Morocco and were allied with the Umayyads. They had extensive naval establishments and contingents of slave and mercenary troops which allowed them to contend with Umayyad Spain on equal terms. Though they had lost Sigilmasa to the latter, they continued to control Wargla and a number of southern Tunisian oases which were also the termini of trans-Saharan caravan routes leading to Kanem and the Niger from which it was possible to tap the Sudan's supply of gold. Their location also enabled them to control the great east-west routes which linked Spain and Morocco with the world of the eastern Mediterranean.

Two states south of the Sahara—Kanem and Ghana—were closely linked with the Moslem west. Kanem was near Lake Chad, and Ghana, whose capital was called Audoghast, was located in the general area of the upper

Senegal and upper Niger rivers. Both were kingdoms ruled by pagan black royal families, and Ghana was especially important as a source of gold which it traded with the north. Both, by the year 1000, were beginning to be affected in a number of ways by the Moslem civilization which merchants were introducing into this part of the Sudan.

Though Arab influences were decisive throughout much of the western Islamic area, thanks to an earlier settlement there of Arab tribesmen and considerable Arabization of town and countryside alike, the entire region also had a distinct Berber flavor. This was especially true of the Kabylie plateau of Algeria, all of Morocco, and parts of Spain and Sicily where large numbers of Berbers had settled in hilly or mountainous regions. In the tenth century many more Berbers also had come to Tunisia and the Iberian Peninsula as mercenary troops and stayed on to give these provinces a special racial mix. At the same time a reverse migration also was taking place as a number of Moslems of native Spanish stock, from Al-Andālūs, crossed into North Africa, some of these founding Fez. The western portion of the Islamic world, then, by the late tenth century was steadily becoming more Arabized in its culture even as the Berber majority and elements of the original Latin population were coalescing to form a rather distinctive civilization. Only in Sicily and Spain did a significant body of Christians still exist, and even here they were adopting so many elements of Islamic civilization that in Spain these Christian Mozarabs, as they were called, had come to differ significantly from their coreligionists in the northern part of the Iberian Peninsula.

The settled world of the west had developed rapidly during the ninth and tenth centuries as the towns grew in population, commerce increased, and a more advanced agriculture made its appearance almost everywhere, along with new techniques of manufacturing and mining. Nevertheless, it faced two serious problems in addition to the rivalries which divided the Umayyads and their client states from those who accepted Fatimid overlordship. One was how to deal with Christian neighbors, especially those living in northern Spain. During the ninth century these latter had advanced south and gained considerable territory from Moslem rulers, especially near the Duero. Abd-ar-Rahman III and Almansor had reversed this trend during the tenth century, but they had not been able to find any long-range solution which could be effective in restraining this warlike society for whom the riches of Al-Andālūs were a constant temptation. There was also a potential problem with the Latin West on the sea where again we find Christian Europeans taking the offensive, often with Byzantine help, to wipe out advancing Moslem pirate bases. Spanish and Sicilian fleets were still able to blunt Byzantium's maritime offensive in western waters in 965, but again the potential danger remained to be dealt with in the future.

The second problem was that of dealing with nomadic tribes who lived in the Sahara and its borderlands. Regularly during the ninth and tenth centuries such nomads had moved north in force to attack settled areas, only to be defeated with considerable difficulty. But they remained a threat to both the Fatimid viceroys who ruled most of the Maghreb as well as to the rulers of Ghana on the other side of the desert—a threat which the next century was to see develop in a rather dramatic way.

A second general area of the Islamic world was composed of Libya, Egypt, most of Syria, and the Red Sea area, as well as the remote Christian realms of Nubia and Ethiopia. This region, which was now almost completely Arabic-speaking, had had a certain overall unity since the time of the Tulunids and Ikhshids who took over Egypt in the last two centuries. By the late tenth it had come to be controlled by a Shia Fatimid dynasty who ruled most of this area directly from its capital at Cairo, and who as caliphs controlled the Hejaz and its holy places, as well as being closely allied to the Shia Zaidids who ruled the Yemen. Since the Fatimids controlled both the Mediterranean and Red Sea sides of that great trade route complex leading to Ghana, Morocco, and Spain on one side and to India, Ceylon, and East African shores on the other, their realm was an extremely prosperous one. Indeed, by now this commerce was beginning to make Cairo and Egypt, where trade centered, more important than Baghdad and Iraq, as can be seen when one examines in detail the Geniza documentation, important Jewish merchant archives in Cairo which allow us to survey the economic life of the Islamic world with considerable precision.

The Fatimids maintained a large fleet in Egyptian and Syrian ports and could count on contingents maintained by their western viceroys as well. They also had a well-organized standing army of Berber, Negro, and Turkish mameluk and mercenary troops. They were served by an effective administrative force of civilians in which Coptic and Jewish bureaucrats played an important role.

Nevertheless, they, too, faced a number of serious problems. First, the majority of Moslems in the areas which they controlled were Sunni and refused to accept their Shi'ism, despite the very effective propaganda machine which they maintained both inside their realm and outside it. Second, their empire, as has already been noted, had to face the intermittent hostility of the Bedouin tribes of the Arabian Peninsula, who were organized under Qarmathian heretical auspices and regularly raided the settled peasantry of Syria and Palestine and the holy places as well. Fatimid efforts to curb these tribes were only partially successful by the end of the tenth century.

Finally, the Fatimids had every reason to fear another external foe, the Byzantine Empire, which, as has been noted, had been able to advance southeast to take Crete, Cyprus, Cilicia, and northern Syria during the late tenth century. Initially, this Byzantine advance had helped the Fatimids by distracting their Moslem enemies while the Fatimids were capturing Egypt. But once established there and in Syria, they found themselves in turn threatened by Byzantine success on the land and sea, especially since the areas taken by Constantinople's forces contained the most important nearby timber resources for maintaining an effective navy. They were able to halt the advance of Byzantium into central Syria in a series of naval actions that took place about the year 1000. At the same time they managed to bring the Shia Hamdanids of Aleppo and Mosul into their network of alliances. But their control over a restive Syria remained as uncertain and insecure as their arrangements with the Bedouin tribes of Arabia and their authority over the Sunni majority whom they ruled, their wealth and their effective government notwithstanding.

A third, eastern region of the Islamic world extended from Aleppo and northern Syria to the borders of eastern Turkestan and Hindu India. It centered in the west around Baghdad and in the east around the cities of Khorasan. Except in northern Syria, deserts separated it from the central portion of the Islamic world where the Fatimids held sway, and in general this area represented the region which an earlier Sassanian empire had ruled with a few additional regions like Turkestan and Sind added to it. By the late tenth century it had come to be divided into a number of principalities, most of which were hostile to one another.

The first of these was a state controlled by the Hamdanids in northern Syria and Iraq. This Shi'ite family of Arab descent served as border emirs along a sensitive frontier that faced Byzantium. They had been unable to stop the advance of Byzantine forces into Cilicia and northern Syria, and by the end of the tenth century were very much on the defensive and relied on an alliance with Fatimid Egypt to maintain their authority in the area they governed.

More important was the realm of the Buyids (or Buwayids), which included most of Iraq and western Persia. The Buyids were an Iranian family of moderate Shi'ites who had become powerful during the first half of the tenth century. They controlled Baghdad, where the orthodox Abbasid caliph had his residence, as well as a large Sunni population in Iraq and Iran by making use of armed forces composed of Turkish mameluks and Persian Daylamite tribesmen. These troops enabled them to keep their Hamdanid rivals in check, to dominate the Armenian uplands in the face of a Byzantine advance, and to protect southern Iraq from Qarmathian invasion. By the year 1000 they were using them to expand their authority to the east at the expense of their principal rivals, the Saminids. One of the more interesting features of their governmental system was their use of iqtà, which were grants of rights of taxation over certain local districts made to important officials and military officers, which allowed the latter to raise revenues to pay their own salaries—a kind of incipient feudalism which was to be taken over and elaborated during the next century by their successors, the Seljuk rulers. The tensions which existed between the majority of their subjects, who were Sunni, and their own Shia claims and pretensions made their power insecure, as did the lack of adequate revenues in their treasury to pay their armed forces and their administrative officials.

The last important state in the east was ruled by the Saminids and included within its boundaries eastern Iran, Khorasan, and Moslem Turkestan. The Saminids, who like the Buyids were of Persian origin, had appeared at about the same time as these latter and about 950 were at the height of their power. Their rule was based upon a well-organized bureaucracy centered in their capital, Bokhara, and an army of Turkish mameluks. By the late tenth century, they were staunchly Sunni as were almost all of their subjects. Despite the lack of religious conflict within their realm, which strengthened their authority, by this time they were in serious trouble for other reasons.

Part of this was the result of their loss of territory, already noted, to their western neighbors, the Buyids. But perhaps more important as a cause of weakness was the sudden appearance of a new Turkish ruling family, the Gaznavids, at Gazna in Afghanistan. This family, though it still recognized the Saminids as overlords, was beginning to chart an independent course of its own. Perhaps because of this, the Saminids began to lose control of their eastern provinces and by 983 seem to have been unable to keep the great Hindu Kush silver mines in operation—mines which were the source of much of their revenues. Even more ominous for them were developments to the northeast where a new powerful Turkish tribal confederacy, that of the Karakhanids, had arisen in eastern Turkestan. These latter were fervent new converts to Islam and were pushing inexorably toward the Oxus-Jaxartes river basin. Also by this time the Saminids seem to have lost control over those Turkish tribes who lived to the northwest between Kwarezehm and the lower Volga. Some of these tribes, such as the pagan Cumans and Po-lovtzi, were already moving westward toward the steppes of southern Russia. Others who had accepted Islam and whom we are to know later on as the Seljuks were more active to the south and were beginning to encroach upon the oases in which Bokhara and neighboring cities were located and were soon to inaugurate a new era.

The tenth century also saw a number of other important changes take place in these eastern provinces of Islamic civilization. The first of these was a renaissance in the use of Persian as a language of literature and general culture. This took place especially in Saminid domains where a new Arabized Persian called Farsi emerged to take the place of Arabic and Daric, the older Persian which was still used in western Iran. A large number of scholars in Bokhara and elsewhere used Farsi as a language for poetry, history, and culture in general and even translated the Arab historian Tabari into Farsi to make his works more accessible to a wider public. Since this literary Persian was adopted by Turkish dynasties like the Gaznavids almost at once, its domination over much of eastern Islam was assured for centuries to come—even though Arabic continued to be used both by the ulema class and the *diqans* who formed the proprietary and administrative elite.

Second, this period saw a rivalry, not yet resolved, between heretical Shi'ism and Sunni orthodoxy. As we have pointed out, a large number of the rulers of eastern Islamic lands, especially toward the west, were moderate Shi'ites as were some of their subjects. Most of those to the east, rulers and ruled alike, were Sunni. The conflicts between the two groups seriously weakened the governments of the region and helped to make possible important future political changes.

In the third place, it is important to emphasize that by the late tenth century this whole region faced serious economic difficulties, unlike central and western Moslem areas which were remarkably prosperous. In an Iraq dominated by Baghdad and the general Persian Gulf area, these problems had begun as a result of the great slave revolts of the ninth century which were followed by disorders attendant upon Qarmathian incursions. No doubt Byzantine encroachments in Armenia and northern Syria made the situation worse.

One result of all this was the financial difficulties in which Iraq and Baghdad, in particular, found themselves and which caused their Buyid overlords to use iqtàs to provide money for their troops who could no longer be supported by the public treasury. Still another was the decline of Siraf as a major center of maritime trade to the Indic world and a general shift of this trade to a Red Sea–Cairo route dominated by the Fatimids.

Still worse conditions, though, were to be found further to the east in Saminid lands. Here the closing of the silver mines, the end of trade going to Itil and the Volga, Karakhanid encroachments, and the raiding activities of other Turkic tribes all combined to compromise seriously the prosperity of cities like Samarkand and Bokhara. Irrigation works and walls needed for the defense of the settled population decayed, the prosperity of the *diqan* gentry declined, and centers of economic life moved southwest toward Nishapur and the cities of Khorasan. A serious crisis began to affect the economy of eastern Islamic lands whose full effects were not to become apparent until the next century.

Finally, before ending our analysis of Islamic civilization, we need to examine the Moslem world's maritime strength and organization by the end of the first millennium. Its influence extended into two quite distinct areas— the Indian Ocean and the Mediterranean. Moslem maritime activities in the Persian Gulf, Red Sea, and Indian Ocean areas were essentially an aspect of Indic maritime development in every sense of the word. This meant the ships found there were built in the Indic fashion using teak and coconut palm logs sewn together without the use of nails. It meant the extensive use of monsoon routes to carry merchants to East African shores as well as to Indian coasts and beyond that to East Asia. It also meant that in these waters where no organized navies existed, except perhaps around Aden, traffic by sea was essentially peaceful in character—a peace interrupted only by intermittent piracy of a minor sort.

In the Mediterranean, on the other hand, the Moslem world faced well-organized Byzantine fleets in eastern and central waters and a potential threat from western Christian flotillas based in Italy and Catalonia, as well as Vikings who could sail freely along Atlantic shores. As a result, not only do we find ghazi pirate fleets at Tortosa, in the Balearics, and in Sicily, we also find well-organized navies maintained by the Spanish Umayyads, Ziridite North Africans, and the Fatimids of Egypt and Syria. Though such fleets were not able to prevent the Byzantines from regaining Crete, Cyprus, and Cilicia, they were able to prevent any further advance of their sea power and, until after the year 1000, kept Latin Westerners penned up along their own coasts where they could not interfere with Moslem Mediterranean commerce.

By the last years of the tenth century, this commerce which brought prosperity to the central and western provinces of the Islamic world made use of a number of different kinds of ships built in the Mediterranean fashion using nails and timber which often had to be imported from Latin or Greek Christendom. Some of these ships were small lateen-rigged craft similar to those in use elsewhere in the Mediterranean. Others were oared, carvel-built galleys, which were particularly useful in war. Most Islamic bulk cargoes, however, seem to have been carried in towed barges or in large round ships which sailed in convoy between the eastern and western Mediterranean—ships that were the prototype of the Italian round ships of the High Middle Ages. Such was the Moslem naval and maritime organization in the Mediterranean on the eve of the great changes which were to take place there in the course of the eleventh century.

Byzantine-Russian
Civilization

The fourth great civilization of this period, the Byzantine-Russian, is more difficult to grasp, since at the end of the tenth century it was still in the process of being formed into a relatively coherent whole. It was made up of three quite distinct regions. One of these was the Byzantine Empire itself as it had emerged by the year 1000 under the rule of the powerful Basil II. The second was a broad expanse of plains and steppes which lay north of the Caucasus and west of the Volga along the shores of the Black Sea. The third region, Kievan Russia, was composed of rolling wooded hills and pine forests north of the southern Russian steppes. It lay between the Urals and the Pripet marshes and was inhabited by Finnish tribes and Slavs who were the ancestors of the present Great Russians, White Russians, and Ruthenians.

The boundaries of this Byzantine-Russian complex were by no means as distinct as those of Islamic, Indic, or East Asian civilizations. Though those facing the Islamic world to the south and southeast were relatively fixed, the same cannot be said of those which separated the South Russian steppes from Moslem Turkestan to the east.

If it is hard to discern any clear boundaries between the Russian steppes and those of Turkestan, those separating the Byzantine-Russian world from Western Europe were even more difficult to discern by the end of the tenth century. For instance, in Italy considerable Byzantine influence was exercised beyond its southern Italian themes, in Campanian cities, Lombard duchies, papal Rome, and a Venice which was expanding along the Dalmatian coast with Constantinople's blessing. And what was true of Italy was also true of boundaries in the Balkan Peninsula as well, where, after absorbing the first Bulgarian empire, Byzantium had reached a Serbo-Croatian-Hungarian zone where it competed with Latin Christendom. The same situation prevailed to the north where Pecheneks met Hungarians and Poles were in contact with Kievan Rūs and Baltic pagan tribesmen were subject to both Scandinavian and Russian influences.

Nevertheless, despite the amorphous nature of some of its boundaries, especially to the west, and despite a climate which varied from the cold weather of the Russian north to the Mediterranean warmth of the Byzantine Aegean littoral, one geographical feature served to tie this entire Byzantine-Russian world together. The Aegean and Black seas network formed its heartland and was of particular importance to the great city of Constantinople which lay between them. It was by way of the Black Sea that the tenth-century Byzantine world communicated with the steppes and forests of Russia. To the south the Aegean played a similar role and knit together the Byzantine Empire on the Mediterranean side, providing easy access east to northern Syrian ports and west to Italy and the Adriatic. The central bastion of this maritime-fluvial complex, the walled capital of the Byzantine Empire, Constantinople, having resisted all earlier attacks, by the year 1000 seemed stronger than ever as Byzantine flotillas dominated these waters and kept Moslems and other potential enemies at arm's length.

If a central network of seas and rivers lent a certain overall unity to this Byzantine-Russian complex, so too did religion. By the year 1000 most of this world was beginning to share a common Eastern or Orthodox Christian faith. This faith was centered in the Byzantine Empire itself, where the emperor, along with the patriarch of Constantinople as a somewhat difficult junior partner, headed a hierarchy of secular clergy and a large number of monastic institutions which directed the religious life of the empire's population. The Orthodox church had long used Greek as its language of theology and liturgical worship and had developed a monasticism of a decentralized sort which flourished in both the countryside and in urban areas and reached its apogee in the monastic communities of Mount Athos. After a long struggle over Iconoclasm, which helped to alienate the Latin West, a religious consensus had been reached which settled this church's theology and organization and its relationship to the imperial government and which made it a force which promoted unity among most of the Christian population.

Once this religious consensus had been achieved, the Orthodox church began to look beyond its borders in an attempt to convert its pagan neighbors. Generally speaking, except in the Caucasus, it had long lagged behind the Latin church in assuming a missionary role. Now all this changed as a number of missionaries, of whom Cyril and Methodius were the most famous, began a conversion of the Slavs of the Balkans during the late ninth century. This effort continued throughout the tenth century as Orthodox Christianity reached Hungary and made some headway among the Vlachs who lived in the Rumanian uplands north of the Danube.

The greatest success which Orthodox Christianity achieved, however, was the conversion of Kievan Russia. This had begun when Olga, the mother of Prince Sviatoslav of Kiev, was baptized in 957. It was crowned with success when her grandson, Vladimir, accepted Orthodox Christianity for himself and his people in 989. Since Byzantine monks soon arrived in Kiev in large numbers and Vladimir supported their conversion efforts wholeheartedly, Kievan Russia soon became a part of a broader cultural area which Dmitri Oblensky has called the Byzantine Commonwealth.

Two things helped to spread Orthodox Christianity into pagan Slavic areas in addition to the zeal of its missionaries and the support of the imperial Byzantine government. One was a decision to present the scripture and the liturgy of its Greek Orthodox Christianity to new converts in Slavic instead of Greek and the invention of a special Cyrillic alphabet for this purpose. The second was that churches and hierarchies beyond the empire's borders were allowed a large measure of autonomy under the general supervision of the patriarch of Constantinople. The first decision made it easier for converts to accept the Christian faith. The second meant that independent Slavic rulers felt they could accept the Orthodox Christianity without having their church hierarchies under the direct political control of the Byzantine emperor.

It is worth emphasizing that this Orthodox Christianity which spread so rapidly among the Slavs during these years made little headway in the steppe zone of southern Russia, except among the Vlachs of Rumania and a few of the Khazars. There were, perhaps, two reasons for this. One was that Christianity with its hierarchical priesthood and sedentary monasticism was not adapted to the nomadic life of the steppes. But more important was the fact that the Khazars, who dominated this area, were controlled by a ruling class who had accepted Judaism, which not only kept Christianity from spreading among the tribes of this region but also limited Islam's appeal.

Within this Byzantine-Russian world, however, there were religious forces which represented a potential or an actual threat to its overall religious unity. One of these was an independent Armenian church located in the Armenian uplands along the eastern borders of the empire. Though most Armenians who lived inside the empire were in communion with the Orthodox church as well as serving as the empire's most dependable soldiers—some even rising to become its emperors—a segment of them felt quite differently. These latter, living near Lake Van in small semi-independent principalities, had long preferred to accept the caliph of Baghdad as their overlord and to maintain a separate Armenian church under a *catholicos* or primate who lived in this area. This churchman steadfastly refused to subordinate himself or his church to either the emperor or the patriarch of Constantinople on theological, organizational, and linguistic grounds. Increasingly, however, during the tenth century as Byzantium expanded east, the Armenians loyal to their catholicos came under Byzantium rule, but they were unwilling, nevertheless, to give up their religious independence. Thus, a potentially dangerous threat to religious unity had come to exist along a frontier which a few years later was to be of great importance for the future of Byzantine-Russian civilization.

Similarly, during the late ninth and tenth centuries a second threat developed in the Balkans which affected the religious orthodoxy that tended to unite the Byzantine-Russian world. This came about as the result of the appearance and spread of a dualistic heresy known as Bogomilism. This heresy, which masqueraded as a Christian faith and which indeed had appropriated many Christian elements, was actually a set of dualistic beliefs which had developed out of Persian Manichaeanism. It struck new roots in Balkan Slavic territory, especially in Bosnia, and was one reason why the Bulgarian empire was able to resist the armies of Basil II for so long a time. It was to remain a source of religious disunity in the years to follow.

The Latin papacy to the west, however, was a much greater threat than the Bogomils or an independent Armenian church. This papacy continued to claim an overall control of Christendom which conflicted with that exercised by Byzantine emperors and patriarchs of Constantinople over the Orthodox church. Second, many areas in Italy and along the Adriatic, which Byzantium dominated directly or indirectly, acknowledged the pope as head of their church. In the third place, Latin missionaries were competing with the Greek Orthodox in the conversion of the Slavs, Hungarians, and Russians. And finally, after 962 papal Rome supported western German emperors who claimed a parity with their rivals, the *basilei* of Constantinople, who had a better claim to the imperial title. There were also a few doctrinal differences of a minor sort between the Latin and Orthodox churches, but these points of conflict were less important than those mentioned above.

Despite all these areas of friction and potential conflict that existed between them, in the late tenth century an uneasy peace prevailed between the two communions. The power which Byzantium could muster in its Italian themes and in Adriatic and southern Italian waters made popes slow to break with the Orthodox church and the emperors who controlled it, while marriage alliances, both actual and projected, between the Macedonian and Ottonian imperial houses tended to neutralize all-out papal support for the latter. So did Byzantine use of a local Roman aristocracy to periodically choose pontiffs there who were not Ottonian candidates. Basil II could even believe he had ended papal claims to control over *both* Latin and Greek Christendom by negotiating an agreement in which the patriarch of Constantinople was recognized as supreme over the Orthodox church in return

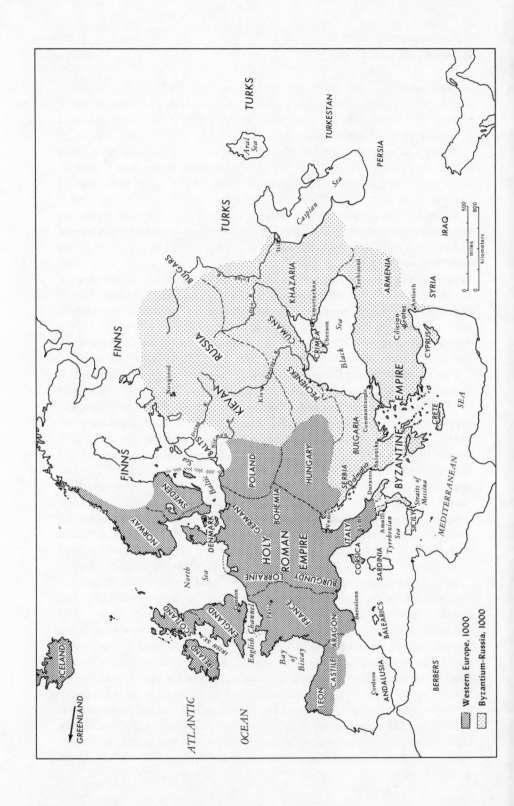

GREENLAND

ATLANTIC
OCEAN

ICELAND

FINNS

FINNS

TURKS

TURKS

TURKESTAN

Aral Sea

Caspian Sea

PERSIA

IRAQ

500
miles
800
kilometers

0

SYRIA

ARMENIA

Trebizond

Antioch
Cilician
Gates

CYPRUS

Black Sea

CRIMEA

Cherson

Tmutorakan

KHAZARIA

Volga R.

BULGARS

RUSSIA

Novgorod

Don R.

CUMANS

PECHENEGS

KIEVAN

Kiev

Dnieper R.

Constantinople

BYZANTINE

Oka R.

Dvina R.

BALTIC

Niemen R.

Baltic Sea

SWEDEN

NORWAY

DENMARK

North Sea

SCOTLAND

IRELAND

IRISH SEA

ENGLAND

English Channel

London

Bay of Biscay

FRANCE

Paris

GERMANY

POLAND

HOLY
ROMAN
EMPIRE

LORRAINE

BURGUNDY

BOHEMIA

HUNGARY

SERBIA

BULGARIA

Durazzo

Salonika

Dalmatia

Venice

ITALY

Amalfi

Tyrrhenian Sea

CORSICA

SARDINIA

SICILY

Straits of Messina

CRETE

EMPIRE

MEDITERRANEAN SEA

LEON

CASTILE

ARAGON

Barcelona

ANDALUSIA

Cordova

BALEARICS

BERBERS

Western Europe, 1000

Byzantium-Russia, 1000

for accepting a similar position for the pope in the West. Despite all of this, however, the potential threat of the papacy to the Byzantine-Russian world remained a reality, as did the threat of a hostile Bogomilism or a stubbornly independent Armenian Catholicism.

A third basis for unity in the Byzantine-Russian world was economic. This complex contained, as has been noted, three interconnected trade systems, one based on Constantinople, another in Khazaria, and a third in Kievan Russia. Of these the first was by far the most important and matched those of Baghdad and Cairo in nearby Dar-es-Islam. Constantinople lay at the heart of a network of maritime routes which passed south through the Aegean and reached the northern Syrian coast by way of Rhodes and Cyprus in one direction. In the other direction these southern routes reached Amalfi and Venice by way of the Straits of Messina and the Adriatic, respectively. On the Black Sea side a number of maritime routes were active as well. One of them followed Anatolian coasts to Trebizond. A second crossed the Euxine to Cherson in the Crimea or Tumortarkan in the Sea of Azov, and a third set went to the mouth of the Danube or to ports leading up the Dnieper to Kievan Russia.

Though maritime routes were the most important of all, there were two important land routes which reached Constantinople as well. One went southeast diagonally across Asia Minor to the Cilician Gates and northern Syria, and was to be used by Latins during the First Crusade. The other proceeded northwest from Constantinople to the lower Danube by way of Adrianople and Bulgaria. The only rival to Constantinople for economic dominance in the empire was the nearby city of Saloniki, which communicated by sea with Aegean trade routes and by land with a commerce which passed along the Vardar Valley to reach Nish, Belgrade, and Hungary. Except for Saloniki, almost all other important trading centers in the Byzantine world were located at the termini of trade routes: Antioch in northern Syria, Trebizond on the borders of Armenia, Cherson and Tumortarkan which faced the steppes of Khazaria, and Venice and Amalfi-Naples in the west.

The much less important trade complex of Khazaria, which for several centuries had been politically and economically linked with the Byzantium network, centered at Itil on the lower Volga. From here trade routes went north of the Caspian to Turkestan. Others went up the Volga to the land of the White Bulgars and northern Russia, followed the Don to central Russia or reached Tumortarkan or Cherson on the Black Sea by way of the Sea of Azov. By the late tenth century, however, Russian attacks on Itil and the White Bulgars seem to have resulted in an interruption of trade to the north just as steppe nomads to the east did the same with trade reaching Turkestan. Nevertheless, Khazaria was still able to maintain some commerce, though it was diminished in volume, with northern Persia by way of the Caspian and the Caucasus and with the Black Sea coast by way of the Sea of Azov.

The Kievan Russian trade complex was only beginning to expand in importance and to reach a certain level of trade maturity in this period. It was centered in a number of relatively new and growing urban centers in northern and central Russia, of which Novgorod and Kiev were the most important. Kievan Russia traded with Khazaria and the land of the Bulgars by way of the Volga and the Don, with Byzantium and Black Sea ports by way of the Dnieper, and with the Baltic by way of the Dwina or a series of lakes and rivers which emptied into the Gulf of Finland. Though these fluvial routes were the most important ones, a terrestrial complex also existed which began at Kiev and went west to Prague and southern Germany by way of Galicia or branched off to reach Hungary and the Danube by way of the Carpathian Passes. As noted above, Russian trade reaching Khazaria had by the late tenth century declined considerably, while that which went to the Black Sea, the Baltic, or central Europe was very active indeed.

In examining the products which followed these trade routes and which tended to knit these trade complexes together, we should begin by noting that Kievan Russia formed a very backward agricultural area. It produced on its scattered agricultural lands, which were hacked out of the forest, only enough foodstuff to feed itself with little surplus available for export. Nor did it produce much in the way of exportable industrial wares. On the other hand, its forests were an important source of honey, wax, and furs, and its people produced slaves who were in great demand in the Moslem world and in Byzantium as well. It also exported to Turkestan fine Frankish swords which it imported from the West. In return for these products for several centuries the Russians had received from Khazaria and the Moslem world oriental wares and silver dirhems and, after 911, silks and other specialized industrial products directly from Byzantium. After 965 when a weakened Khazaria could no longer maintain regular trade with Turkestan or to the north, Kievan Russia found itself looking more and more to Constantinople as the source of needed Eastern wares and industrial products which it could exchange for its wax, slaves, and furs, though it also began to ship some of them to central Europe over land routes as well. In this same period its commerce with the Baltic also lost importance since it now had fewer dirhems to exchange for goods reaching the east and there was no longer any market in Turkestan for Frankish swords. Hence the supreme importance of a Byzantine market, as far as Kievan Russia was concerned, as the tenth century drew to a close.

The second trade complex, Khazaria, can be dismissed rather summarily as far as products are concerned, for its limited local economy produced nothing for export except an isinglass made from Volga and Caspian sturgeon. Rather, it depended completely upon a transit trade for its prosperity—indeed, for its very existence. That is why, when trade routes leading to

Kievan Russia and to Moslem Turkestan all but ceased to function during the late tenth century, Khazaria began to disappear as well as a viable state.

With all this in mind, let us turn our attention to the Byzantine trade complex, whose system of economic exchanges both inside the empire and outside its borders was so important that by the year 1000 it tended to dominate the entire Byzantine-Russian world, especially now that Khazaria had lost importance. It is frequently stated that this Byzantine world formed a great intermediary trading system which linked less advanced Russia to the north and Europe to the west with the products of China, India, and Islam. We have already noted that this statement applies with great accuracy to Kievan Russia, especially as the latter lost trade contacts with the Moslem east after 965. It is also true that Western Europe was able to find in Constantinople silks, spices, and other luxury wares which were in great demand and which Europeans did not produce for themselves. But it is equally important for us to understand the nature of Byzantium's economic life and commerce, both internal and external, for these dictated how it played its role as an intermediary. This role differed profoundly from those we have examined in studying both the Islamic and Indic worlds and was indeed much more like that played by China than anywhere else throughout the civilized world of the period.

Historical experience since the time of Constantine had led the Byzantine Empire to consider itself a Christian Roman Empire under siege. It had successfully weathered German barbarian and Sassanian attacks in the fourth and fifth centuries, Avar and Persian assaults at the time of Heraclius, and expeditions launched by the Arabs and the Bulgars. During these same years it had also had to deal with what it regarded as hostile Carolingian and Ottonian efforts to challenge, with papal help, the exclusiveness of its Roman imperial tradition. All of this explains why it adopted a fortress mentality toward the outside world in which its economic life and its internal and external commerce tended to be organized, like its army, navy, government, and religious life, to defend itself against foreign foes.

It regarded a rich, healthy, balanced internal economy maintained at the highest possible level as one of its bastions of defense, for it allowed the empire to maintain an effective government and bureaucracy, to pay the cost of a well-organized army and navy, and to have ample funds to use as a diplomatic weapon against actual or potential enemies. Byzantium had no interest in a free commerce which flowed into and out of its empire from neighboring regions or in a powerful merchant class which, like those found in the Islamic or Indic worlds, would range throughout its length and breadth, bringing wealth to its cities or its rulers. Nor was it willing to allow its large or small landowners to become so involved in the world of trade and finance that they ignored what it felt were their primary functions;

namely, to serve as soldiers, sailors, or diplomats at the disposal of the empire, or to act as priests or monks testifying to the glory of its Christianity, or scholars and artists who celebrated its noble and civilized accomplishments. It regarded its merchants and skilled artisans and the commerce they helped to foster as necessary to maintain the strength of its Christian empire, but only if they were severely and carefully controlled.

Fortunately for Byzantium, within the area which formed its heartland or in the Black Sea area which it controlled sufficient resources and technical expertise were to be found so that it could be almost completely self-sufficient, in contrast to the Moslem world nearby. Maritime and terrestrial routes could be utilized to bring to Constantinople everything needed to maintain a healthy and balanced economy on which the empire relied as an important element in its defense. There were even a few surpluses available which could be used in controlled external commerce with its neighbors within the Byzantine-Russian complex and beyond.

From the rich farming land of Thrace and Asia Minor came supplies of grain and livestock which fed the populace of Constantinople—supplies which were now more abundant as the threat of Moslem and Bulgarian attacks receded. From the Aegean area came wine and olive oil, while the Black Sea contributed a special kind of salt fish, so prized that its export was forbidden. Other necessary natural products were wool and hides from the flocks and the herds which ranged Balkan and Anatolian uplands, raw silk from the Morea and central Greece, and flax and honey which the Bulgarians had long furnished to the empire and its capital in return for trading privileges. War horses used by the *cataphracti* who formed the empire's elite cavalry were raised in large numbers in Asia Minor. And timber, so necessary for fuel and ship construction, was plentiful everywhere, although probably the Pontic forests were the source of the most important supplies which found their way to the Sea of Marmora where the major imperial shipyards were located.

Other natural products important to the empire were salt and metals which were produced in salt pans or which came from mines operated by the state as government monopolies. Byzantium again was fortunate in having abundant supplies of iron and copper in the Balkans and Armenia, as well as lead produced in a number of locations, and alum, so necessary for the manufacture of woolen cloth, which came from large deposits near Smyrna in Asia Minor. Silver, largely a by-product of lead production, was in shorter supply but local production could be easily supplemented with silver imported from Russia or the Moslem east by way of Trebizond or other border trading spots, while gold probably reached the empire in considerable amounts from Dacia, the Caucasus, and the West, as will be noted later on. Stone, especially fine grades of marble, came from quarries which were controlled by the state and were located in many parts of the empire, especially around the Aegean.

Byzantium, however, not only produced this wide range of natural products; it also could boast a well-organized industrial establishment. Woolen, linen, and silk cloths were woven in a number of urban centers, especially in Constantinople, where the imperial government maintained special workshops which produced clothing for its armed forces and fine textiles of silk or brocade which were distributed on a regular basis to the court and its officials. Some of these fine textiles were exported under strict governmental control. In Constantinople and other cities like Saloniki we also find skilled jewelers and workers in ivory and artists who produced a variety of luxury wares in great demand among the upper classes, churchmen, and abroad as well.

There were only a few products lacking within the empire which had to be imported from the outside world to maintain a high level of prosperity and a balanced economic life. They included wax, furs, and slaves which could most easily be procured from the Kievan Rūs; spices, perfumes, jewels, some raw silk, and cotton cloth which came from the Islamic world; and gold which could be brought in from a number of places. Otherwise, everything necessary to maintain a high level of prosperity and economic autarchy was locally available to Byzantium.

This combination of fortress mentality and an unusual degree of economic self-sufficiency explains how the empire chose to organize its economic life. Internally, Byzantium grouped its merchant and artisan classes into guilds which, as that manual of government regulation called the *Book of the Prefect* reveals, were under strict governmental control. This included an extensive system of price fixing, especially as regards foodstuffs necessary to provision the capital. While money lending was permitted, bankers and the rates of interest they could charge were regulated by the state. Such controls not only limited the profits of the merchant and artisan class, but the extensive network of state factories may have also helped to discourage the rich from investing in commercial ventures. Instead they tended to invest their surplus capital in land, in contrast to the Islamic world, where landlords were commercially minded and tended to mingle with and be absorbed by the urban business elite.

All of this seems to have had an important effect upon Byzantine technical development. Byzantium showed herself capable of real technical advances during these years, especially in the fields of ship construction and military architecture and in the development of Greek fire—all of which had military and naval applications. The golden throne and singing birds made for the palace of the Emperor Theophilus illustrate the same technological virtuosity. But the fact that the state exercised so much control over mining and manufacturing, both direct and indirect, seems to have discouraged technical progress in this area of economic life to an extent not found in nearby Islamic regions. Similarly, the fact that its landholders had few commercial interests meant that the agriculture they practiced remained essentially traditional and that we find little evidence of the kind of innovations that distinguish the agricultural practices of contemporary Sung China, Islam, or the Carolingian and Ottonian West. Without an improved agricultural technology, the yield of Byzantium's forests, fields, pastures, and mines could not be improved, nor could its population become more numerous.

Finally, since Byzantine traders were discouraged by the government from venturing beyond the empire's borders and the export of gold was forbidden, this tended to turn over the empire's external commerce to foreign traffickers and merchants living near its borders who either traded directly with Constantinople or Saloniki or with border commercial outposts like Trebizond, Cherson, Antioch, Venice, or Amalfi. Merchants from these outposts also tended to control the trade between their home cities and the capital itself by the tenth century, especially Amalfians and Venetians who maintained special quarters on the Golden Horn, Armenians who dominated traffic to and from Trebizond and other Black Sea ports, and Syrians who trafficked along trade routes between the capital and the Islamic world. The passive nature of the empire's foreign commerce then, noted by so many scholars, was the direct result of both overall governmental policies and the way its internal economy functioned.

Byzantium, as we have said, felt it especially important to control all export trade as a means of maintaining its economic strength and as a defense against its enemies. In the course of the tenth century, therefore, it negotiated a series of trade treaties with the Kievan Russians which regulated how the latter's merchants could bring their wares to Constantinople, how long they could stay there, and what products they could export, such as silks and other manufactured and luxury wares. Probably as early as the tenth century Trebizond had been set up as the main controlled-entry port for Islamic wares such as spices, perfumes, raw silk, and cottons, although some Syrians may have been allowed to trade directly with Constantinople. Late in the tenth century after the Byzantine conquest of Cilicia, Cyprus, and northern Syria, it seems probable that Antioch replaced Trebizond as the main entrepot trading with the Islamic world. At least we now find trade treaties regulating commerce with the Hamdanid emirs of Aleppo and the minting of a special gold *nomisma* coin, similar in weight to the dinar, which could only have been designed to facilitate such commerce. And since at this time the Hamdanids temporarily recognized Byzantine overlordship, such trade treaties had a political as well as an economic purpose.

That political considerations often dictated Byzantine trade with the Moslem world can further be seen by the fact that, at the very same time she was encouraging trade with a friendly and vassal Hamdanid principality, Byzantium forbade the shipping of timber and arms to an unfriendly Fatimid empire. Thus we can see here a policy of attempting to purchase those wares which were needed from the Islamic world in such a way that the resulting commerce was directed toward friendly Moslem states and away from those which were hostile.

It was, however, much more difficult for Byzantium to deal with Venice and the Amalfi-Naples region than with either the Kievan Rūs or nearby Moslem regions. There were a number of reasons for this. In the first place the Venetians and the Amalfians by the tenth century had come to control much of the trade between Constantinople and the West. Second, this trade very much benefited the empire since the goods exported from Constantinople by these Italian traders, such as silks, much exceeded in value those they sold there and the difference was paid in gold which the empire very much desired. And third, since Byzantium wished to maintain its influence in an Italy where the Ottos and the papacy were a potential menace, it needed to strengthen the nominal allegiance which these cities owed to the empire. In the case of Venice, Basil II, who wished to use the Venetian fleet upon occasion to transport troops to Italy, even allowed the Venetians to take over Dalmatia and lowered customs duties charged those Venetian merchants who traded with Constantinople.

On the other hand, both Amalfi and Venice had economic interests which were dangerous to Byzantium. Both had long traded with Italian regions which were hostile to Byzantium and were unwilling to end this trade. Even worse, they regularly supplied arms, timber, and slaves to the hostile Fatimids of Egypt, Syria, and the middle Mediterranean, and the arms and timber they traded were used against Byzantium. They used this trade to procure for themselves the gold which they used to buy Byzantine silks and other luxury wares in Constantinople. Byzantine authorities made efforts to get Amalfi and Venice, especially the latter, to cease sending arms and timber to Moslem ports, but were unable to force them to acquiesce. The result was that these Italians continued to supply Byzantium with valuable gold supplies, but at the cost of their increasing measure of control over the commerce between Constantinople and the West and assistance to hostile Moslem powers which endangered Byzantine interests—a cost which was to increase as the next century wore on.

In examining the economy of the Byzantine-Russian world, we need to emphasize that during this period Byzantium continued to maintain an abundant gold coinage whose value was kept uniform. This was supplemented by silver coins whose value remained equally steady, though their importance was not as great as that based upon gold. The imperial government regarded the purity of its gold money as an important basis of its power and made every effort to increase the amount at its disposal. Hence, it continued during these years to forbid any gold exports and to accumulate a hoard of nomismata in its central treasury. During the reign of Basil II this resulted in the piling up of a great gold reserve larger than that maintained by Emperor Theophilus during the ninth century or Emperor Anastasius in the sixth.

All of these economic policies had important effects upon the rest of the Byzantine-Russian world and its Islamic and Western neighbors as well. For instance, as we have already noted, now that the Kievan Russians could no longer count on oriental wares reaching them from the Moslem world, thanks to the breakdown of commerce reaching Khazaria from Turkestan, they found that Byzantium was an indispensable market. This explains why Sviatoslav was so eager to expand southwest and set up a new capital on the Danube in the years 968–71 and why Vladimir a bit later sought an alliance with Constantinople and accepted Orthodox Christianity for his realm. Since Byzantium's trade policies forbade export of gold, this helps to explain why Russia during this period continued to use silver money as it had earlier in the form of Moslem silver dirhems. And finally since the Byzantine Empire discouraged its own merchants from proceeding north beyond ports which it controlled, like Cherson, it meant that Rūs merchants had to continue to travel to Constantinople or other special trade portals to procure the goods they desired. Hence, the importance for the Russians of maintaining control over routes which passed through the southern Russian steppes where nomadic tribesmen like the Pecheneks were a constant threat to trade—a problem that Kievan Russia found increasingly difficult to solve in the years to come.

As for Khazaria, Byzantine trade policies and patterns of control proved decisive here also by the end of the tenth century. Once the Kievan Russians had thrown off the Khazar yoke and begun to trade directly with Constantinople, Byzantium had no further need of the Khazars as favored trade partners. Byzantines could get furs, wax, and slaves directly from Kiev and procure the Islamic products which they needed more cheaply via Trebizond and Antioch than by way of Khazaria, and they no longer felt the need of a Khazar alliance to restrain Moslems who had ceased to threaten their Armenian and Syrian frontiers. Khazaria, earlier of great importance, now ceased to represent a vital economic or political element in the Byzantine-Russian world with important results which were to be apparent in the next century.

Byzantine economic policies also affected Western Europe in a number of ways. This part of the world produced very little that the Byzantines needed to maintain a high level of prosperity and a balanced economy, for, as we have noted, most of what they did need could more easily be procured from the Russians than from Latin Westerners. They did, however, welcome the gold which Amalfian and Venetian traders brought to Constantinople and exchanged for silks, spices, and other luxury wares, and they desired to keep these Italian cities friendly to help maintain their dominant position in Italy—that is all. So Byzantium's role as an intermediary with the West was very much limited by its own needs and policies down to the end of the tenth century.

Overall, the Byzantine-Russian world's economy profited from a favorable balance of trade with its neighbors. The thousands of silver coins which still circulated in Kievan Russia and which have been found in so many coin hoards emphasize that, despite the primitive nature of its economy, the Russian trade balance with the Moslem world was favorable. We have every reason to believe that it found commerce with Constantinople almost as profitable as long as it could keep trade routes to the Black Sea open. It even seems possible that commerce which now began to flow to the West along reopened trade routes to Hungary, Poland, and Germany took up some of the slack from the diminution of commerce with Moslem Turkestan and from its decreasing Baltic trade. At any rate, we have every indication that the year 1000 saw Kievan Russia unusually prosperous.

As for the Byzantine Empire proper, the fact that it kept its gold coins unchanged in value and was able to increase the size of the gold hoard at the disposal of its rulers attests both to its prosperity and to a continuing favorable balance of trade with its neighbors, the Russians, Amalfians, and Venetians. There is no evidence either that its commerce with the Islamic world via Trebizond or Antioch was unfavorable and drained gold eastward. Instead, trade treaties with the Hamdanids dating from this period, which specify an import of coins, seem to point in the other direction. We have every reason, then, to believe that the Byzantine-Russian complex remained prosperous, with a unique trading system directed from Constantinople that enabled it to maintain a special place in the civilized world of the late tenth century.

Last of all, a word about the culture of the Byzantine-Russian area as a factor making for a certain overall unity. During Macedonian times the Byzantine Empire began to enjoy a distinct and unusual civilization of its own. This civilization was characterized by a magnificent art and architecture once Iconoclasm had ended, an intellectual elite who prized and preserved classical Greek literature, a legal system which was embodied in codified form in laws knows as the *Basilics*, and use of Greek as a language of religion and general culture. It is true that Byzantine civilization was in many ways backward-looking and may have lacked the speculative, scientific concerns which characterized nearby Islam, but nevertheless it was powerful in other ways. And it was beginning to mold the culture of the Kievan Russians who had just accepted its Orthodox Christianity, while it was also able at this time to spread its art and architecture to Italy via Rome, Amalfi, and Venice. Nor was Western Europe beyond the Alps unaffected by Byzantine culture, for one cannot examine tenth-century Germany or Anglo-Saxon England without being aware of strong Byzantine influences, especially in the field of art. Such influences were to remain vital as Western Europeans, about the year 1000, began to form a new civilization of their own.

Despite its wealth, its power, and its distinctive civilization, this Byzantine-Russian complex had a relatively small population compared to East Asia, the Indic world, Islamic civilization, or even Western Europe. It lacked densely settled fertile plains comparable to those found in the Yangtze and Yellow river valley complexes of China, along the Indus and Ganges, and in Egypt, Iraq, and Andalusia. Its only really large city, Constantinople, had a population of between 200,000 and 300,000, about the same as Baghdad, but then its next two important ones—Saloniki and Antioch—were only in the 30,000 to 40,000 range. Then we find a few smaller ones like Trebizond whose populations may have reached 5,000 to 10,000. In short, the Byzantine Empire lacked cities in the middle range.

Beyond the empire, Itil in the tenth century may have had a population as large as that of Trebizond, while in Kievan Russia, where city life was only beginning to become important, only Kiev had a substantial population—perhaps numbering 10,000 to 15,000 in all. The other Russian towns were smaller with 5,000 to 10,000 inhabitants. Unlike the Islamic world, city life was not demographically important to this region.

As for its total population, perhaps the best estimate is that by the year 1000 the Byzantine Empire had some 20,000,000 inhabitants, of which 8,000,000 lived in Asia Minor and the empire's eastern provinces and 12,000,000 in the Balkans and those parts of Italy which Byzantium controlled. The Kievan Russian population, which was spread over a vast area, probably numbered at most 4,500,000 at this time, according to recent estimates. The steppe region between the Danube and the Volga was even more thinly populated, and so its total could not have exceeded 1,000,000 or 1,500,000 at the most. If we add this population to that of the Byzantine Empire, then we arrive at an overall figure of 25,000,000 to 26,000,000 for the entire Byzantine-Russian complex or roughly one-half of that found in Greater India or the Islamic world and one-third that of East Asia.

We have already noted in some detail the economic, religious, and cultural factors which gave strength to the Byzantine Empire proper. But we also need to note another factor which had ominous overtones for its future: the rise of large estates owned by its fighting aristocracy, especially those who lived in Asia Minor.

Until about 900 Byzantium had managed to survive in the face of heavy outside pressures by organizing its defenses in a special way. Its outlying provinces or themes, as they were called, were defended by landholders who were guaranteed their property as unalienable freeholds in return for service in local armed forces or naval contingents commanded by governors or *strategoi* who combined military and civil functions. These themal levies were backed up by contingents of professional soldiers and naval flotillas located near the capital itself which could easily move to threatened frontier areas. The entire system was supervised by a well-organized bureaucracy centered in Constantinople which was paid in money and controlled both finances and the intricate system of economic controls we have already described, making sure that the imperial government had an ample supply of money.

In the course of the tenth century, however, the empire ceased being on the defensive and began to advance its frontiers eastward at the expense of the Arabs and westward at the expense of the Bulgars. As this happened, the older defensive provincial levies lost their importance, and a new striking army and a new fleet emerged. The new navy made possible the reconquest of Crete and Cyprus and cooperated with the new striking army which was led by generals and emperors chosen from the great warrior families of Asia Minor like Nicephorus Phocas or John Zimisces. To strengthen this offensive army, the government encouraged the development of estates large enough to provide the new type of mounted armed forces it found necessary and closed its eyes as small landholders began to find their freeholds illegally absorbed into the estates of the warrior nobility. The fact that landholders were discouraged from investing their wealth in anything but land markedly increased this tendency. Thus by the late tenth century the empire and the imperial office itself increasingly came to be controlled by warrior magnate families. Small landholders who were losing their lands seemed helpless against them, though both the imperial bureaucracy and the church still resisted, backed at times by an imperial navy.

Finally the whole crisis came to a head during the reign of Basil II when revolts by Bardas Phocas and Bardas Skleros threatened to deliver the empire into the hands of warrior aristocratic families. Basil II, however, using a mercenary force of Scandinavian Varangians imported from Russia, was able to put down these revolts and then proceeded to curb the power of the great landed aristocrats by forbidding any further absorption of small landholdings and imposing a financially crippling taxation on them. His stern policies resulted in a temporary balance between the central government which used mercenary forces and the warrior aristocrats who still served as cavalry in his armies. But he was unable to revive the small landholders as an essential buttress of the empire and left the basic problem, unresolved, to his successors.

Furthermore, by this time a special problem had come to prevail in the empire's western provinces which the great Basil II was not able to solve either. Only in its themes of Calabria and Langobardia did Byzantium have any forces of consequence, and these few in number, while the imperial navy was far away indeed. Byzantine rulers thus had to rely upon diplomacy

and the use of semi-independent naval levies from Venice or Amalfi to maintain their position. As has been pointed out, such fleets in practice were
controlled by local authorities whose interests seldom coincided with those
of the imperial government. Instead, as has been emphasized, these Italians
tended to use their maritime strength to protect their own trade with the
Moslem and Western European worlds, both of which were often hostile to
Byzantium. Thus in western waters, too, an ominous situation had arisen
by the year 1000. It was to have important consequences for the empire
when the strong hand of Basil II was removed from the imperial helm.

The tenth century brought change also to Khazaria. The Khazars for some
centuries seem to have controlled southern Russia using a system of taxation
and military force, later to be used by the Golden Horde, and had thus
insured peaceful trade throughout the steppes. Yet they were never able to
recover from the blow dealt them by Prince Sviatoslav of Kiev in 965 when
he sacked their capital of Itil. We have already noted the important economic
consequences of this Khazar decline, but we also should emphasize its political results. Not only were the Khazars now unable to control the nomadic
tribes of southern Russia, like the Pecheneks, but they also were equally
powerless to deal with nomads to the east over whom the faltering Saminids
had lost control by the year 1000 in the Khirkiz steppes. These tribes, the
Cumans and Polovtzi, now began to press westward and to move toward
the Danube, helping to create a chaotic state of affairs in the steppes of
southern Russia.

The fortunes of the other part of the Byzantine-Russian civilization, Kievan
Russia, were considerably brighter in the tenth century. Its power was the
result of a triple alliance between the prince and his warrior *druzina* or
bodyguard, many of whom were of Scandinavian origin like the ruling house
itself, merchants of the Russian *grodys* or towns, some of whom were Slavs,
others Scandinavian, and the Russian and Finnish tribes of the region. The
power of the princes, which was based on this alliance, had made it possible
for them to throw off the Khazar yoke and to organize the commerce of their
area so that their merchants could reach distant markets of the Islamic world,
in Byzantium, in the Baltic, and in central Europe. Trading and raiding
could often be combined as a source of revenue for the princes and their
state. At the time of Sviatoslav, who succeeded Igor as Prince of Kiev in
959, for example, raiding predominated, as his attacks on Khazaria, the White
Bulgars, and the Danube area prove conclusively. His successor, Vladimir,
turned to a more constructive policy which led to an alliance with Basil II
and the acceptance of Orthodox Christianity. Byzantine civilization accompanied Orthodoxy and thus made it possible for Vladimir to copy some
aspects of Byzantine law and administration and to regularize internal arrangements with both the tribes and town merchants who more and more
began to resemble the urban *veches* or militias of the later Kievan period.

Vladimir seems to have understood that it was vital to his interests to keep trade routes open to the south where his merchants could procure needed outside goods in exchange for their own wares. After 989 his close alliance with Byzantium assured him the vital market of Constantinople, but perhaps he was also attempting to cooperate with the remnants of Khazar authority when he occupied Tumortarkan in 988. Be that as it may, his policies did not permit him to solve the problem of controlling steppe tribes like the Pecheneks who were already being pushed to the west by the even more savage Turkish tribes to the east of them. This problem he left for his successors in the course of the next century.

Finally, we need to examine maritime matters as they affected the Byzantine-Russian complex. By the late tenth century this entire complex was dominated by the sea power of an empire which was now unchallenged in the Black Sea, in the Aegean, along the southern coasts of Asia Minor, and to some extent in the Ionian Sea to the west. This sea power consisted of an imperial navy with its main base in Constantinople headed by an admiral or *drungarios* and a number of smaller fleets under provincial naval *strategoi*. The main themal fleets were those of Cephalonia, Crete, Cyprus, and the Cibbyrhoets area of southern Asia Minor, as well as some Black Sea areas, whose main function now was to police the seas and keep down piracy. Innumerable small dockyards existed along most of the empire's coasts— wherever ship timber could be found—but the main naval arsenals and shipyards were in or near Constantinople. Other dockyards, which may have served both as naval bases and repair facilities, were at Saloniki, Rhodes, Attalia, Cyprus, northern Syria, at Cherson and Trebizond in the Black Sea, and at Durazzo and along the Dalmatian coast.

The main warships of the period, *dromons* or *chelandia*, were large narrow warships, lateen-rigged, and also propelled by oars. Galleys were also found in Byzantine waters by this time, but these were simply a smaller kind of *dromon* or *chelandia*. There were also a number of heavier ships very much like the round ships of the Arab Mediterranean. Some of these, like the *katena* and *pamphylia*, used oars. Others, called *ousias* or *hussiers*, were built much the same way but used only sails. There were also a number of different kinds of merchant ships of various sizes called *nefs* which were often much like *ousias* in design and which could be impressed into service and used as transports when needed by the authorities. We find also a number of smaller craft adapted to the island-studded seas that surrounded the Byzantine Empire and which carried most of the commodities which knit the empire together economically.

Maritime conditions found in Adriatic and Tyrrhenian waters were somewhat different, for here, as has been noted, Byzantium could muster little maritime strength except when special fleets arrived from Constantinople. Themal authorities in Langobardia and Calabria maintained small squadrons which, on occasion, they could stiffen with vessels contributed by merchants of seaports like Bari. They could also probably do the same along the shores of Dalmatia where we find a maritime tradition often linked with piracy. But the main fleets available in the west were those of Venice in the Adriatic and of Amalfi on the west coast of Italy, both of which were only nominally under the empire's control. Venice's naval establishment now included galleys copied from those found in Byzantine war fleets and some heavier merchant vessels as well. In Basil II's time, as we have said, this fleet was closely tied into the maritime system of the empire by a special treaty with the doges of the Orseoli family, who in return were given the right to take over Dalmatia as a Venetian preserve. It not only patrolled the Adriatic but also seems to have been used to protect commerce going to distant shores including those of the Moslem Mediterranean.

We know much less about the fleets of Amalfi and nearby Naples, except to note that they seem to have operated more freely than Venetian fleets and to have traded extensively with Sicily, North African ports, Egypt, and Syria as well as with Constantinople. Probably Amalfi's ships were built more along Moslem lines than the essentially Byzantine Venetian ships. At any rate, it is clear that Amalfi, unlike Venice, despite its trade with Constantinople, was never really part of the empire's naval system but stood outside of it.

Shipping in the rest of the Byzantine-Russian world was apparently much less developed. The Khazars operated ships in the Caspian Sea, but we know little about them except that they traded with Azerbaijan and Persian Caspian ports. The Kievan Rūs during the tenth century used river craft called *karabos* which seem to have been made of hollowed-out logs and which could be carried along portages around river rapids found on the Danube and perhaps the Don and Volga as well. Perhaps these boats were used to sail in large flotillas along Black Sea shores to trade with Constantinople or to sail in the Caspian. If so, this explains why Byzantium found it so easy to deal with the maritime threat of such craft in the Black Sea during the early tenth century. It is possible, of course, that the Kievan Rūs increased the size and improved the construction of the ships they used in the Black Sea by the last years of the tenth century, but we have no basis for such an assumption, for Kievan Russia down to the end of the first millennium remained a fluvial rather than a maritime power and left the Black Sea to a Byzantium which was able to control it with a minimal naval establishment.

The Civilization of
Western Europe

The fifth and last great civilization of Eurasia and Africa was that of Western Europe. Having just begun to achieve a measure of overall unity in the eighth and ninth centuries, it was distinguished from the others by being by far the most geographically remote and underdeveloped of them all. Nevertheless, by the year 1000 the varied peoples who formed its population were beginning to enjoy a civilization that had a number of unique features and a great potential for future development.

The first basis of its overall unity was geographical. It lay completely within the temperate zone, although its climate varied from the cold that prevailed in the tundras of northern Scandinavia to the warmth of its Mediterranean shores. Thanks to the Gulf Stream, the prevailing westerlies, and the effect of the waters of the Atlantic, however, its overall climate was much more moderate than one would expect, considering its latitude. These maritime influences also provided almost all of Western Europe with abundant winter rainfall and most of it, except for Mediterranean areas, with summer rains as well. This assured a long growing season for its crops as well as considerable forest growth. Its forests generally were deciduous, except along the northern fringes of Europe where conifers predominated. There were also some moors and fens about the North Sea where trees were not to be found. These forested areas tended to be very extensive, so that many agricultural areas had to be hacked out of what was still essentially primeval growth.

Although unified by a climate favorable to agriculture and timber growth, Western Europe was divided by a number of mountain ranges along its southern and southeastern borders, forming three relatively distinct regions: along the Atlantic, along the Mediterranean, and in central Europe. These mountain ranges were the Cantabrian-Pyrenees system in northern Spain, the Massif Central in France, the Alpine chain which ringed Italy, and a complex of mountains which surrounded Bohemia in central Europe.

The North Atlantic region was the largest of the three and consisted of land which surrounded the five northern seas of Europe: the Bay of Biscay, the Irish Sea, the English Channel, the North Sea, and the Baltic Sea. Offshore islands from the Hebrides to Iceland were part of this complex, too. In some areas like northern Spain, around the Irish Sea, and in Norway, mountains came right down to the salt water. Elsewhere, from southwestern France to Russia on the continent and in eastern Britain as well, the northern seas were bordered by flat plains which were drained by a number of rivers including the Garonne, the Rhine, the Elbe, the Vistula, the Thames, and the Humber.

The Mediterranean region of Western Europe was much smaller and consisted of a series of plains along the shores of the Adriatic and the western Mediterranean. In much of this area the mountains which separated this region from the other two came right down to the sea. Elsewhere we find coastal plains and a number of river valleys: the Llobregat in Catalonia; the Aube and Rhone in southern France; the Arno, Tiber, and Po in Italy. Of these rivers the Rhone and the Po, both of which were navigable, were the most important. Coastal plains and river valleys in this part of Europe were fertile areas, but their fertility was limited by scant summer rainfall, so the growing season for food crops could not be extended through the summer months without irrigation.

The central European area consisted of a Bohemian plain ringed by mountains and the upper and middle Danube valley. This latter was relatively narrow in southern Germany but broadened out to form a large Hungarian plain which was drained by a network of rivers that flowed into the Danube on its way to the Black Sea. In this plain were to be found Western Europe's only steppe lands. Also it is worth noting that throughout this entire central European region there was sufficient winter and summer rainfall so that it had the same long growing season enjoyed by the Atlantic region.

Despite the geographic distinctness of these three regions, communication between them did not present any insuperable problems. Though Moslem fleets still barred any regular maritime connection between the Mediterranean and Atlantic areas by way of the Straits of Gibraltar, a number of other practical routes existed which connected them. Passes across the Pyrenees, for instance, linked both Catalonia and northwestern Spain with France, while both the Aube and the Rhone valleys provided routes from the Mediterranean to the Atlantic side of France. In the same way a number of Alpine passes, which were impassable only in winter months, led from northern Italy to France, Germany, and Austria. As for central Europe, it also communicated with Atlantic Europe by way of a number of passes which pierced the mountain shield surrounding Bohemia or one could follow the Danube River which linked Bavaria to Hungary. This region also was linked to Italy via passes over the eastern Alps. In short, Western European regions were not, at this time, isolated from one another, although the difficulties presented by some of the routes outlined above limited the type of traffic which could easily move along them.

It is equally worth noting that, although every part of Western Europe was able to feed itself using locally produced foodstuffs, a combination of climate, rainfall, and terrain dictated the particular foods which prevailed in various parts of the continent. For instance, although grain grew in all the plains areas of Europe without exception, there was a tendency for most of northern Europe to concentrate on rye instead of wheat, since rye tended to be more dependable and yield greater harvests in more northerly latitudes. Beyond the areas where wheat and rye grew, barley and oats served as the main breadstuffs for similar reasons.

Regional differences were also revealed by the types of drink produced in Western Europe. Wine from vineyards originally introduced by the Greeks and Romans and extended northward in Carolingian times could not be produced north of the Loire and Champagne or beyond the Moselle, the upper Rhine, the Main, or the Danube valley in central Europe. Beyond this wine line, cider made from apples or pears was used in place of wine, or the population drank beer made from grain. And beyond the cider-beer line, on the fringes of Europe the local drink was a mead made from honey.

Similarly, we have a difference between those areas of Western Europe which used olive oil and those depending upon lard and butter. In general, olive oil was to be found only in Mediterranean areas. Northward, butter was used except where pigs were especially numerous. There was a similar difference in the way fruit trees were distributed. In general, apple, pear, peach, cherry, and plum trees were not grown beyond the old boundaries of the Roman Empire except in Germany, and vegetables and root crops had much the same range. Nut trees, on the other hand, were more widely distributed, especially oaks whose acorns were a favorite food for the swine who roamed forest areas.

A wide variety of domestic animals was also raised in every part of Western Europe at this time. Cattle, sheep, goats, and pigs were plentiful, although to some extent terrain and climate dictated where various species were to be found in the largest numbers. There was a tendency, then as now, for goats to be concentrated in Mediterranean regions where they could browse in the dry uplands during the summer season. Cattle, on the other hand, prized for their meat, milk, and hides and used as draft animals as well, were found mainly in plains areas or in regions having abundant rainfall. Sheep had an even wider range and were especially numerous in the south where goats flourished and in more northerly coastal wetlands, upland moors, and remote areas like Iceland, where few other domestic animals did very well. They were used for meat, as a source of wool, and furnished sheepskins for an export market.

In general, pigs did best, as we have noted, in forest areas, and everywhere we find horses of various kinds which were used for riding, as draft animals, or as beasts of burden. Most horses were small, but in northern plains areas and in Lombardy by the tenth century there was a breed of large horses, probably originating in Anatolia, which were used as war horses. To such domestic breeds we should add the numerous wild animals that roamed the forests and wastes of the period. Some were an important source of meat. Others in the north and the Baltic area produced the furs much prized locally or in foreign markets beyond the boundaries of Western Europe itself.

Fish were plentiful, too, and were to be found in both fresh water and the sea. Perhaps already by this time Basque and British fishermen were beginning to catch the whales which abounded along their coasts. By this time as well, the two main concentrations of herring—those which spawned off Scania and those found in the North Sea—were attracting fishermen from nearby coasts, although exploitation of this resource, like the cod of Norway, was certainly much less intense than it was to be later. But it is interesting to note that by the tenth century Arctic products like reindeer hides and walrus tusks were beginning to reach the Baltic and North Seas areas in appreciable quantities.

If Western Europe had available such a wide variety of products from its fields, forests, pastures, and the sea, it also could count on other natural products of importance. Salt, for instance, was now already being produced in the lagoons of the Adriatic or along the shores of Languedoc, and its distribution was an early basis of Venetian trade. Equally important was the salt which was refined from salt springs or mined in Austria, England, Germany, and elsewhere.

Along with salt, metals of various kinds were available in many different regions, for Western Europe was particularly fortunate in this respect. Iron, for instance, was found in parts of Europe as diverse as Tuscany, northeastern Spain, the Massif Central, Lorraine, the Rhineland, Austria, Britain, and northern Scandinavia. Copper, less widely distributed, came from the British Isles, Bohemia, the Tyrol, Sweden, Hungary, and the Balkans. The main deposits of tin were located in Cornwall and Bohemia, while zinc came from Belgium.

Turning to more precious metals, we should note that silver deposits, like iron ore, were widely distributed throughout Western Europe, with the most important mines being located in Sardinia, France, Britain, and Germany. Lead was produced as a by-product of silver smelting everywhere. In fact, only gold and alum were in short supply among the metals needed by Western European civilization at this time, for alluvial gold had been exhausted, and the alum deposits of Italy had not yet been discovered. In contrast to the Islamic and Indic worlds, what seems remarkable about Western Europe is that it was blessed with an unusual variety of natural resources which were at least potentially more extensive than any we have so far been able to catalogue.

Western Europe's civilization at the end of the first millennium was also unified by a Latin Christianity common to all of its people. By this time only a few pockets of Basques, Scandinavians, and Baltic peoples were still pagan. The process of Christianization which had begun during the fourth century and continued during the sixth had been particularly rapid in the course of the tenth when the majority of Scandinavians and the Poles, Czechs, and Hungarians finally accepted a Latin Christian faith, at least in a nominal fashion.

This Christianity was in theory headed by a pope who lived in Rome and by a hierarchy of archbishops, bishops, and priests responsible to him as well as a widespread network of monastic establishments. Except in Ireland, these monasteries followed a Benedictine rule as modified by Carolingian reformers. In practice, however, the papacy had long shared control over the church hierarchy and monastic groups with rulers like the Western emperors or English kings who were perhaps affected by the imperial Caesaropapism of nearby Byzantium. In the year 1000, for example, Emperor Otto III and Pope Sylvester II collaborated in an attempt to develop a Christian Europe in which each of them would work together for a common Christian ideal.

Looking back over earlier centuries in the history of the Western church, one becomes aware of how difficult church control tended to be. Occasionally, powerful popes like Gregory the Great in the sixth century or Nicholas I in the ninth were able to exercise overall leadership and control. At other times, a Charlemagne, an Alfred the Great, or an Otto I was supreme over at least that portion of the church located within his own realm. By the year 1000 it was still not clear whether pope or secular rulers would end up as victors in a competition for church leadership. And the situation was further complicated by the fact that in many parts of Europe and especially in Spain, France, and Italy, secular church officials and monastic leaders alike had come to be appointed by noble families who dominated local areas—which threatened the church with absorption into the secular militarized society of the time. This was true despite the first faint stirrings of a new spirit of monastic reform at Cluny and in a few other localities.

Finally, as has already been noted at this time, the Latin church had an ambiguous relationship with the Orthodox church in the Byzantine East. Although by now the earlier schisms of Carolingian times had been healed and the two churches were in full communion with each other, all was not well. Despite the fact that Byzantine emperors exercised a measure of influence over papal Rome, basic differences and deep suspicions helped to poison the relationships between the two churches and were to lead to serious troubles in the future.

This Western church which controlled the religious life of almost all peoples who shared in Western European civilization, used Latin almost exclusively and had developed a common doctrine and theology based upon the fifth century ideas of Saint Augustine and other Latin church fathers with some later Carolingian modifications. It possessed a body of church law more nebulous than that governing the Greek Orthodox church but which was binding upon its hierarchy, its monks, and its communicants. Thanks to its considerable landed endowment accumulated over the centuries, it was extremely wealthy. And in a society which was still largely rural and illiterate, it had a monopoly of learning, exercised an important role as the chief patron of the artist and the architect, and furnished administrators who formed the rudimentary administrations in the governments of the time. Since the church was not only believed to have the keys to salvation but handled all education and social welfare, it controlled everyday life in myriad ways. In short, with all its limitations it was already Western Europe's most important and universal institution.

Closely related to a shared Latin Christianity was a new common Western European culture in which most of its upper-class population participated in varying degrees. This culture was a mixture of Roman, Germanic, and Celtic elements with some Byzantine ones added to them which had begun to take on real form and substance within the confines of the Carolingian empire. There a new blend of learning, literature, music, art, and architecture had appeared which combined classic, Christian, British, and Continental culture in a special way. Though subsequently the Carolingian empire which gave this culture birth disintegrated, by the tenth century it was more widely diffused than ever to regions like Christian Spain, Anglo-Saxon England, Ottonian Germany, and northern Italy.

Turning from the common Christianity and culture of this new Western European civilization, let us examine still another factor which helped make for unity—a common economy. The situation in this regard by the end of the tenth century was a complex one. One aspect of this economy was a common silver currency which circulated widely. It consisted of silver pennies first issued by Carolingian rulers and then copied by Anglo-Saxon monarchs during the eighth and ninth centuries. By the late tenth, similar coins were being struck in Ireland, Scandinavia, and central Europe as well. On the basis of evidence provided us by coin finds the most active mints issuing such money were those which were located in England, Germany, and northern Italy—many of them completely new mints—though there were also a few in northern France controlled by local authorities which were striking a considerable volume of coins. Less active were the surviving mints which were to be found in southern France or in the Rhone valley whose money only circulated very locally. The overall region in which such Caro-lingian-type silver money circulated extended from Galicia to central Europe and from the British Isles to the eastern Baltic.

In addition to Carolingian-type money, still another form of silver currency had a wide circulation throughout much of northern Europe and is often found in coin hoards along with Anglo-Saxon and Ottonian silver pennies. This was Arab silver dirhems, generally of Saminid origin, which seem to have reached Western Europe by way of Russia. Coin hoards dating from these years suggest that such coins circulated most widely in Baltic areas, for thousands of them have been unearthed here. But they were found elsewhere as well and were remarked upon by a traveler from the Islamic world who saw them in Cologne during the tenth century. Thus it would seem that Western Europe, from a monetary point of view, was linked economically much more closely with Kievan Russia than it was with any of its other neighbors. On the other hand, monetary evidence indicates that Christian Spanish areas south of the Pyrenees and Cantabrian mountains were economically connected with the Islamic world of Spain since they used Spanish Moslem silver and gold coins almost exclusively.

Moslem gold dinars circulated in Christian Spain and were not uncommon in Italy, especially in Venice and Amalfi, but the rest of Western Europe seems at this time to have possessed very few dinars or Byzantine nomismata, despite assertions to the contrary by a number of historians. In fact, only a handful of such coins have been unearthed in finds dating from the tenth century. Some gold pennies, it is true, were minted by contemporary Anglo-Saxon rulers using supplies of gold which were probably procured from Wales or Ireland, but these did not circulate widely.

From the eighth century on, Western Europe had begun to develop an agrarian system which was much more productive than any it had possessed earlier. One aspect of this was an extensive clearing of virgin or abandoned land, particularly noticeable between the Loire and the Rhine. Here noble proprietors, religious establishments, and peasants alike began to cut down the great forests, clear brushland, and dike and drain marshy areas around the North Sea. By the late ninth century this effort had spread into Saxony, central Germany, the middle Danube valley, and England. In Scandinavia, Poland, and Bohemia the same process went on, although at a slower rate. It was even marked by the settlement of some 20,000 to 30,000 Scandinavians in Iceland between the years 870 and 930.

We can trace a similar development in the French Midi and in Christian Spain as well. In this latter area both the plain of Ausona, located in Catalonia, and the deserted lands of the Duero basin began to be colonized from the late ninth century on by mixed bands of peasants, noble proprietors, and religious houses, while in northern and central Italy we find the same thing happening, especially in the Po valley.

In many parts of Europe, however, clearing of new land for agriculture temporarily ceased during the late ninth and early tenth centuries. Viking attacks and local disorders halted it in much of France and England, while a combination of Moslem raids and advanced pirate bases along with a collapse of local governments did the same along Mediterranean shores between Catalonia and the Tiber. A bit later the same thing happened in parts of Germany, Austria, and northern Italy subject to Hungarian raids. But this slowdown of agricultural clearing did not last very long. By 911 the worst of Viking raids were over and more effective rulers in Scandinavia and newly Christianized central Europe brought sufficient order to this part of Europe so that agricultural progress was again possible.

Elsewhere things improved at a much slower pace. But after Otto I had defeated the Hungarians in 955, it became possible to resume clearing activities in northern Italy and along the Danube. The same thing happened in the Iberian Peninsula where, despite the campaigns of Abd-ar-Rahman III and Almansor, Catalan and Aragonese peasants and pastoralists edged down toward the Ebro valley and others to the west completed the settlement of the "Desert of the Duero." Even western Mediterranean shores saw Moslem pirates cleared from Provence in 972, and authorities began to bring a new public order to the area—a process repeated in Languedoc, in Liguria, and Tuscany. By the year 1000 Western Europe had laid the bases for a continued expansion of the area devoted to agriculture, making possible an increase in both its food supply and its population.

More than putting new land to the plow, however, was involved in this agricultural advance, for clearing was accompanied by what can only be described as a revolution in agricultural techniques. This revolution was marked by the appearance of a new kind of plow over a wide area, a new use of horses as draft animals, and a new system of crop rotation which we call the three-field system.

The new plows were heavy, wheeled, mould-board affairs with late Roman and Slavic antecedents but which only in the late eighth century began to spread throughout Europe from northern France to Poland and to make their appearance in Britain and Scandinavia as well. Such plows, which turned a deep furrow and required considerable animal power, could break the soil of the heavy, fertile clay bottom lands more effectively than the plows used in Mediterranean areas where the soil was light and cross plowing was the normal practice. They also demanded a more cooperative agricultural system since labor had to be pooled to operate them effectively.

To pull such plows, more efficient draft animals were needed, and this led directly to the use of horses instead of oxen in many parts of Western Europe. Use of horses led to the development of horseshoes and a new system of rein attachment which had originated in central Asia. So effective did these prove to be that they soon spread throughout the heartland of the Carolingian empire. Horses, however, one should hasten to say, did not at once replace yoked oxen as draft animals, especially in western France and in England, for it took some time for the advantages of horse power to become fully apparent, but where they were used they proved especially efficient.

The three-field system used in place of the older two-field system represents still a third example of agrarian technological advance. In Mediterranean and Roman Europe the traditional two-field system dictated that half of the fields of a village be planted in crops each year with the other half left fallow to recover its fertility. In much of southern Europe such a system of cultivation was necessary because, as has been noted, rain was only abundant during winter months and thus crops could not be grown during the dry summer period. In the northern and central European plains, however, it was possible to utilize summer rain as well as winter precipitation to grow an additional crop on the same land if a proper rotation system was followed. This led, then, to a rather intricate system of tillage using three fields instead of two and provided twenty-five to thirty-five percent more food to the cultivator using the same amount of land.

This system of tillage which seems to have spread rapidly across northern Europe, however, did more than increase crop yields. Since much land was still uncultivated, it proved easy to add a third field to the two great fields already in use in most villages. Since legumes and root crops were the favorite second crop raised each year on the same land, it increased their production and thus provided a better balanced diet for the peasantry. Since the three-field system spread plowing, planting, and harvesting activities more evenly throughout the year than the older system did, it made for greater efficiency in the use of peasant labor. And finally, since its rotation system provided oats in large amounts, as well as legumes, from its second or spring sowing, it produced a grain ideal for horses, but not for cattle, thus increasing the horse population wherever it became popular. In short, the spread of the three-field system resulted in a more productive, balanced, and efficient agriculture in which horses proved especially useful as draft animals.

It is important for us to emphasize, however, that this full-scale agricultural revolution which included the three-field system was not possible everywhere in Europe. It has already been made clear that in the Iberian Peninsula, Italy, and other Mediterranean lands a combination of light soils and lack of summer rain precluded the use of the heavy plow or of the three-field system. In extreme northern and western areas like Brittany, Ireland, or northern Scandinavia hilly conditions, acidity of the soil, prevailing patterns of pastoralism, and some other factors, such as cold, wet climate, limited the spread of such changes also. In other places, like western France, disorders in the countryside probably inhibited its development. In short, the full effect of this agricultural revolution tended to be concentrated in the great northern plains of Europe which stretched from Poland and Bohemia to the Atlantic and included most of eastern Britain and southern Scandinavia.

Closely related to these technological changes were the development and spread of a more cooperative agricultural system which we call the manor. Though this system was to be found in both the French Midi and northern Italy, it was most characteristic of the agriculture practiced in the plains on either side of the English Channel and the North Sea. The manor, as a type, varied considerably in detail, but in general consisted of a village surrounded by great open fields, pastures, and woodland areas. These open fields, generally now three in number, were divided into strips which were cultivated by the villagers in cooperative fashion, and the pasturage and woodlots were similarly exploited cooperatively. The produce from about one-third of the strips went directly to the lord of the manor or his agents. Whatever was produced on the rest belonged to the peasants themselves, after the payment of a variety of dues. Village custom dictated how land was to be utilized, what crops were to be planted, how labor services were to be apportioned, and how the game, the animals, and the wood which common land provided were to be divided between the lord and his peasants, most of whom were now serfs tied to the soil. What needs to be emphasized, however, is the cooperative nature of manorial agriculture, especially during the seasonal plowing, planting, and harvesting of crops. Such cooperation was vital to realize the full potential of the new agricultural techniques.

Nevertheless, by the end of the first millennium neither the cooperative manorial system nor the new agricultural techniques had spread widely enough to change definitively the whole of Western European agriculture. Their full effect lay in the future. What had happened was that new land was now being exploited which had not before been cultivated, and Western Europe's fields, forests, marshes, and pasturelands were beginning to pour out a surplus of foodstuffs making possible a considerable increase in population almost everywhere. For instance, it has been estimated that by the year 1000 England had a population of 1,000,000 to 1,500,000, which was double or triple what it had been able to support in Roman times, and similar increases are to be found in most other areas of the continent as well. The demographic tide had turned so dramatically that it would not be amiss to estimate Western Europe's total population as somewhere in the neighborhood of 30,000,000 to 40,000,000—decisively in excess of that found in the nearby Byzantine-Russian complex. And it is even more significant that the *rate* of population growth had accelerated so greatly that within the civilized world only China could match it. A demographic basis had been laid for all later progress.

By this time Western Europeans had also begun to exploit more effectively their store of other natural resources. Iron mines located in France, Germany, the Alps, Britain, and Scandinavia now began to produce ore in appreciable quantities, as did the copper mines of Wales and Germany and the stannaries of Cornwall and Bohemia. An increasing volume of lead and silver from mines at Melle, in the Mendips, or at Goslar in Saxony made possible the abundant silver coinage of the times. Salt production was active in Venetian lagoons and at Salzburg, Luneville in Saxony, and in Britain. Everywhere mineral wealth was actively exploited.

At the end of the first millennium some parts of Western Europe had also managed to achieve considerable industrial production, especially of woolen textiles. England and the Low Countries, for example, both began to produce woolens which were prized in distant markets, while Ireland's looms made both linens and a coarse woolen cloth which were shipped overseas as well. Everywhere that we find iron deposits being exploited we discover that arms were being produced, the most famous being the Frankish swords of the Rhineland and those from the Alpine regions of Austria which were highly regarded in Islamic lands. Glass was made in the Rhineland and metalware in Britain and Belgium. Fine jewelry was a specialty of the Scandinavians, the Irish, and the British. The list continues to grow as the spades of archaeologists turn up more and more evidence of a nascent vigorous industrialism sprouting up in many parts of Europe alongside an improved system of agricultural production.

A special facet of this industrialization was the technological virtuosity it displayed. For instance, the Frankish swords of the Rhineland have been shown to have been made using a technique which gave them a sharpness and a temper unknown except in Japan, India, and the Near East. The water mill, known since Roman times, had by now spread so widely that in the eleventh century over 5,000 of them were in use in England alone. By the late tenth century we find that power from such mills was used to full cloth mechanically, while a few decades later Venetians built mills which were operated by using tides to turn their wheels. As early as the ninth century, other mills used rotary grindstones with a crank attachment to grind grain.

Still another interesting example of improved technology was the appearance of a prototype of the stagecoach in Slavic central Europe by 965 and its spread to England, in a somewhat different form, a few years later. Equally important was the use of the stirrup, which, once introduced after the seventh or eighth century, revolutionized warfare, as did the motte and bailey castle which became well known in Italy and parts of France somewhat later. And finally we have a whole category of northern European merchant ships and warships, which were clinker-built and quite different in their design from Mediterranean craft. These were employed, as we will note, by Scandinavian, Frankish, and Anglo-Saxon mariners and some others as well. Indeed, the more one examines the evidence, the more one is struck by Western Europe's technological advances by the end of the first millennium.

All of this activity helped to increase the volume of commerce as the products of its fields, forests, mines, and workshops were transported along European waterways and across the narrow seas which linked its people together. What emerged was a great northern European trading area, where silver money was used, stretching from the eastern Baltic to Iceland, Ireland,

and northern French shores. Here natural products like salt, metals, wine, and wheat along with woolens, linen, metalware, and the like were sent north and east in exchange for honey, wax, horses, slaves, furs, and Moslem silver coins from Russia. And it is probably significant that the areas in which this trading activity centered by the late tenth century were those where agriculture was most productive and the food supply and population were growing most rapidly.

All of northern France and most of Germany, which formed a part of this great trading area, were linked via Alpine passes with northern Italy, which was equally precocious from an economic point of view, especially the Po valley and Tuscany as far south as Rome. Here, too, a variety of crops and a considerable amount of industrial wares were exchanged—especially those which reached Venice.

The flourishing commerce in these two areas of Europe had still another consequence, too—the appearance of new urban centers within the regions where trade was active. By this time a number of trading places called *portuses, wicks,* or *grodys* had grown sufficiently large to become towns, of which London, which could boast a population of 10,000 to 15,000 was certainly the most important. Others were smaller like Dublin in Ireland, York in England, Hedeby in Denmark, Birka in Sweden, Cologne and Hamburg in Germany, Ghent in Belgium, or Verdun in Lorraine. Even smaller trading centers were much more numerous; more than fivescore are known to have existed at this time scattered across this entire northern trading area. Nor was all commerce yet centered in such nascent towns, for Frisians, who were active traders, often lived in rural villages during nontrading months in the winter, and Icelanders and Gotlanders, who traveled widely as merchants, had no towns at all in the islands which they inhabited. The great northern trading area of Western Europe, then, was still backward and only just beginning to form the kind of urban centers which had long been found in the civilizations of Byzantium, Islam, Greater India, and East Asia, which shared the Old World with it.

The second region where urbanism was now a significant factor was Italy. There, in addition to Venice and Amalfi which, at this time, might well be considered Byzantine rather than Western European in character, we find two other important towns—Rome and Milan—and a series of smaller centers, like Pavia, Bologna, and Ravenna, which were growing rapidly. Christian Spain, too, had its Leon, Burgos, Compostela, Barcelona, and Gerona which had all achieved a modest urban growth.

Despite all this development, however, we must emphasize that two areas of Europe still failed to share in this urban growth by the end of the tenth century. One such region was along the middle Danube, where a combination of Hungarian raids and Byzantine attacks upon Bulgaria had stifled Danubian traffic upon which towns might have been based. This was true despite some overland trade with Kievan Russia or that which crossed eastern Alpine passes into northern Italy.

A second and more significant area which lagged behind the rest of Europe lay south of the Loire and included all of southern France, northwestern Italy between the Apennines and the sea, Sardinia and Corsica, and the shores of northern Spain between Corunna and Gascony. This region was, as we have noted, little affected by the agricultural and commercial growth which had changed northern Europe or the progress made in Christian Iberia and Italy.

For a short period of time during the reigns of Charlemagne and Louis the Pious, it had seemed probable that this entire region was destined to develop as rapidly as other parts of Europe. But after 840 all such progress ground to a halt for a century and a half. Perhaps the chief cause of this was a collapse of Carolingian authority which not only resulted in internal chaos and an end of agricultural growth but left the coasts of this part of Europe open to Viking and Moslem attacks. Such raids on the Atlantic side could not be stopped by weak local rulers who possessed no shipping of their own, while on the Mediterranean side neither Byzantium's western viceroys nor Carolingian emperors nor popes were able to protect Christian shores or to persuade the only considerable local naval forces—those of Amalfi and Naples—to resist Moslem attacks. As a result, it was not until 972, when Islamic pirates were expelled from Fraxinetum, that a semblance of order returned to these shores. And by that time little economic activity was to be found in a region which seemed to be backward politically, agriculturally, and economically and unaffected by the growth we have described in the rest of Europe.

Turning from these two depressed areas of Western Europe, let us now consider what we know about the merchants who in the tenth century were beginning to play an active role in its economy and its commerce. By this time it is clear that the most important of them came from England, Frisia, Germany, and Scandinavia and ranged widely along northern trading routes. A few of them, largely English and German, also traveled south to Pavia and Rome to procure eastern wares brought there by Venetians and Amalfians. There were also a few merchants whose trade was more local in character, like those from northern France and Belgium who trafficked with England, those from central Europe who traded with Russia, and Italians who peddled their wares throughout the Po valley.

By this time also, it is worth noting, Jewish merchants had lost much of the importance they had had in Carolingian times. A few still were to be found at Amalfi, and some still carried slaves with them from Verdun to Umayyad Spain, but the important trade of both Italy and the maritime north proceeded without them. Indeed the only area whose commerce they now dominated was central Europe which led to the East. And even in this part of Europe the fact that there were no considerable Jewish communities within the Byzantine world suggests that their role in trade was a restricted one.

We know very little concerning how merchants were organized in tenth-century Western Europe nor how they carried on their commercial activities. Later saga evidence suggests that some Scandinavian traders were already forming partnerships in their pursuit of profit, as did Jewish merchants and those of Amalfi and Venice who were much influenced by the more advanced trading practices which were to be found in the Islamic and Byzantine worlds.

Most other merchants, however, seem to have begun to organize themselves into guilds, especially those from England, Frisia, Scandinavia, and Belgium, for guilds were particularly useful for those engaging in long-distance trade. Some of these guilds had begun to be centered in specific towns, and some had begun to coalesce to form *hansas*, especially those whose merchants traded with England. There were also by now a few artisans in textile trades who were forming artisan guilds to regulate the way in which they produced and sold woolen cloth.

It is important to keep in mind that while an active commerce was taking hold in many parts of Western Europe, it remained relatively isolated from the more advanced economies of the Byzantine Empire and the Islamic world, an isolation which has already been emphasized in our reference to the silver money which was its essential medium of exchange. Both the Venetians and Amalfians carried on an active trade between their home ports and the Byzantine Empire and Moslem Mediterranean shores, exchanging slaves, arms, and timber for oriental and luxury wares, but they did so on a very small scale. Equally unimportant was traffic linking Umayyad Spain with Western Europe through the enterprise of a few Jewish traders. And although commerce reaching Russia by way of the Baltic or central Europe was appreciable, it, too, as we have noted, was limited by the decline of Khazaria and Byzantium's own trade policies.

Thus any view of the economy of Western Europe at this time must emphasize its essential isolation from Islamic and Byzantine markets as it developed a more active commercial life of its own. Its indigenous new merchant class was beginning to develop in certain regions and to reap profits from a growing commerce, a progressive agriculture, and a much improved technology, but all of this was still self-contained. And this was to remain true as long as broad expanses of underdeveloped and politically disorganized territory existed along western Mediterranean shores or along the middle Danube, for such territory made it difficult for merchants and others to establish fruitful contacts with the advanced economies of Byzantium and Islam.

There remains one last feature common to Western European civilization of this period: its militarization. By the late tenth century Viking, Moslem, and Hungarian invasions, coupled with a breakdown of local order in many areas, had produced an intensely militarized society. The fortress had become its central reality; whether privately controlled castles or fortified abbeys or *wicks, burgs*, and *grodys*, they were located across the length and breadth of the land. This, of course, is in sharp contrast to the situation which we have noted in all the other civilizations of the time where such fortifications were almost entirely concentrated along frontier zones, and the interior remained relatively unfortified. In Scandinavia, England, Germany, central Europe, Castile, and a few northern French principalities castles and fortresses were controlled by the rulers. Elsewhere they belonged to local strongmen and castellans, who considered them their private possessions. But overall the effect was the same—a profound militarization which affected every segment of society.

One of the results of this militarization was that now all secular landholders, large and small alike, and most merchants and other freeborn men found the profession of arms necessary to protect their interests. In France, Italy, and Germany the same was true of the clerical hierarchy as well. Some peasants also tended to be warriors when the occasion demanded, except in areas where privately constructed fortresses resulted in their being disarmed and controlled by the new class of castellans and *milites*.

Within this pattern of overall militarization, we can discern differences of a regional sort in the way in which military forces were recruited and organized. In Scandinavia, much of Germany, Slavic central Europe, the British Isles, and to some extent in northwestern Spain there was a reliance upon the freeborn foot soldier who was mustered for war by his prince or ruler. And here, except along frontiers, fortresses tended to be relatively rare. France, Lorraine, Italy, and Catalonia, however, depended on the mounted cavalryman or *miles* who lived in fortresses which dotted the countryside.

In these latter areas the expense of maintaining the equipment of a heavily armed cavalryman and of constructing the fortresses themselves tended to restrict effective military power to a small class of men who could afford the cost. This class steadily increased in number throughout the tenth century and tended to be formed from elements of the old Carolingian landed aristocracy and some peasants who were able to join this aristocracy by acquiring the necessary military skills and equipment. Merchants from the towns also were often able to acquire military power. In certain parts of northern France and Lorraine, such warriors were beginning to organize themselves into a feudal society which emphasized a network of personal relationships on a local level that provided them with military protection and justice of a rudimentary sort. In still fewer localities certain rulers, like the dukes of Normandy or the counts of Anjou and Flanders, were beginning to organize this warrior class and the castles in which they lived into workable patterns of government. Elsewhere, efforts were made to control them using a church-inspired Peace of God movement. Most regions with this sort of

society, however, experienced a militarized anarchy in which church, peasantry, trade, and orderly government were at the mercy of a new, fluid
militarized class of warriors who lived in private fortresses and dominated
the life of their local areas.

Nevertheless, it is important for us to realize that this militarization had
by now produced a class of warriors whose skill in battle, honed to a fine
edge by their constant feuding, was of a very high order. Their battle tactics,
using the lance and the stirrup in shock combat, were the equal of any in
the world, and their castles, especially those of the motte and bailey type,
were unusual in that they could be easily built and effectively defended.
Too, this class now was filled with a warrior mystique which gave them a
special *esprit de corps* different from that found among similar warriors in
nearby civilizations. In the next century these warriors, along with elements
drawn from the churchmen, merchant class, and peasantry who shared their
militarization, were to expand their bases of operation as they carried their
banners across the Channel into England and throughout the northern seas
of Europe or crossed the Alps and Pyrenees in large numbers into Spain,
southern Italy, Sicily, Syria, and Palestine to succeed at the expense of
Byzantium and Islam where Charlemagne and Otto I had failed. By the year
1000, for good or ill, Western European development was closely tied to a
militarism in which most of its population shared and which distinguished
it from the other great civilizations of this period.

Despite the disorganized state of affairs to which we have referred above,
we need to emphasize that many areas had managed by this time to develop
effective governments. In the north the best organized ones were found in
Anglo-Saxon England and in the Holy Roman Empire of Germany along
with new kingdoms in Scandinavia and central Europe which were also
beginning now to exhibit a measure of political order and stability.

Of all these realms, England was in many ways the most precocious and
advanced, politically speaking. Here from the time of Alfred the Great on
an able line of kings had defeated Danish invaders and advanced slowly from
Wessex to absorb their settlements in the Danelaw into a united English
realm. In doing so, they had managed to establish a national defense system
based upon fortified boroughs and regular naval levies and reorganized their
government and legal system along national lines. Sheriffs, who were paid
in money and could be removed by the king, appeared as did shire and
hundred courts where a national law prevailed. Agriculture, trade, and considerable industry flourished, and a national network of mints issued silver
pennies of uniform weight and relative purity. Great churchmen like Dunstan continued Alfred's reorganization of the church and the founding of
monasteries, which made for a high level of culture. Unfortunately, however,
during the last decades of the tenth century this well-organized English
realm came to be ruled by a weak monarch, Aethelred the Redeless. His
rule encouraged new Viking raids which he unwisely attempted to end

through the payment of massive Danegelds. Though these laid the basis for later national taxation, they so encouraged the pirates to which they were paid that by the year 1000 their attacks intensified and were to lead a little later to a conquest of England by Kings Swein and Canute of Denmark.

A second powerful northern European realm was the empire of the Ottos of Germany, which differed profoundly from England. This realm was the creation of a Saxon line of rulers who by 960 had united the great German duchies under the personal direction of a monarch who had strong church backing. Otto I was the second of this line and proved to be an able monarch. He not only absorbed Lorraine, to which French monarchs laid claim, and advanced into Denmark and across the Elbe but also in 955 defeated the Hungarians at Lechfeld. Secure north of the Alps, he then marched into Italy where he was crowned by the pope as Holy Roman Emperor in 962, an event which seemed to revive the power and prestige of Charlemagne in all of Western Europe.

Otto's realm was a prosperous one with many new markets and trading places, new mints, and some pretensions to a culture based on progress made by the Carolingians, but it lacked any effective central institutions of government. Instead it remained essentially Carolingian in many ways with emperors who were forced to depend upon their church to furnish them with administrators or troops they could use on distant campaigns. Unlike England, Germany developed no system of national law, taxation, or administration. It was particularly weak in Italy where imperial authority could be exercised only intermittently and to the north and east where rulers like the kings of Denmark or the princes of Poland and Bohemia accepted overlordship only reluctantly. As a result of this, during the reigns of Otto II and Otto III the prestige of the empire declined as the first met a severe defeat in southern Italy in 982 and the latter saw Denmark and Slavs living beyond the Elbe loosen the grip which Otto I had fastened upon them. By the year 1000 this empire was still powerful but less so than had been the case somewhat earlier.

The other important political units of northern Europe were the national monarchies which had arisen in Denmark, Norway, and Sweden by the late tenth century, and a trio of newly Christianized states in central Europe—Poland, Bohemia, and Hungary. In the year 1000 Denmark seemed to be the strongest Scandinavian realm with kings who were extending their power over Norway and south Baltic shores. They freed their realm and the church from German control and were reaching out for England, which they were soon to conquer. In central Europe at this same time the princes of newly Christianized Poland and Hungary had just received crowns from Otto III and the pope and were beginning, like Bohemia, to join in Latin Western civilization. But these states, like those of Scandinavia, were often still tribal and backward politically, slow to form central administrations which could guarantee a more orderly society.

West of these states lay the more remote Atlantic lands of Iceland, Ireland, and Scotland which were now only beginning to become of some importance. Iceland, nominally tied to Norway, as were the Orkneys, Shetlands, and Faroes, was actually an anarchical republic run by peasant aristocrats. Scotland had just emerged as a monarchy which was endeavoring to unite its population of Britons, Angles, Picts, and Scots. And Ireland consisted of a coastal fringe of Norse and Danish settlers surrounding an interior of Celtic tribesmen ruled by a High King. None of these three had advanced far along the path of orderly government.

The situation in France was no better. Here by 987 the Capetian family had triumphed over Carolingian rivals to become the kings of West Francia, but in the course of this struggle had lost control of most of the realm their Carolingian predecessors had ruled. Their authority was hardly recognized by the great nobles south of the Loire, and to the north of it they had little power except in their own personal domains. Thus the principal authority in northern France—which formed part of the great northern trading area— was exercised on a local level by princes like those who ruled Normandy, Anjou, and Flanders. Elsewhere in the rest of France and in Catalonia and northwestern Italy, despite the efforts of individual noble houses, nothing like true principalities had yet emerged. This part of Western Europe formed, instead, a welter of ecclesiastical and secular lordships dominated by castellans and milites who controlled local areas and shared little in the political progress noticeable elsewhere.

Three southern Western European states, however, were already revealing some special features of government which were to be important in the future. They were the Asturian kingdom of northwestern Spain and the maritime republics of Venice and Amalfi. The Asturian realm, now divided into a kingdom of Leon and a county of Castile, had managed to colonize the Duero plain and, despite attacks by Almansor, had laid the basis for later advances south at the expense of the Moslems of Al-Andālūs. Its rulers were able to maintain control over both their border fortresses and their warrior nobility, and so avoided the feudalism that took hold in northern France.

In Italy both Venice and Amalfi, which we have already examined in relation to Byzantium, had also developed some special features by this time. Venice, which was under the nominal suzerainty of the Byzantine Empire, was ruled by a doge and had emerged as a commercial state depending upon a naval fleet for both trade and war. Its commercial contacts with Byzantium and Moslem Mediterranean ports were extensive and profitable, as we have already noted. At the same time, it had begun to dominate the Adriatic and the Dalmatian coast, which opened up opportunities in the next century for its merchant class. Amalfi was equally important from a commercial point of view. It had established a colony of merchants in Constantinople, while other Amalfian merchants were especially active in Syrian and Egyptian ports, and maintained peaceful relations with the Moslems of Sicily and the

Maghreb, which brought great profits in trade. Like Venice it was ruled by a doge and nominally attached to the Byzantine Empire. But unlike Venice it seems to have had little interest in fighting. Instead its fleets remained resolutely neutral in the maritime struggles which affected this part of the world. The next century was to prove that such a policy was less successful for the Amalfians, economically advanced though they were, than the more aggressive course chosen by the Venetians.

We can sum up the political situation in Western Europe during this period, then, as follows. Three well-organized states had emerged in southern Europe: Asturian Spain, Venice, and Amalfi. Between them and the north was a broad band of territory composed of anarchical and disorganized lordships. In northern Europe a number of large and better organized realms had appeared; the most important were England, the German empire, Norway, Denmark, Sweden, Poland, and Hungary. Northern France produced three smaller feudalized principalities—Normandy, Anjou, and Flanders—which were to be very important in the future. Western Europe, increasingly prosperous, Christianized, and militarized, was on the threshold of a great future.

Last of all, we need to consider the maritime power which this civilization had managed to develop by the end of the first millennium. Along Mediterranean shores, as we have shown, the sea was still controlled by the organized fleets of Byzantium and the Islamic states. Amalfi and Venice were the only Western European communities capable of any maritime strength of their own. Venice's flotillas, as we have already pointed out, were organized for both war and trade and relied on swift galleys and merchant ships which were much like those of the Byzantine Empire. Indeed, Venice's shipping could almost be considered a provincial themal fleet over which Byzantine authorities at times still exercised some control.

We are much more in the dark about Amalfi's flotillas. It does seem probable, however, that they resembled Moslem commercial fleets which were active along sea lanes linking Al-Andalūs and North Africa with Syria and Egypt. The Amalfians carried olive oil, timber, slaves, and grain from southern Italian ports to Islamic shores and procured in return the gold and Eastern wares which they traded in Constantinople and the West, respectively. Amalfi remained an essentially commercial maritime center, displaying few warlike propensities.

In northern Europe quite a different maritime tradition had developed by this time. Here Denmark, Norway, Sweden, and England all possessed war fleets based upon territorial levies or quotas of ships imposed by ruling authorities. These war fleets used ships of various sizes, the most important of which were small craft similar to the Viking vessels which have been unearthed at Gokstad in Norway and a few other locations in Scandinavia. Some of these longships in time evolved into huge vessels built for the rulers of the period and in this case they were known as *drekkars* or dragon ships.

Those built at Nidaros in Norway, like the *Long Serpent* of Olaf Trygvason, were the most famous, though we have some evidence that there were also a number of huge Anglo-Saxon-type war vessels constructed during these years. The pirates of the northern seas, including seagoing Wends, generally employed oared, clinker-built longships. So, too, did the mariners who lived along the English Channel, if the depictions of the later Bayeux tapestry are accurate.

Side by side these warships, however, were other vessels which were primarily employed for commerce and long sea voyages. The most important of these was the *knorr,* a sailing ship without oars which could be sailed far from land using sun stones and lodestones as navigational aids. It was the knorr which was employed in voyages to Iceland, Greenland, and North America during the late tenth century and in commercial voyages from Scandinavia to the British Isles or eastern Baltic shores. Probably most Anglo-Saxon vessels used for commerce during this period were similar to the knorr. On the other hand, along Frisian and northern German coasts somewhat different types of ships had developed which were used by merchants who trafficked with Scandinavia or sailed across the North Sea to Britain. These ships were the ancestors of the *cogs, hulks, keels,* and *busses* which were to appear in such numbers in these waters later on. And at this same time we have some indication that along the shores of the Bay of Biscay mariners were using still another kind of vessel for commercial purposes, the *barca* or the barge, which differed considerably from the ships used in the North Sea or along the coasts of Scandinavia.

In short, by the year 1000 an important and quite distinct maritime tradition had appeared in the north in which Scandinavian, Anglo-Saxon, Frisian, German, Gascon, and Wendish mariners participated and which helped to link together the entire northern European trading area. Ships from this region were even bold enough to venture out into the Atlantic as far west as North America. This tradition helped provide a number of different seagoing merchant vessels which in Scandinavia and England were used to form war fleets nearly as effective as those of the Mediterranean.

Nomadic and Western
European Expansion

The Assault of Western European and Nomadic Peoples, A.D. 1000–1100

The century following the first millennium saw great changes take place in North Africa and Eurasia which were primarily the result of the aggressive activities of Western Europeans and of a number of nomadic peoples inhabiting the arid wastes between the Atlantic and the borders of Chinese Turkestan. By the time the warriors of the First Crusade had reached the Holy City of Jerusalem in 1099, at least three of the five great civilizations to which we are giving our attention had been considerably changed, and not always for the better.

The very first steps in these momentous changes took place in two rather restricted regions: to the east in southeastern Russia, Turkestan, and Persia; and to the west in Iberia and Italy. Let us first consider the eastern area. Here the collapse of Khazaria and the disappearance of the Saminids by 999 had set in motion a series of movements by nomadic Turkish tribes who had heretofore been restrained by Khazar and Saminid might. Immediately the Karakhanids, a Turkic-speaking people newly converted to Orthodox Islam, advanced to seize all territory east of the Oxus, as well as the former Saminid capital of Bokhara. West of the Oxus other Islamicized tribes of Turks, who were to become the Seljuks, began to wander freely between the Aral and Caspian seas and to press south toward the Persian cities of Khorasan. Still other Turkish tribes, the Cumans and the Polovtzi, who were still pagan, began to move directly west past Khazaria and the lower Volga into the steppes of southern Russia. From the Pamirs to the Don, then, the first two decades of the eleventh century saw a number of Turkish tribes begin to move, unrestrained by the Khazar and Saminid authority which had long kept them in place.

South of the Oxus, however, the Saminids' demise brought quite a different state of affairs, for here they were succeeded by their former vassals, the Gaznavids, who in 998 had pushed across the Khyber Pass into the plains of northern India. From here between 998 and 1030 Mahmud of Gazna was to launch a spectacular series of raids against the Hindus from his newly conquered base of Lahore in the Punjab. His raids were successful and profitable for a number of reasons. First of all, Mahmud recruited a large army of ghazi warriors, who flocked to this frontier in response to the lure of booty and a militant Islamic spirit filled with hatred for all Hindus whom they regarded as idolaters. Second, the principal objectives of his raids were temple complexes which were both rich and unfortified. And in the third place, the Hindu rajas who opposed Mahmud were both disunited and, according to the historian Biruni, incapable of dealing effectively with Gaznavid cavalry contingents, since their troops were not accustomed to fighting on horseback. So year after year Mahmud led his armies out on destructive raids and plunder poured into his twin capitals.

Mahmud's victories in northern India seemed at the time to be spectacular and gained for Islam a secure base in the upper Indus valley for future operations, as well as providing the Indians with a view of a frightening new set of intolerant conquerors. Nevertheless, the Gaznavid realm which arose as a result of all this was to prove rather disappointing. One reason was that Mahmud's warriors, who were highlanders, found it hard to acclimatize themselves to the summer heat of the Indian plains—a fact that restricted their conquests considerably and limited them to the upper Indus region. Also, back in Persia in former Saminid territory, Gaznavid rule, based upon slave and mercenary troops like that of their predecessors, was especially unpopular with those who lived in the cities. Thus, despite their riches, their orthodoxy, and their role as patrons of that Persian cultural renaissance which had begun somewhat earlier, by 1040 they had been driven out of Khorasan and most of eastern Persia by the Seljuks. Under their next ruler, Sultan Ibrahaim, they ruled a smaller, less important principality extending from the Punjab to eastern Iran with two distinct capitals located at Lahore and Gazna. In the world of eastern Islam the initiative had now passed to the Seljuk Turks and the Cumans, each of whom were now moving west toward new objectives.

To the west what seems to have set in motion a new series of events was the weakening of Fatimid authority in the Maghreb and Sicily and the collapse of the caliphate of Cordoba, both of which occurred during the first decades of the eleventh century also. Fatimid weakness seems to have co-

incided with the reign of the mad caliph Al-Hakim which loosened the bonds
between Cairo and the Ziridites of Medhia and between the Hammadids of
Bougie and the Kalbite emirs of Palermo as well. The Ziridites, however,
were unable to use this weakness to tighten their control over Algeria and
Sicily and delayed until 1048 a formal breach with their Fatimid Egyptian
overlords. But the confusion which ensued gave an opportunity to the Christian mariners who lived along western Italian shores to recover an initiative
on the sea which they had not enjoyed since the time of Louis the Pious.
They began to send flotillas from Genoa and Pisa to clear Corsica and Sardinia
of Moslem pirates, defeating Mugahid of Denia in 1016, thus gaining control
of the valuable silver mines of Sardinia, which became definitively theirs by
midcentury. And soon thereafter in 1034 the Pisans felt strong enough to
raid Bone on the shores of North Africa itself.

It was probably this Islamic maritime weakness in western Mediterranean
waters which caused the Byzantines to attempt a last campaign against Sicily
between 1038 and 1043—an attack led by the able George Maniaces and
supported by a considerable fleet. Though this campaign ended in failure
after some initial successes, it did have one important result worth noting.
The armies assembled by Byzantium for this venture included a large number
of Norman Frankish mercenaries who thus became thoroughly acquainted
with southern Italy and Sicily—a knowledge they were to put to profitable
use soon after 1043.

Finally, these decades saw an increase in the power of Venice in the
Adriatic. Its Orseoli doges, who were allied with Byzantium, began by gaining control of the Dalmatian coast and soon thereafter intervened successfully
in Hungary, with whose royal house they intermarried. Though they were
expelled from Venice by political opponents in 1026, the expansion they
helped inaugurate was to continue under their successors. In the Adriatic
as well as the Tyrrhennian Sea a new breed of aggressive Italian merchant
adventurers was now becoming active.

What was happening in Italian waters was matched by events unfolding
in the Iberian Peninsula where the caliphate of Cordoba was collapsing.
Here the slave and mercenary contingents who had served Abd-ar-Rahman
III and Almansor so well proved disastrous under the weak rule of their
successors and tore the fabric of the state apart. As a result of this, by 1031
the Ommayad caliphate had disappeared and its place was taken in Al-
Andālūs by a score of unstable, warring principalities known as *taifas* and
in Morocco by a number of weak Zenata Berber lordships.

These new taifas of Islamic Spain were ruled by kinglets, of Berber origin
in southern mountainous areas, of slave background in eastern regions, and
of Arab or Muwallid origin in Andalusia and areas to the west. And, though
there was a tendency for stronger taifas to absorb their weaker neighbors as
time went on, none of them was very strong militarily speaking. This made

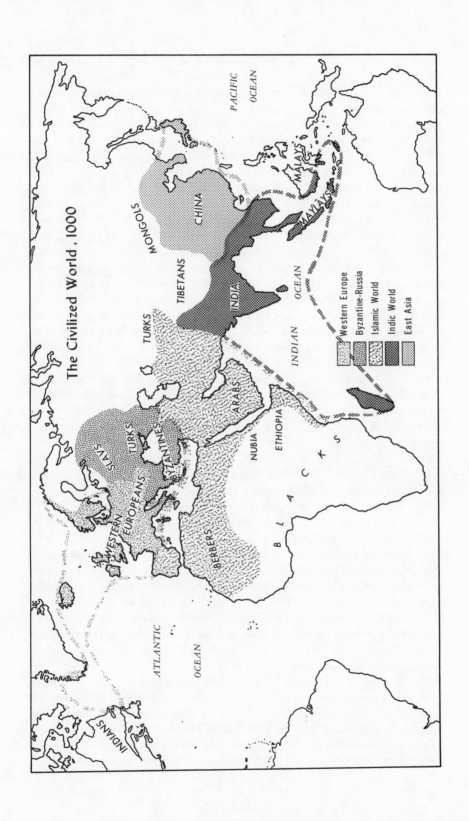

The Civilized World, 1000

Western Europe
Byzantine-Russia
Islamic World
Indic World
East Asia

PACIFIC OCEAN

MONGOLS

CHINA

MALAYS

MALAYS

TIBETANS

INDIA

TURKS

INDIAN OCEAN

SLAVS

TURKS

BYZANTINES

WESTERN EUROPEANS

ARABS

NUBIA

ETHIOPIA

B L A C K S

BERBERS

ATLANTIC OCEAN

INDIANS

it easy for the Christian princes of the north to recover the military initiative they had lost to the last Ommayad rulers and advance south again. Under Sancho el Mayor of Navarre (1000–1035) at first, and then under Sancho's son, Fernando I of Castile, and Count Ramon Berengar I of Barcelona, Christian Spanish armies moved deep into Moslem territory, expanding their frontiers to the south and extorting both plunder and regular tribute from their Islamic neighbors. The Reconquista, so long stalled by Moslem resistance, had been resumed.

These Latin Christian offensives, which grew out of local Italian and Spanish initiatives through the year 1043, coincided, interestingly enough, with a last great Viking explosion in northern Europe. Scandinavian pirates were again active along the shores of Iberia, western France, and Ireland. Swein and Canute of Denmark used such freebooters to create a Danish maritime empire which included England, most of Scandinavia, and the south shores of the Baltic. At the same time Poland grew powerful under Boleslas I, and in Kievan Russia Yaroslav the Wise (1015–1056) forged a European-wide network of marriage alliances which linked his family with the reigning houses of France, Germany, Scandinavia, and Hungary.

Even more important, this initial stage in western European expansion coincided with the beginnings of a religious revival which took various forms. A new reformed monasticism of Cluny, in the heart of militarized French society, freed itself of lay control to expand across France and into northern Spain the system of daughter houses under the direct control of Cluny's abbot, in the process making religion more important to the nobles and the rulers of the Latin West. The spreading influence of Cluny paralleled another movement in this part of Europe. Known to us as the Peace of God movement, it was an effort on the part of leading churchmen and laymen to curb the excesses of the new class of castellans and milites, especially as they affected church establishments.

If Cluny and the Peace of God demonstrate a revival of church influence in France, we find similar tendencies elsewhere too, which in various ways represented efforts to free the church of corruption and secular control that were dangerous to it. We find such efforts in Lorraine, in Tuscany and Lombardy in northern Italy, in England, where St. Dunstan's reforms had begun to bear fruit, and in the Holy Roman Empire, where Henry II and Henry III were making serious attempts to improve the quality of the clergy—including the distant popes of Rome.

Finally, during these same decades, we find a growing interest in pilgrimages. Some of them were basically local in character—like those which drew Scandinavian rulers of Ireland to Iona, Norwegians to St. Olaf's new tomb at Trondjeim, or Slavs to St. Adalbert's final resting place at Gneizno. Others were more international, like the pilgrimages which attracted so many Frenchmen and other northern Europeans to Santiago de Compostela or which caused a Canute or an Emperor Conrad II to travel to Rome. And what was to prove more important, we now find a number of nobles and other notables who ventured in large groups on the longest pilgrimage of all to the holy places of Palestine via the Danube or the Mediterranean— often stopping at Rome or Constantinople on the way. By the mid-eleventh century a new spirit of religious reform was spreading throughout the Latin West, causing those who were affected by it to begin to purify their monastic institutions and secular church establishment of lay control, to curb the warlike propensities of their milites, and to travel in increasing numbers to local or distant shrines in the hope of acquiring religious merit.

Let us now turn our attention back to the nomadic peoples of the East who, after 1040, were continuing their advance westward. By the 1050s the Seljuks, for example, having taken over most of the Iranian plateau and having been accepted as overlords by the cities of Khorasan had begun to move in two new directions—toward Baghdad and Iraq and toward the Armenian frontiers of the Byzantine Empire. The Seljuk advance into the Iraqi plain was triggered by appeals sent to them, as fervent and orthodox Moslems, by the Abbasid caliph who wished to use them to rid himself of the heretical Buyids who were his masters. Their movement toward Armenia, on the other hand, was not so much on the initiative of their rulers as in response to their tribesmen, who were attracted to the cool upland plateaus and pastures of Armenia, Kurdistan, and Anatolia, where their flocks, their hardy central Asian ponies, and their mountain Bactrian camels could provide them with a good livelihood.

The Seljuk conquest of Iraq proved swift and easy. By 1055 they had managed to destroy the Buyids, their leader Tughil Bey had been proclaimed sultan or chief of the secular government by a grateful caliph, and they had begun to move into northern Syria, which was their next objective. The almost simultaneous advance of Turkoman tribes toward Armenia, however, was more amorphous and undirected. And when they arrived there, they met with opportunity along Byzantine frontiers.

Here, by the late 1040s, Emperor Constantine IX had managed to conquer the last independent princes of Armenia and to annex the territory they controlled. These princes and their followers were disarmed and a diaspora followed—some Armenians moving north into Georgia and others into the mountainous uplands of Lesser Armenia. At the same time this part of Armenia, which had clung to an independent church ruled by its own patriarch or catholicos, found itself at odds with a Byzantine Greek Orthodoxy determined to force all Armenians to accept control by the patriarch of Constantinople.

To make matters worse, the years since 1025 had seen the Byzantine Empire's military strength decline disastrously. Basil II's imperial successors, all of them members of the civil aristocracy, who one after another married the frivolous Empress Zoë, were extravagant wastrels. Fearful of losing out to the military aristocrats of Anatolia, they relied almost exclusively on expensive and often undependable mercenaries. Their policies ended up destroying the effective themal armies and themal administration and inflating the coinage.

When the Macedonian line came to an end in 1056, the next emperor, Isaac Comnenus, who belonged to that military aristocracy which had so long been ignored, might well have remedied this state of affairs. Unfortunately, Isaac quarreled with the patriarch of Constantinople and was bitterly opposed by the civil aristocrats. When his short reign ended, he was succeeded by an emperor who represented a return to the worst features of civil aristocratic rule noted earlier. Nothing was done to strengthen the empire's eastern border defenses or to reform its armed forces. Indeed, futile negotiations with independent Armenian churchmen in 1064 increased religious bitterness along Byzantium's eastern frontiers. The Seljuk tribes then arrived and began to push across borders which were largely undefended.

Faced with this crisis, the Byzantines selected as their new emperor a certain Romanus IV, who was a military aristocrat and was determined to halt the Seljuks and drive them back across the empire's borders. He gathered a large, motley army of mercenaries, ill-armed themal levies, and other troops and in 1071 reached Manzikert, deep in eastern Armenia. Here a great battle took place. Romanus's troops were unprepared for Turkish tactics, which employed mounted archers and lightning attacks that destroyed enemy communications. His themal troops were badly led, and, worse, he was deserted during the battle itself by contingents under the command of civil aristocratic leaders. The result was a total disaster—the destruction of the entire Byzantine army and the capture of the emperor himself. Asia Minor lay open to Seljuk incursions.

There was still an opportunity to remedy the loss at Manzikert, for the Turkish sultan, Arp Arslan, was less interested in advancing into Anatolia than in seizing Syria, so he offered Romanus IV generous peace terms. Unfortunately, however, the Ducas family, who now controlled the empire, refused to accept either these terms or the return of Romanus as emperor. The chance for a favorable peace was lost, and Turkoman tribes pushed deep into Asia Minor during the next two decades until they had reached the Aegean and laid the foundations of a sultanate of Rum with its capital at Iconium. A frontier which had held firm for centuries in the face of Persian and Arab assaults had at last been breached by the new pressures and tactics of aggressive, nomadic Turkish tribesmen with important consequences for the future of Byzantine civilization.

As the Seljuk Turks advanced into Syria and Asia Minor, their pagan Turkish counterparts, the Cumans and the Polovtzi, were also moving west through the steppes which lay north of the Black Sea. As long as the powerful Yaroslav ruled, however, it seems probable that their activities were not dangerous to Kiev, which continued to control Tumortarkan on the Sea of Azov and whose contingents could reach the Black and Caspian seas in sufficient strength to raid Turkestan in 1042 and Constantinople itself in 1043.

The situation changed, however, when Yaroslav died in 1054 and his realm was divided among quarreling heirs. Immediately, the Cumans drove the Pecheneks toward the Danube and ranged throughout the southern Russian steppes virtually unchallenged. In 1068 they badly defeated the Russians at about the same time the Poles attacked Kiev from the west. And in 1094 they were again victorious in a battle fought with the Kievans. By the last decades of the century, they and their allies controlled all of southern Russia and had cut routes to the Black and Caspian seas which had for so long linked the Russians with Byzantium, Khazaria, and the Islamic states. At the same time their continuous pressure had driven the Pecheneks west to the lower Danube where the Pecheneks began to attack Byzantine Bulgaria across the river. The nomadic world of central Asia had reached southern Russia and the Danube valley in force.

By the middle of the eleventh century, nomadic pressures, which were so important for the future of Byzantium-Russia and the world of eastern Islam, had also begun to impinge upon the peoples living in central and western Moslem areas of the world. We have already noted how, in the course of the tenth century, bedouins of the Arabian Peninsula had become dangerous to their more settled and civilized neighbors as they interfered with caravan routes across the desert, threatened Mecca and Medina, and raided the agricultural population on both sides of the Fertile Crescent. For reasons which are still obscure to us, by the early eleventh century some of these same tribes seem to have reached Egypt itself despite Fatimid efforts to contain their movements. Here they ranged through the Libyan and Nubian deserts, where they were joined by more southerly nomadic tribesmen who were already attacking settled Christian Nubian farmers who lived along the banks of the Nile south of the First Cataract.

To be rid of these bedouins and at the same time punish their Ziridite vassals for throwing off their yoke and accepting the caliph of Baghdad as their spiritual leader, the Fatimids encouraged two of the most dangerous of these tribes, the Beni Solaim and the Beni Hilal, to move westward into the Maghreb. They were eager to oblige and by the 1050s had overrun most of Tripolitana and pushed into southern Tunis where they cut the caravan routes which led east to Cairo and south to Lake Chad and Ghana.

The Ziridites attempted unsuccessfully to halt the Hilalians outside Kairouan with an army of slave and mercenary troops. As a result of this victory, these bedouins were able to sack this old Tunisian capital and religious center and to overrun the fertile countryside nearby upon whose peasantry and crops all of Tunisia depended for its prosperity. Though coastal cities and plateau regions were able to resist nomadic pressures with some degree of success, the Ziridite and Hammadid realms both now found themselves in serious trouble in the interior at the very moment when they faced dangerous Latin Christian maritime initiatives in the western Mediterranean.

These years saw another burst of nomadic activity in the western Sahara which was to have equally important consequences for Islamic civilization. This was the sudden appearance of a new confederacy of nomadic, camel-riding Berber tribesmen whom we know as the Almoravids. These Almoravids, unlike the Seljuks, the Cumans, or the Hilalian Arabs, seem to have been suddenly fused into a formidable force by a religious leader called Abdullah Ibn Yaseen, who lived near the Niger River. In 1054 Abdullah led his Toureg followers in a successful attack against Ghana, only to be killed two years later during a raid upon southern Morocco. His successor, the puritanical Yusuf Ibn Tashfin, proved more successful. In 1064 the latter led Almoravid warriors north again and overran Atlantic Morocco and founded the city of Marrakesh which he made his capital. A few years later in 1069 Fez submitted to him as well, and he led his Almoravids east to conquer all of Algeria up to the borders of Hammadid Bougie.

Yusuf's military successes now attracted the attention of the Moslem kinglets who ruled Al-Andālūs and who were under intense pressure from the north. So in 1086 a number of them invited him to cross the Straits of Gibraltar and come to their assistance. He did so with a large army and won a great victory over the Castilians at Zallaqa, just northeast of Badajoz. Yusuf returned to Morocco immediately after the battle, but in 1089 he was back in Spain and during the next few years conquered and deposed most of the local rulers of Moslem Andalusia, one after another. By the time of his death in 1106 he ruled all of Moslem Spain except Saragossa and controlled Morocco and eastern Algeria as well. The Almoravids, like the Seljuks in the east, had managed to build a large empire and one which for a time blocked any further Christian advance.

As nomadic Turkish, Arab, and Berber tribes began to conquer settled areas of the Islamic world during second half of the eleventh century using forces which neither Spanish taifas, Maghrebi rulers, Fatimid caliphs, nor eastern Moslem potentates were able to defeat with traditional slave or mercenary armies—and did the same in the Russian-Byzantine world as well—Western Europeans were not idle. Indeed, the crises which these years brought to their more civilized Byzantine and Islamic neighbors provided them with opportunities which they hastened to exploit.

The area which lay most open to them turned out to be southern Italy. Here, where weak Byzantine *catapans*, Lombard dukes, and independent city-states shared a growing anarchy, bands of Norman adventurers from northern Europe made their appearance. Between 1043 and 1071 these Normans, led by Robert and Roger Guiscard, were able to create a new Norman principality which soon received recognition from the papacy and the Holy Roman emperors of Germany. Even before the Guiscards had completed their conquest of southern Italy, however, they began to attack Moslem Sicily. Led by Count Roger Guiscard, they first took Messina in 1059, and continued with the capture of Palermo in 1072 where they were helped by the Pisans and Genoese. Despite considerable assistance given Sicilian Moslems by the Ziridites, the Guiscards they were able to complete their conquests in 1091 when the last Islamic stronghold on the island fell into their hands, as did the nearby island of Malta. A solid block of territory south of Rome, soon to be known as the kingdom of Two Sicilies, had come into Western European hands.

Even before Roger Guiscard had managed to complete the conquest of Sicily, however, his older brother Robert had displayed a strong desire to expand Norman authority in another direction—across the Straits of Otranto toward the heart of the Byzantine Empire. Robert and his able son, Bohemond, launched attacks on these shores in 1081 after enlisting the help of a number of flotillas manned by Dalmatian pirates. They were resisted by the new Byzantine emperor, Alexius Comnenus, who persuaded the Venetians to help him. By the year 1085, following the death of Count Robert, the enterprise ended in failure despite some initial successes, but it served as a warning of what the neighbors of Norman Sicily could expect in the future for, between 1043 and 1091, these adventurers had managed to build a powerful state which controlled the waters linking the western and eastern Mediterranean and were able to threaten the Byzantine Empire itself as well.

The appearance of this new Norman state in the central Mediterranean coincided with continued successes enjoyed by the Pisans, Genoese, and Venetians. As we have noted already, the Genoese and Pisans helped Roger Guiscard in conquering Palermo and were rewarded by being given considerable commercial privileges in his realm. Even more important than this was the great raid they launched in 1087 against the Ziridite capital of Medhia—a raid which brought them and the Amalfians, who joined them for a change, considerable booty and which made it clear that control of the waters of the western Middle Sea was now in Latin Christian hands.

On the other side of the Italian peninsula, the Venetians were equally successful. Their flotillas not only were able to limit Dalmatian piracy but also helped drive the Normans from Albanian shores during the years 1081–85. Thanks to the success gained in this enterprise, they were rewarded by the grateful Byzantine emperor, who gave them the Golden Bull of 1082, guaranteeing them a privileged trading position in Constantinople and much of the rest of the empire—privileges that were to serve as the basis of much of their future commercial success.

As Normans, Genoese, Pisans, and Venetians began to exercise a mastery over these western Mediterranean waters, which had so long been a Byzantine or a Moslem maritime preserve, in the Iberian Peninsula events were unfolding in a way which was also favorable to the Latin Christian side. Here, after 1050, Christian power increased as King Alfonso VI of Castile continued to levy heavy tribute upon the Moslem taifas and in 1085 captured the important city of Toledo as well. At the same time his rebellious vassal, the Cid, was busy making a name for himself as a soldier of fortune operating along the frontiers of Moslem Saragossa to the east, where the kings of Aragon were attempting, with less success, to expand their frontiers as well.

As we have already pointed out, Castilian success caused Moslem rulers to invite the Almoravids to come to their assistance, and this resulted in a great Moslem victory at Zallaqa in 1086. Curiously enough, however, this defeat did not result in any loss of Christian territory. Instead, despite the return of the Almoravids in 1090, the Castilians kept their earlier conquests, the Cid was able to capture and hold Valencia until his death, and the Aragonese were able to resume a slow, steady advance at the expense of the emirs of Saragossa. Despite Zallaqa, until 1100, in Iberia as in Italy, the picture was one of Christian expansion and success.

It is important, however, to note a difference between *this* Christian expansion in Spain and that which took place during the first half of the century—namely, that it was accompanied by considerable help and encouragement from Europe north of the Pyrenees. Not only did Cluny now actively support the Reconquista, but so did Pope Gregory VII, who in 1073 had his legates in southern France proclaim what was almost a crusade to encourage French noblemen to assist their Spanish Aragonese coreligionists. And now, too, we begin to find large numbers of northern and southern French warriors crossing the Pyrenees to seek adventure, booty, and religious merit in warfare against the Moors. A new crusading spirit was appearing in the West and in Spain several decades before the First Crusade itself.

All of which brings us to the matter of the overall growth of papal power in the late eleventh century, which was to affect profoundly the expansion of Western Europe during the next two centuries. This increase in the influence and the authority of the Roman pontiff owed a great deal to that new impulse toward religious reform which during the reign of Pope Leo IX (1049–53) resulted in a number of churchmen gathering at the papal court who were eager to free the papacy and the church in general from corruption and lay control.

One of these churchmen, Cardinal Humbert of Lorraine, was responsible for leading a delegation to Constantinople in 1054 which broke with the patriarch of Constantinople and proclaimed a schism between the Greek and Latin churches. A second member of this group, who became Pope Nicolas II in 1059, freed the papacy from lay control by giving the College of Cardinals the exclusive right to select a new pope. A third member, Hildebrand, as Pope Gregory VII, not only encouraged Christian expansion in Spain and the western Mediterranean but was also responsible for beginning the Investiture Struggle with the emperors of Germany which ended with a pope who was much more powerful and princes who were much less able to appoint high churchmen than had previously been the case.

This new papal independence and the increase of papal authority which accompanied it throughout the Latin West were both closely linked to successful efforts to expand Western European power—especially in the Norman realm of the Two Sicilies. Thanks to this expansion, popes in Rome no longer had to rely upon Byzantium for protection against Moslem attacks. Nor did they need to fear, as much as they had at one time, the intervention of German emperors in their affairs. And this explains why, as the century drew to a close, the papacy took the crucial step of proclaiming what we know as the First Crusade.

It is true that in a certain sense this crusade was the result of an appeal by the Emperor Alexius Comnenus for a thousand Latin mercenary knights whom he could use to drive the Turks from Asia Minor, as well as a reaction to tales reaching Europe of how the Seljuk Turks were interfering with Latin pilgrims who were traveling to the Holy Land in increasing numbers. But it would probably be more accurate to regard this movement as an essentially Western European one invented by Pope Urban II, who was both a former Cluniac and the scion of a noble French family.

In preaching this crusade in 1095 and 1096, Urban managed to combine a number of diverse elements to form a project which assured Western European expansion in a special way. These included the aggressiveness which native Spanish Christians and those from across the Pyrenees had long displayed in Iberia, as well as that which animated Normans and Italian mariners around Italy; the growing impulse toward pilgrimages; and a strong feeling for religious reform which was prevalent throughout the Latin West. At the same time the pope could rely for support upon those who saw in a reformed and powerful papal office the true leader of Western Europe— and one which could even hope to use such a crusade to persuade the schismatic Orthodox church of Constantinople to accept papal overlordship.

That Urban judged his flock aright can be seen from an examination of the First Crusade itself, which represented a remarkable, spontaneous effort by most of Latin Europe. Although the main crusading forces were composed of nobles from France and Norman Italy, it soon attracted Pisans and Genoese to its ranks who sailed their ships to Syrian shores in large numbers. Others were added a bit later from the North Sea and Scandinavia, joining in the attack after a long sea voyage by way of the Straits of Gibraltar—and in so doing managed to fuse an older Viking spirit with a new Christian zeal. By the year 1100, as the Holy Land began to pass into the hands of the Franks, Western Europe from Norway and Britain to the borders of Moslem Spain and Byzantium became united in an expansion which was to continue, with the church's blessing, for many decades to come.

Of the Byzantine-Russian, Islamic, and Western European civilizations, it was the first which was most severely affected by this century of nomadic incursion and Latin Christian expansion. By 1071 it faced a crisis as dangerous as any it had known. This is especially true of Byzantium proper, which, having lost both Asia Minor and southern Italy, found itself attacked by the Pecheneks along the Danube and by Normans along its shores facing the Ionian Sea. The empire's religious unity had been compromised by a mid-century quarrel between its emperors and the patriarchs of Constantinople, and because of this it had severed all ties with the papacy and the Western church, while failing to reach any settlement with the Armenian church to the east. Bogomilism remained a powerful force in its Balkan provinces, while many of its most important monastic establishments, located in Anatolia, were being destroyed by the Seljuk Turkish advance.

Equally important, by the time Alexius Comnenus had become emperor in 1081 the empire's machinery of government was in a state of collapse. The last emperors of the Macedonian house and their successors, as has been noted, had helped to bring this about by debasing their gold nomisma coinage and by weakening the taxation system of the state through tax-farming and grants of feudalistic *pronoias* to favored aristocrats.

The decline in the empire's military strength was even more serious. The themal system was now moribund and could no longer provide effective soldiers for battle. At the same time the naval themes were so disorganized that by the late eleventh century, instead of the flotillas of earlier years, they were able to muster only a few ships for guard or patrol duty.

Unfortunately, nothing had been done for some decades to create a new system to replace such themal levies. The civil aristocrats who from 1025 on had tended to control the central government and the imperial office itself were afraid to allow a striking army which might have been used by the military aristocrats as a springboard to power, and they built only *one* fleet, that used in the Sicilian campaign of 1038–43. As a result, the only trained troops available were foreign mercenaries: Franks, Varangians from Russia, Scandinavia, and England, and motley collections of Turks—all eager to serve the empire for gold. Such mercenaries were expensive, turbulent, rebellious, and unreliable as defenders.

It is difficult to form an accurate impression of the empire's economic status by the last years of the eleventh century. Certainly, the agricultural surpluses which had been sent to Constantinople from nearby areas of Europe and Anatolia were no longer so abundant, as Asia Minor found itself invaded by Turkish nomads and the Pecheneks raided across the Danube. And no doubt the productivity of the peasants declined even in areas which were not subject to outside attack but which felt the weight of heavy taxation and the encroachments of noble and ecclesiastical landlords. It is also clear that the weak post-Manzikert government found it difficult to control the empire's external and internal trade and to regulate its factories, mines, and quarries as it had done until 1025. In short, economically, religiously, politically, and militarily, Byzantium faced a profound crisis.

Nevertheless, many historians may have overestimated the difficulties which the Byzantine world faced at this time and underestimated its power of regeneration, for by the year 1100 things were much improved. The first steps in this process were taken by the emperor Alexius, who, although a military aristocrat, came to terms with his old rivals, the civil aristocrats, by allying himself with the Ducas family. This was followed by an improvement in relations with the church which ended imperial rivalry with the patriarchs of Constantinople. Now military aristocrats, civil aristocrats, and church hierarchy were at last prepared to work together.

During the next two decades Alexius also effected a reorganization of the civil administration and the taxation system of the empire so that they functioned in a more efficient fashion, and he tapped church resources on a temporary basis to pay for his armies and the expensive diplomacy he used to divide his nomadic enemies. He also used a policy of granting lands on a lifetime basis in the form of *pronoias* and *charisticums* to tie aristocrats to his person and use them in the service of the empire as warriors and administrators.

The results were soon apparent. By 1085 the Norman threat to the empire had temporarily ended and vassal Slavic princes along the middle Danube had returned to their allegiance. Soon thereafter the Pecheneks ceased to be a threat as the Cumans, egged on by Byzantine gold, attacked them from the rear, and the survivors crossed the Danube and settled in Bulgaria as imperial allies.

With his European provinces secure, Alexius then turned his attention to the Turks in Asia Minor whom he had prevented from consolidating their gains by a diplomacy which kept them in constant turmoil. Needing outside help to reconquer Asia Minor, he appealed to the pope for western aid—an appeal which helped precipitate the First Crusade.

The First Crusade, as is well known, brought thousands of armed Westerners to Constantinople, some of whom, like the Norman Bohemond, the Byzantines had every reason to distrust. But the emperor was able not only to survive this danger but to use it to his own advantage, for, thanks to the Crusaders and the new army and fleet which he had formed, he was able to recapture almost all coastal areas of Asia Minor and restrict the Seljuks to the less fertile interior. If he was less successful in Lesser Armenia and Cilicia, where the Armenian upper class remained hostile, or in Antioch, which the Crusaders refused to return to him, by 1100 he had managed nevertheless to use this Western European expansionism to check the Seljuks' advance and to revive the power and cohesion of the Byzantine world at the same time. The schism between Latin and Greek churches was still unhealed; Venetians had begun to use the provisions of the Golden Bull to exploit the economy of the empire in a systematic fashion; Pisans, Genoese, and Franks were establishing themselves in Syria and Palestine in a way that could seriously threaten the empire's future; and Greek and Latin suspicion of each other had been heightened, but Byzantium had weathered the storm. It was now prepared to face a brighter future under its Comneni rulers than had seemed possible two or three decades earlier.

But what of the rest of the Byzantine-Russian world? By 1100 the steppes between the Volga and the Danube were completely under the control of the Cumans and their nomadic allies who had reduced to a trickle all commerce moving across them. Perhaps a few Cuman chiefs had begun to accommodate themselves to their Russian neighbors toward the end of the century by contracting marriage alliances with princely families like that of Vsevold of Kiev (1078–93). But if so, only a few instances of such arrangements are known to us.

The more northerly Kievan Rūs were now in a much weaker position than they had been during the first half of the century. Their princes divided power amongst themselves according to an intricate succession system which gave a special primacy to the ruler of Kiev. Their towns, in which political power was shared with merchant *veches* and the *druzinas* or bodyguards of the prince, enjoyed considerable autonomy. Both their religious establishments and their culture—influenced by Byzantium—continued to develop along lines which had been laid down by the year 1000. But the Kievan Rūs found their economy considerably altered as older profitable commercial contacts with Byzantium and the Moslem south were curtailed. Despite tenuous contacts with central and northern Europe, the Russian economy had to develop in an isolation greater than any it had faced for several centuries.

The changes which had taken place in the Islamic world were equally important but of a somewhat different character. Most obvious was a loss of territory in Spain, Sicily, Sardinia, and Syria to the Latin West which almost balanced Islamic gains in Asia Minor and northern India. Then there was the movement of nomadic peoples in significant numbers into settled areas—Berber Touregs into Morocco and Al-Andālūs; Arab bedouins into Tripolitana, Tunisia, and parts of the Fertile Crescent; and Turkomans who took over much of Transoxiana and reached Syria, northern Persia, Azerbaijan, Armenia, and Anatolia.

Even more important, these nomadic invasions and Western European pressures helped bring about certain military and governmental changes. Again and again during this century Islam's border defenses, based on ghazi warriors and pirate flotillas, had proved incapable of an effective defense against Latin Christian attacks in Italy, Spain, or the Near East, while its slave and mercenary troops showed themselves equally unable to protect the sedentary population, whether we are referring to the Spain of the Ommayads and taifas, the Maghreb of the Ziridites, or the areas governed by the Gaznavids, the Buyids or the Hamdanids in the east. Indeed, by the end of the century, only two realms still were making use of slave and mercenary contingents, Fatimid Egypt and Gaznavid Persia and northern India. And in the case of the former, such levies had a very spotty record in combating bedouin tribesmen or Crusaders in Palestine—as well as displaying a dangerous turbulence when they rose in a great revolt in Cairo in 1076 which almost destroyed the Fatimid government.

Equally noticeable during these years was a precipitous decline in Moslem sea power in the Mediterranean. In western waters by 1100 the organized navies which the Ommayads of Spain and the Fatimids of Sicily and North Africa had long maintained simply disappeared, leaving only a scattering of ships which could be mustered for warlike purposes. In the eastern Mediterranean, while something remained of Fatimid sea power, it had been considerably reduced to a small force capable of little more than defensive operations along Egyptian and Syrian shores. The Mediterranean seemed to have become a Latin Christian lake from the Pillars of Hercules to the coasts of Syria.

As navies, border ghazis, and internal slave and mercenary forces all proved inadequate to the tasks assigned them, these years saw a new military system take their place, especially in eastern Islamic areas ruled by the Seljuks and the Karakhanids. This system was one which depended upon a combination of tribal levies and a new body of professional soldiers, often Turkish, who were rewarded by grants of iqtà lands and who were tied to their military commanders by bonds of personal loyalty. Such a military aristocracy, now to be found in the very heart of the Islamic world, gradually began to adapt itself to the older unarmed elite of ulemas, merchants, and scholars who continued to live in the cities, serving as bureaucrats, jurists, and literary figures of note, as well as running the businesses and industry of the period. This new military elite, however, was frequently hostile to those elements of the older upper class who lived on estates in the countryside, for its soldiers coveted such lands for themselves and quite frequently took them over as iqtàs. They were also hostile to Christian and

Jewish elements among the settled population to whom they were unwilling to accord full toleration or a privileged status in the bureaucracies which continued to function everywhere.

In the third place, these years saw an important change take place in the religious life of Islam—a steady growth of Sunni orthodoxy and a decline in Shia power. This began in the west as early as 1048 when the Mahgreb and Sicily renounced Shi'ism and when the Almoravids, despite their unorthodox ideas, supported the narrow views of orthodox Sunni ulema within their empire. In the east, where both the Gaznavids and the Seljuks were fervent Sunnis, the same thing happened. These Seljuks made it a policy to suppress Shi'ism, both by their victories over the Shia Buyids and Hamdanids and by establishing orthodox schools knows as *madresas* throughout their domains. Such *madresas* were especially dear to the heart of the great Persian vizier of the Seljuks, Nizam-al-Mulk. As a result of such policies, by the early twelfth century Shi'ism found itself restricted to small sects like the Ismailis or the Druzes who often took refuge in inaccessible or remote regions, like the Elburz and Lebanon mountains, the hills of the Yemen, and the swamps of Iraq. Even in Fatimid Egypt, which remained Shia, we find during these years a considerable growth of Sunni sentiment among the ruling and business elite. By 1100, Sunni orthodoxy steadily widened its appeal and became the doctrine accepted by most Moslems everywhere.

Changes in economic trends were much less sweeping or decisive than in the other areas we have discussed. It is true that the eleventh century could not equal the boom times and expansiveness of the tenth throughout the Islamic world. It is also true that the movement of nomadic tribesmen into settled areas as well as Latin expansion in the western Mediterranean had some deleterious effects upon the prosperity enjoyed by most Moslems. Both of these movements at times harmed the settled peasantry and the rural elite and temporarily cut off trade routes upon which the prosperity of a particular region depended. Witness the effect of Turkish invasions upon Transoxiana and western Persia during half a century and what nomadic tribes did as they spread all the way to the Mediterranean and Black Sea soon thereafter. There is also little doubt that the Hilalian Arabs undermined the rural prosperity of much of the eastern Maghreb and interrupted caravan routes leading to Egypt and the Sudan. Almoravid attacks upon Ghana, like their conquests of Morocco and Spain, also did considerable damage, just as the Norman seizure of Sicily had its destructive side.

Nevertheless, the evidence now available to us suggests that few of these events had any long-range significance or destroyed in any way the basic fabric of the Islamic world's economic life as it had developed during the ninth and tenth centuries. For instance, Geniza documentation from Egypt shows us that the vital international trade route which centered in Cairo and linked Spain, Sicily, and North Africa with India and East Africa was never interrupted. If Hilalian Arabs severed *land* routes to the east and to the Sudan, it simply meant more *maritime* commerce reached Tunisia and that traffic over western Saharan caravan trails to Sigilmasa increased to make up for that which no longer reached Gadames or Wargla to the east. Similarly, when Norman attacks disrupted Sicilian commerce, we know that the Amalfians who handled products similar to those of Sicily were more active than usual in the entrepots of Syria, Egypt, and North Africa.

In the Moslem east, again, it is significant that once the Gaznavids, the Karakhanids, and the Seljuks had managed to stabilize their borders, economic conditions improved almost at once. El-Bekri and other Moslem geographers then tell us of trade reaching the lower Volga, of Baghdad and Iraq reestablishing profitable contacts via the island of Kish with Indian shores, and of Seljuk and Gaznavid rulers accumulating sufficient stocks of gold to strike gold dinars, though often of inferior quality. It is also worth noting that when the Franks reached Syria they found an abundant store of oriental spices and oriental wares in its ports—goods that could only have reached there by way of the Persian Gulf. By 1100, then, except along the borders of Armenia or in Anatolia which were both much affected by Turkish nomadism, the basic economic structure of the world of Islam had survived this time of troubles relatively intact.

What then of Western Europe during this century of changes? How was it affected? We have already commented upon one important development— the rise of the papacy to a position of overall leadership in the Latin West. But there were other changes, too. One of them was a steady, almost inexorable spread of the militarized world of castles and milites which had originated in the area between the Tiber, the Pyrenees, and the Rhine, to new regions—first of all, to England and southern Italy both conquered by the Normans and then to Sicily, Christian Spain, and Syria and Palestine of the Crusaders. As this took place it is worth noting that the Normans, who played so important a role in all this, showed an amazing ability to combine the militarized governments they established in England and Sicily with preexisting nonfeudal indigenous institutions—a fact which had important implications for the political future of Western Europe.

Equally important was a spread of towns into areas like northwestern Italy and the French Midi where they had been rare or weak earlier and the growth of some urban areas in northern Italy and Flanders into autonomous communal centers with a distinct political life of their own.

The spread of towns and of the new militarism had important economic implications for the Latin West as a whole, and especially for those two backward areas which we have mentioned earlier—the upper Danube valley and the area between the Loire and the Mediterranean. In Austria peasants again began to clear the soil of river valleys for their crops, and connections were reestablished with the Byzantine Empire, via a newly Christianized

Hungary, which were used not only by merchants but also by streams of pilgrims and Crusaders on their way to Constantinople. In the other backward area we now find Genoese, Pisans, and Christian Spanish accumulating so much wealth at the expense of their Moslem adversaries that this booty helped to revitalize ports from the Llobregat to the Tiber and to stimulate commerce and agriculture in the interior as well. By 1100 this activity had helped integrate the economies of these two regions with those of the northern seas and of northern Spain and Italy, uniting all of Europe into a single and increasingly prosperous economic region.

This economic revival, however, did not extend to every part of the Continent during the last years of the eleventh century. This was especially true of the Baltic area, which until about 1050 had been the scene of considerable economic activity. Now, despite some traffic still reaching Russia by way of Gotland, this part of Europe saw its economic life steadily decline in importance—a decline which was probably related to Kiev's failure to maintain commercial contacts with Turkestan or Constantinople.

The decline of commerce in this part of the Latin West, however, had its compensations, for the resulting tilt of Western Europe toward the south and southwest made it possible for the Genoese, Amalfians, Pisans, and Venetians to exploit trade with the Moslem and Byzantine worlds of the Mediterranean. By 1100 they and a number of Norman and Frankish noble adventurers were firmly established in Sicily, Syria, Palestine, and Constantinople where they could exploit the commerce of the Mediterranean. Western European civilization which had so long lagged behind its neighbors had at last come of age.

Perhaps the most decisive and dramatic symbol of this new state of affairs was represented by the Latin West's new strength on the sea—a matter which can only be briefly sketched here. By the first years of the twelfth century, as we have already pointed out, the Mediterranean had all but become a Latin Christian lake. The Genoese, Pisans, Venetians, and the inhabitants of the Two Sicilies dominated its western waters, controlled the straits past Sicily, and were in the process of establishing bases in the Near East from which they could challenge Byzantine and Fatimid naval establishments.

Of equal importance as a portent of the future was the fact that during the last years of the eleventh century the maritime peoples of northern Europe began to sail their ships south along the shores of Atlantic Iberia and Morocco, where organized Islamic fleets had disappeared, and enter the Mediterranean—first as pilgrims and then as Crusaders sailing their fleets to the Near East. A Western European maritime establishment had begun to emerge to match the common purpose of its Crusaders, the institutions of its towns and its class, those who dominated its castles, and the fusion of its economic life into a more prosperous and unified whole.

The Eastern civilizations of Eurasia, with a few exceptions, were affected only indirectly by the changes which were so important to the peoples of Western Europe, Islam, and the Byzantine-Russian area. Northern India, for instance, experienced a feudalization which some historians believe took place in response to the raids of Mahmud of Gazna and which may have helped halt any immediate advance of Islam after his death. It is also possible that economic troubles in northern India during this same period resulted from Gaznavid attacks upon the Hindus of this part of the Indic world.

Perhaps the most important result of these changes, however, was the general decline of commerce which reached East Asia by land in the course of the eleventh century and an increase in that which followed maritime routes. This change was certainly the result of the dislocations which we have noted were taking place in Moslem Turkestan and southern Russia for some decades after the year 1000 and which certainly affected the silk routes which passed through this part of central Asia.

With all this as a general background, let us turn our attention first of all to China proper and attempt to sketch in some detail the changes which took place there during this period. This century saw China's economy grow spectacularly until, by the year 1100, it had developed what can only be regarded as the most advanced form of economic life to be found in all of Eurasia. One basic aspect of this growth, to which we alluded briefly in an earlier chapter, was a sharp increase in agricultural productivity, which seems to have been closely linked to the introduction of a new strain of early ripening rice from Champa. A second was the construction of a number of new reservoirs and dams along Chinese rivers which improved irrigation. The combination of these two made it possible to produce as many as three crops a year in fertile river valleys. Third, we now find considerable improvement in the empire's canals—especially the Grand Canal which linked Kaifeng, the Sung capital, and the Yellow River complex with that of the Yangtze to the south. This meant agricultural surpluses could be moved more easily and cheaply to areas which needed them.

This agricultural revolution, which occurred mainly in central and southern China, was matched by a remarkable industrial development in northern China—the appearance of a new iron and steel industry. This industry, centered in Kaifeng, made use of coal and coke in the smelting of ore and during these years managed to reach a production level of 125,000 tons of iron and steel annually. And as iron production boomed in northern China, so did the mining of copper and other metals, mainly in the south and southwest, as well as much salt and various clays for making fine porcelain. China had not only become increasingly productive in its agriculture but had also become a kind of medieval industrial colossus.

Naturally enough, all of this resulted in a considerable increase in China's population, two-thirds of which was now located in the Yangtze valley and

in southern China in the very areas where the rice revolution had increased
the food supply so dramatically. Much of this population surplus now found
homes in towns and cities creating an urban explosion in which small towns
became cities and cities became metropolises. Thus by the first years of the
twelfth century Kaifeng's population had risen to at least 1,000,000 or more,
making it the largest city in the world, and Hangchow, the most important
city in the Yangtze valley, had reached a size of 600,000 to 700,000.

A new class of capitalists presided over this economic development in
towns and countryside. These were the merchants and the industrialists of
the period, who also invested their profits in land and improved methods
of agriculture. They also served as bureaucrats who were chosen by examination to staff the imperial administration. They formed a class not unlike
the elite who ran the businesses and served as bureaucrats in the Islamic
world to the west. And like them, this Chinese elite continued to show little
interest in the martial arts, preferring to rely upon foreigners and mercenaries recruited from the lower classes to defend the empire. Consequently,
the northern Sung remained on the defensive during this century in relations
with their Kitan and Tangut neighbors who were aggressive warriors and
who prized well-trained cavalry contingents not available to the Chinese.

The efficient Sung bureaucrats have provided us figures which summarize
the results of this growth in China's economy from an internal point of view.
These years saw the money supply increase so markedly that in the year
1067 the government issued some 37,000,000 strings of copper cash, in
contrast to less than 2,000,000 strings produced annually in late Tang times.
And some decades later during the first years of the twelfth century the
Chinese authorities could count on revenues that quadrupled to include
17,000 ounces of gold and 1,146,723 ounces of silver as well. To such money
and specie which had a wide circulation we should add paper money, first
issued on a private basis by merchants of Szechwan in 1024, which became
very popular and a government monopoly soon afterward, and which was
used to facilitate credit and commerce or to pay taxes of various kinds.

This economic surge had an effect upon the carefully regulated trade with
regions beyond imperial borders—a trade which consisted mainly of tea and
silks exchanged for horses from Hsi Hsia and Liao and for other seaborne
goods as well. By this time maritime traffic had become much more important
than overland traffic—amounting to about seventy percent of the total. It
was stimulated by governmental construction of warehouses and port facilities and by the establishment of a number of commissariats of foreign maritime trade, one located in Shantung, one in Canton, one in Fukien, and two
at Hangchow and Ningpo near the mouth of the Yangtze River. The maritime
trade consisted mainly of cotton textiles, spices, and other tropical luxury
products which were imported in exchange for the porcelains and Chinese
industrial wares highly prized in the rest of East Asia and in the markets of

the south. One interesting feature of this traffic was that throughout this century an increasingly large share of it was handled by native Chinese mariners with larger and more efficient seagoing junks—some of which now began to be equipped with compasses of a rather crude sort. It was also facilitated by imperial policies that encouraged Chinese merchants to establish themselves abroad and by treaties which were negotiated on their behalf with South Indian, Srivijayan, Cambodian, Javanese, and Champa rulers.

Despite all of this activity, however, China's foreign trade, had some important limitations and special characteristics. First of all, Chinese society remained essentially self-sufficient, throughout this century, like tenth-century Byzantium and unlike the Islamic world. It was able to produce, within the borders of the Sung empire, all the foodstuffs, all the timber, and all the metals and industrial wares which it needed to support a high standard of living. And since it relied upon a copper cash currency or paper money, it did not prize gold or silver coins which were deemed essential by the other great civilizations of the time. Its imports, except for horses, were of a tropical or luxury character and its exports were rather similar—being essential neither to the Chinese who sold them nor to the foreigners who bought them.

In the second place, although such commerce increased in volume and in value so that between 1087 and 1098 customs duties levied upon it realized an average of 400,000 strings of cash a year, such revenues never amounted to more than one or two percent of the government's current total receipts—and were, therefore, a minor element in its financial balance.

And last of all although the Chinese authorities favored maritime enterprise, they did not think it worthwhile before 1125 to build a navy to protect it. Instead, in the case of the one naval operation of which we have knowledge—an attack on Annam in 1077—they used a fleet of impressed Fukienese merchant vessels, which did not prove very effective. Down to the end of the eleventh century, then, the northern Sungs saw foreign commerce grow, especially maritime commerce, but the increase hardly matched internal economic growth. In addition, this traffic consisted mainly of non-essential or luxury goods which did not seem important enough to warrant the building of a navy to protect it.

China's East Asian neighbors experienced few important changes of either a political or an economic nature. Though the northern Sungs perpetuated the fiction that all their neighbors were their tributaries, only the Korean kings and the rulers of Nan-Chao actually played the part. Neither the Japanese emperors nor the monarchs who controlled Annam, Hsi Hsia, and Liao were ever willing during these years to accord this sort of respect to a Son of Heaven whose armies and navies struck no terror in their hearts. The economic impact of eleventh-century China was equally limited. Annam and Nan-Chao benefited somewhat from the expansion taking place nearby in the south and southwest of China. On the other hand, Hsi Hsia and Liao found their prosperity diminished during these years, although, as far as the Tangut realm was concerned, an increase in Sung tribute payments may have compensated in part for this.

We have too little information concerning the economies of Japan and Korea to hazard more than a few generalities. Probably trade with China increased—via its Shantung trade portals—much of it now carried in Chinese ships. But we have no evidence that this commerce strengthened the Korean merchant community, which continued to be subordinated at home to its landed aristocracy. Japan saw some increase in the power of its imperial house located in Kyōtō, using a system which stressed the power of ex-emperors of the imperial family over court rivals like the Fujiwara. But there is nothing to indicate that this coincided with any increase in internal trade or in the development of a true money economy. Instead, it was its feudalized warrior bands in the provinces who continued to grow in power and who now, for the first time, intervened in Kyōtō in matters which heretofore had been the preserve of powerful court aristocrats or the great Buddhist shrines.

For the other great civilization of the east, that of Greater India, the most important development which took place during this century was not the Gaznavid invasion nor an increased Chinese trade to the south, but the appearance of a great Chola maritime empire. During the reigns of Rajarada I (ca. 990–1016), Rajenda I (1012–44), and Kulortlunga (1070–1116), the Chola empire not only controlled the Tamil, Pandya, and Chera areas of southern India but also used its powerful navy to seize control of Ceylon and the Maldive and Laccadive islands for some years, as well as the Andaman and Nicobar islands in the Bay of Bengal. Its rulers were able to intervene at times in Orissa, Bengal, and Burma and to send fleets in 1025 and 1068 to attack Srivijaya. Inscriptions which date from this period and which show that Tamil merchants were active in Java and Malaya and vice versa emphasize the commercial interests of the Cholas, as does the record of their diplomatic and commercial dealings with Burma, Cambodia, and Sung China. So does another interesting southern Indian inscription from about 1050 which tells of its merchants (called *Ayyovole* merchants) who traveled to Bengal, Malaya, northern and western India and Persia in pursuit of gain.

This powerful Chola realm, which seems to have developed an elaborate bureaucracy, a powerful army and navy, a flourishing agriculture based upon irrigation, and considerable industrial production played a vital role in the Indic world as a whole. First of all, it seems to have used its maritime power to monopolize commerce in the Bay of Bengal between the Coromandel Coast and the Straits of Malacca. This kept Arab merchants from venturing east of Ceylon and the Malabar Coast and the Chinese from extending their trading range beyond Srivijaya and Java. Second, the close connections the Cholas were able to maintain with northern India helped to encourage a revival of Sanskrit literature and Hinduism in general in southern India. And in the third place, their empire seems to have helped spread Hinayana Buddhism from Ceylon and the temple of Conjeveran to Burma, which, for reasons still obscure to us, was at the time unusually receptive to Buddhist doctrines.

Important as the rise of this Chola empire was for the peoples of Greater India, there were other developments which took place during these years that were almost as vital. One was the emergence of a powerful Burmese state which controlled the Mons and had its capital at Pagan, and whose great rulers Anawrahta and Kianyettla maintained close ties with both China and the Cholas. A second was the appearance, during the last years of the eleventh century, of an equally powerful royal house in Cambodia which controlled the lower Mekong valley and much of present-day Thailand. Still a third was the rise of a new Kediri realm in eastern Java—one which developed an improved system of irrigation and control over trade with the Spice Islands to the east into a power strong enough to challenge the might of Srivijaya. The Kediri rulers did so, incidentally, in alliance with the Cholas, and their success may explain why the Sungs were so eager to establish good relations with them and settle Chinese merchants in their ports.

All of this seems to have resulted in a decline in the power and prosperity of Srivijaya. Although it was able to maintain some control over the commerce that linked East Asia with Greater India by way of the Straits of Malacca, Sunda Strait, or the Malay Peninsula, increasingly Srivijaya found it difficult to maintain its authority over local ports and rajas within its empire. Down to 1100 Srivijaya remained an important state with close relations with China and the Chola empire, but its decline was at hand. The same is true of Champa, the other older Southeast Asian state which had long served as an intermediary in the commerce of this part of the world. The Chams were now subject to considerable pressure from the Annamese who captured some of the northern Cham provinces. They were also attacked by equally aggressive Cambodians who coveted control of the Mekong Delta. The eleventh century, then, saw powerful realms arise in Burma, Cambodia, and Java which shared a major role along with the Cholas in Indic civilization and began to replace Srivijaya and Champa as leaders in the commerce and economic life of this part of Asia.

We know little about the kinds of ships which the Cholas used to control the waters of much of the Indic world or those employed by their allies and their enemies. We have no reason to believe, however, that Indic vessels were influenced in any way by Chinese shipbuilding methods, which relied on watertight compartments, nails, and oak or pine planking. Instead, it seems that both Indic and Arab mariners continued to ply the waters of the

Indian Ocean in sewn ships made without nails and built of teak or coconut palm. Such vessels still followed coastal and monsoon routes throughout these seas, as of old, on a regular seasonal basis.

By this time, however, we begin to have some firm evidence that traffic *within* the Indic world differed from that with China, carrying more than just spices and luxury goods. Geniza documentation from Cairo and other evidence from Islamic areas, for instance, show us that there was a considerable traffic between Red Sea and Persian Gulf ports which involved foodstuffs, timber, metal, and textiles—much of them of a bulk character. *Ayyovole* merchants operating in the Bay of Bengal used ships which carried cargoes of elephants from Burma or Ceylon and horses from the west. Unlike East Asian overseas commerce, that of Greater India had already assumed a character which was much more basic to the needs of those who shared in it or were affected by it—a situation which was to continue in the years to come.

The Balance Restored:
Byzantium, Islam,
Western Europe, China,
and India, 1100–1195

The years between 1100 and 1195, which form the second period with which we are concerned in this study, represent a contrast with the era we have just finished examining. The eleventh century was a time of considerable change within the five great civilizations of Eurasia and Africa and one which saw an alteration in their relationships with one another. This next age was in many ways a reaction to what had preceded it, as the peoples who made up these civilizations made an effort to overcome the difficulties which they had encountered and to reassert their very different styles or identities.

Each civilization's response to this turbulent time was remarkably similar. The Sungs prized a backward-looking neo-Confucianism, and the Taira clan of Japan behaved like the Fujiwaras. The Indians revived ancient Hindu traditions, while Khmer monarchs used the sculptures of Ankor Wat to appear as heroes from the Ramayana. The Islamic world welcomed the narrow and intolerant religiosity of the Almohads and Saladin. Andronicus Comnenus pretended he was Basil II. And the *Primary Chronicle*, which depicted a Kiev which was no more, was welcomed by the circle which surrounded Vladimir Monomach. Even in rapidly changing Western Europe, which was least subject to such organized nostalgia, we find Charlemagne reappearing as a feudal overlord, Hohenstaufen emperors attempting to act like the Ottos, and Icelanders clinging to the glory of their pagan past. For if there is a common theme or a single thread uniting the civilizations which stretched from the Atlantic to the Pacific during this period, it was their urge to restore the balance between what had been at the end of the first millennium and what had come to be by the year 1100.

Despite the considerable success which each of these civilizations achieved during these years in strengthening its own distinctive economy, institutions, and culture—often in conscious opposition to the other civilizations—such efforts proved illusory and unsatisfactory. Instead by 1195 we find a well-advanced process which was to lead to a very different era with intermingling of cultures rather than separation the order of the day.

The Islamic world had been severely buffeted by nomadic invasions and Western European expansion during the eleventh century. How did its people attempt to recover during the next nine decades? The especially vulnerable western region recovered its vigor and its coherence during the reign of the second Almoravid ruler, Yusuf (1106–1143). From his twin capitals of Marrakesh and Seville, Yusuf was able to organize an effective empire early in his reign. In Al-Andālūs he used his Toureg tribesmen to keep the aggressive northern Spanish Christians in check and to overawe the cultivated Andalusians whose town militias he needed in his army. At the same time he relied upon stern Malekite ulemas to curb the Spanish Moslem upper class who were unsympathetic to Berber masters whom they regarded as both brutal and uncivilized.

In African domains, on the other hand, the Almoravids used a Christian bodyguard, and Andalusians manned their bureaucracy and built fortresses in many parts of Algeria and Morocco. They constructed a powerful fleet which operated out of ports on both sides of the Straits of Gibraltar and kept Christian ships from using these straits, recaptured the island of Majorca after it fell to the Pisans in 1115–16, and kept the naval forces of the Norman kingdom of the Two Sicilies on the defensive. In short, despite the loss of most of the Ebro valley to King Alfonso I of Aragon in 1118–19 and the latter's deep raid into Andalusia in 1125–26, on the whole at first the Almoravids were able to hold their own.

By 1130, however, a new movement had appeared in the Atlas Mountains led by a religious reformer, Ibn Tumart, who proclaimed himself a Mahdi, rallied the sedentary Masada Berber tribesmen to his cause, denounced the Almoravids and their ulema as heretical, and proclaimed a holy war against them. By 1147 the Almoravids had been overwhelmed in Morocco, and their capital of Marrakesh had fallen to the warriors of this movement whom we know as the Almohads. In Spain, however, some of the Almoravids clung to power, which they shared with a number of native Andalusian princes who reestablished taifas in various parts of the peninsula.

The confusion which attended the rise of the Almohads and the decline of the Almoravids gave the Latin Westerners an opportunity to renew their offensive. Almost at once the Normans of the kingdom of Two Sicilies, who had a new monarch, Roger II, and a new, powerful fleet, attacked North Africa and between 1134 and 1148 occupied every important port between Bone and Tripoli. During the same period the Genoese and Pisans showed their armed might by forcing the weakened Almoravids to grant them favorable trading terms in treaties negotiated in 1133 and 1135 and, in the case of the Genoese, to open the Straits of Gibraltar to their ships which could now traffic as far west as Safi in Atlantic Morocco. Soon thereafter these Italian maritime cities joined Christian Spanish rulers in seizing the great port of Almería in 1147 and the northern base of Tortosa in 1148. Meanwhile, in western Spain where both the Castilians and the Portuguese, led by Alfonso Henriques, were advancing their frontiers south, the latter took advantage of Moslem weakness and captured the port of Lisbon in 1147 with the help of a strong flotilla of English and Flemish Crusaders who were sailing toward the Mediterranean as part of the Second Crusade.

This Christian expansion, however, was not destined to last, for the Almohads proceeded to revive Moslem strength. First of all, they crossed the Straits of Gibraltar and established themselves on the European side between 1153 and 1157 and in the process recovered the great port of Almería. Then their forces advanced east in the Maghreb, driving the Normans from the ports which they had seized, occupying that part of Algeria and Tunis which had been ruled by the Hamdanids and the Ziridites, and expelling the Hilalians from southern Tunis.

With the Maghreb theirs, they turned their attention back to the Iberian Peninsula. Here in 1172 they defeated the forces of Ibn Mardanish who ruled Murcia and Valencia and was allied with the Spanish Christians, and annexed his realm to their empire. And finally they opened hostilities against the Castilians and the Portuguese who had taken advantage of their preoccupation elsewhere to form new, powerful crusading orders along their frontiers and to move south to seize cities like Alcantara, Badajoz, and Alcacer do Sol. In the seesaw battle which followed, the Almohads proved powerful enough to drive the Christian princes out of most of the territory which they had seized in southern Iberia, despite the help of English and Flemish Crusaders on their way to Syria during the years of the Third Crusade. And finally in 1195 they badly defeated the Castilians at the great battle of Alarcos. Despite all their efforts, then, the Christian Spanish found their boundaries in 1195 not too different from what they had been in 1100 or 1150. The Islamic west had demonstrated its ability to stand up to their assault.

Almohad successes during these decades were due to more than the fanaticism which their well-trained troops were able to display on the battlefield. Success also came from their use of a powerful fleet which, like that of their

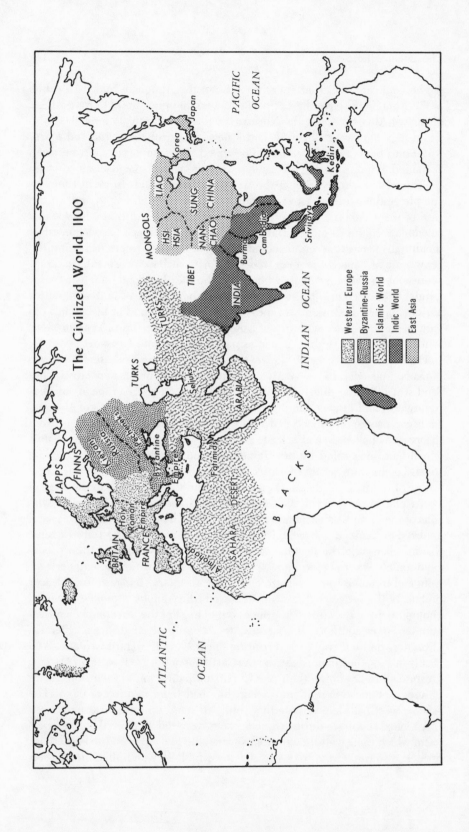

The Civilized World, 1100

ATLANTIC
OCEAN

LAPPS
FINNS

BRITAIN
Holy
Roman
FRANCE Empire
Almohads

SAHARA DESERT

B L A C K S

KIEVAN
RUSSIA

Byzantine
Empire

Fatimids

ARABIA

TURKS

TURKS

Seljuks

TIBET

MONGOLS

HSI
HSIA

SUNG
NAN
CHAO
INDIA

Burma

Cambodia

Srivijaya

LIAO

CHINA

Korea

Japan

Kediri

INDIAN OCEAN

PACIFIC
OCEAN

Western Europe
Byzantine-Russia
Islamic World
Indic World
East Asia

predecessors, they established along North African and Andalusian shores. This navy not only helped them gain victories over Normans, Italians, and Christian Spaniards, but it was also powerful enough to again bar the Genoese from the Atlantic and to keep northern European crusading fleets from attempting to return to home ports from the Mediterranean by way of the Straits of Gibraltar.

The governmental system used by the Almohads to control their large empire was much like that of the Almoravids—even though they emphasized the religious authority of their rulers, set up a special ghazi or *ribat* system along their Spanish frontiers, and relied upon a tribal system which stressed traditions found in settled mountain valleys rather than those appropriate to wandering Saharan nomads. Like the Almoravids, for instance, they maintained twin capitals in Seville and Marrakesh, used a Christian bodyguard, Andalusians in North Africa, and tribal troops in Iberia to keep opponents in check, and employed Andalusians to run the bureaucracy which they organized. Like them, too, they were both intolerant and narrowly religious and on occasion severely persecuted Jews, Christians, and Moslem intellectuals throughout their domains. And, like the Almoravids, they were able to keep their realm prosperous and to balance the interests of North Africans and Andalusians, of Berbers and Arabs, of city and countryside, while encouraging a culture which saw the art, architecture, and literary skills of cultured Andalusians spread across the straits into the Maghreb on a scale more extensive than that found in any earlier period.

The second great area of the Islamic world was the middle region of Egypt, Syria, and the Red Sea, which also developed in an interesting way during these years. Here, though a number of problems existed which its Moslem population was called upon to solve, the most important was the presence of Latin Franks as conquerors and rulers in Syria and Palestine.

During the first four decades which followed the fall of Jerusalem to the Latins, the kings of Jerusalem and their great vassals, the counts of Edessa and Tripoli and the princes of Antioch, were able to conquer much of Syria and Palestine through a steady advance made possible by a number of factors. First, the Latins were able to use newly arrived contingents and overwhelming sea power—mainly Italian—to seize every port north of Ascalon and in the process to destroy the Fatimid navy which attempted to stop them. Second, they built an intricate system of castles and other fortresses which the troops of neither the Fatimids nor the Moslem princes of the interior were able to capture. Third, they benefited from the fact that most of the Moslem population of Syria and Palestine were Sunni Arabs who hated both the Seljuk Turks and the heretical Egyptians and thus would not cooperate with either against the Franks. Last of all, they had the support of native Christian Armenians and Arabs whose backing made up for the hostility which was frequently displayed by the nearby Byzantines.

By 1142, however, the situation began to change, as Syrian Moslems found a new leader in Zengi who ruled Aleppo, Mosul, and other interior cities and who in that year captured the country of Edessa from its Latin ruler. When the Second Crusade failed to regain it and Zengi was able to add Damascus to his realm, the crusading states suddenly found themselves facing a dangerous and united Moslem enemy to the northeast.

Under the leadership of the next two kings of Jerusalem, Amaury I and Baldwin IV, the Latins attempted to deal with the Moslem threat in two ways. First of all, they came to terms with Byzantium by accepting ties of marriage and the overlordship of the Emperor Manuel Comnenus. Then, in great campaigns which took place between 1162 and 1169, they attempted to conquer Egypt. A little later one of their barons, Reginald de Chatillon, even built a fleet on the Gulf of Aqaba which raided shipping in the Red Sea carrying pilgrims to Mecca.

The attempt to seize Egypt, however, backfired, for it caused the Egyptians to seek the assistance of Syrian Moslem leaders. By 1170 this resulted in Egypt falling into the hands of the able Saladin, who soon thereafter added the Syrian lands of Nurredin, Zengi's successor, to it. He developed a new and effective army in Egypt by distributing estates as fiefs to his soldiers, and he rebuilt a powerful fleet. He conquered Nubia and the Hejaz, outlawed Shia doctrines, and recognized the Orthodox caliph of Baghdad as spiritual leader for his realm.

Then in the late 1180s he turned his full strength against the kingdom of Jerusalem whose nobility was disunited, whose new young king was incompetent, and which could no longer count on help from Byzantium, now ruled by weak Angeli emperors. The result was a great victory at Hattin in 1187 in which most of the armed forces of the Latin Westerners were destroyed, after which Saladin was able to advance with his troops to clear the Christians from the interior and one by one capture their coastal strongholds.

Saladin's victories, however, proved inconclusive in some ways because they resulted in a Third Crusade which, though it failed to recover Jerusalem, was able to destroy his fleet and regain most of the coastal area as well as the island of Cyprus which was taken from the Byzantines. But what had emerged by the time this great Ayyubid ruler died in 1193 was a strong state which controlled Egypt, most of the interior of Syria and Palestine, and the Red Sea region and which, like the empire of the Almohads, represented a revival of Moslem unity and purpose in this part of the world. It was also a realm which, by ending Fatimid rule, had reestablished a Sunni orthodoxy which most of its Moslem inhabitants very much welcomed.

The third part of the Islamic world—the east—also saw considerable change during this period. In 1100 this region was, as has been noted, controlled by Seljuk sultans who ruled their empire through a loose family system of appanage fiefs and subordinate *atabegs* who were served by a

centralized Persian bureaucracy. Both the Gaznavids and Karakhanids accepted the Seljuks as overlords, as did the Turkoman tribes who did their
bidding. Gradually, as the twelfth century progressed, however, the Seljuk
sultans began to lose control over outlying areas to their kinsmen, the Seljuks
of Ruñ, to the Zengids of Mosul and Aleppo, to the Danishmends of Sivas,
and to the Ortuqids of Armenia. Their most serious setback, though, was
the result of the arrival of the Kara Khitai in Turkestan. These invaders,
who had been expelled from their Liao realm in northern China by Jurched
Manchurian tribesmen, moved west and began to set up a new empire,
which in 1137 forced the Karakhanids to accept their hegemony and in 1141
was strong enough to defeat the Seljuks. Nevertheless, despite this defeat,
the Seljuks kept a large measure of authority throughout their empire until
the death of their last great sultan, Sanjar, in 1157.

Then a number of changes took place. First of all, a new Afghan dynasty,
the Gurids, appeared and replaced the Gaznavids as rulers in India and
eastern Persia. Then, for the first time in more than two centuries, the
caliphs of Baghdad threw off the yoke of their sultans and became the undisputed secular masters of Baghdad and Iraq. Third, Turkoman tribesmen,
unrestrained by central authorities in the 1150s, became powerful enough
to sack a number of cities in Khorasan and Transoxiana, like Bokhara. And
soon thereafter most of northern Persia came under the control of a new
Persian Khwarazmian shah who was to rule this region until the coming of
the Mongols. What had been in 1100 a Seljuk-controlled empire had become
a welter of warring Islamic principalities, none of which could match the
strength of those ruled by the Almohads or the Ayyubids.

Several features of this state of affairs which had emerged by 1195 in the
world of Islam seem worth noting. First of all, not only had Islamic society
managed to rally and resist the Latin West rather effectively in Spain and
the Near East, but they had also done remarkably well in taming and con-
taining their dangerous nomads. Some nomads, like the Seljuks or the Almoravids, were essentially neutralized by being absorbed into the settled
populations whom they had conquered. Others, like the Hilalians, or bedouins in Egyptian deserts, or Turkomans of Transoxiana, were kept in check
by the power of hill or mountain tribesmen like the Almohads or the Gurids,
or were tamed by warriors who followed Saladin or Khwarazmian shahs into
battle. Even the Franks of Jerusalem played a role in curbing the nomads
of the Syrian desert by building castles along their frontiers and providing
homes for sedentary Transjordan Arab Christian farmers within their borders. In general, then, these years saw the threat of nomads recede temporarily and cease to represent a major problem for the settled population
of the Islamic world as a whole.

In the second place, this age saw a continued spread of new military elites
who were rewarded with grants of land in return for their service. The Gurids

introduced such a soldiery into the realm of the Gaznavids which they conquered, and Saladin did the same in Egypt as well as in Syria where he
thought it wise to eliminate town militias of cities like Damascus, Aleppo,
and Homs and replace them with his own emirs and warriors. In some ways
the military system used by the Almoravids and Almohads resulted in the
presence of a similar military class within their domains, though this class
had more tribal roots than those found elsewhere in the Islamic world. By
the last years of the twelfth century, then, it seems fair to say that the older
system of slave and mercenary troops had completely disappeared, with the
Christian bodyguard maintained by Almoravids and Almohads in Morocco
representing the only vestige of it still to be found anywhere. And everywhere throughout the Islamic world we find a tremendous increase in fortifications, as towns and cities like Cairo and Marrakesh found that the
advantages of fortifications more than outweighed the expenses which they
entailed—and, as a result, found themselves much more secure than they
had been previously.

This new military elite managed to accommodate itself to the older town
elites who still served as ulema, bureaucrats, scholars, businessmen, and
merchants. These elites, though they had no military role except in a few
border areas like Spain and Syria, were able to maintain considerable prestige
and wealth and even continued to include a certain Jewish and Christian
element. But it is worth noting that there was now a growing tendency for
military elites to discriminate against non-Islamic elements. For instance,
both the Almoravids and the Almohads persecuted their Jews and Moriscos
and refused to use them in their civil administration, while in Egypt Saladin
removed such elements from governmental office and made them pay higher
customs dues than were levied upon merchants who were Moslems. Though
there were parts of the Islamic world—especially in the east—where such
discrimination against non-Moslems was still rare—witness the Armenian
minority—this was a growing tendency. And it probably explains why rulers
like the Seljuks and Saladin persecuted Shia heretics like the Assassins so
brutally, and were unwilling to allow freethinking intellectuals who were
influenced by Aristotle to flourish within their domains. For these new
military elites had very narrow religious views which were useful in sup-
pressing rival caliphates and spreading Sunni orthodoxy everywhere, but
disastrous to the cause of the intellectual freedom which had once been so
widespread in the towns and cities of the Islamic world.

In economic terms the Islamic world enjoyed a large measure of prosperity
during this period—more so than during the eleventh century and almost
as much as during the tenth. One aspect of this prosperity was the remarkable
range and vigor of its commerce, both internal and beyond its borders. In
the Indian Ocean we now find that merchants—some Moslem, some not—
could again proceed from Red Sea or Persian Gulf ports past Ceylon to reach

Srivijaya and Java in some numbers, since Chola sea power no longer was able to bar their way. Some of them even sailed on to southern Chinese ports where they were welcomed by the Sung authorities. Still others carried on a more active trade along East African shores where they settled in some numbers in Kilwa and Zanzibar from which they could more easily tap the trade of the interior. And by the last years of the century we find that traffic reaching the island of Kish and the Persian Gulf in general began to grow in volume while that with Aden and the Red Sea suffered some decline, perhaps in part because of the disorders caused by Crusaders invading Egypt, which was the terminus of the Red Sea route. This may also explain why Saladin ceased to coin gold dinars in Egypt and instead minted only silver dirhems.

As the trade of the Islamic world in the Indian Ocean grew in importance, so did that in central Asia. Here, after a midcentury interlude, we find merchants moving in large numbers to reopen trade with northern China along the old silk routes. We find them trafficking with the Kievan Rūs of the upper Volga by way of the land of the Black Bulgars and carrying goods to Trebizond on a scale which assured the prosperity of Greater Georgia through which they passed.

Even more remarkable was the economic recovery which quickened commerce in the Islamic west during these same years. Here caravan routes which led from the Sudan north to Sigilmasa and a new Tlemcen in Algeria were unusually active. And by 1160, after the Almohads had cleared the nomads out of southern Tunisia, those caravan routes included more easterly ones which had their termini in Wargla and Gadames. Even more interesting is the fact, to which Idrisi, the Moslem geographer, attests, that these years saw a considerable Atlantic commerce develop between Moroccan ports and the Canaries and the Guinea coast—anticipating Portuguese activities in these same waters some three centuries later.

The major economic question which needs to be answered, however, is, how active was Islamic trade in the Mediterranean along that great trade route which stretched east-west from Egypt to Iberia and the Maghreb by way of Sicily? The evidence which we possess from Geniza and other Egyptian documentation shows that it remained an active one indeed and that Moslem merchants participated in full measure. So true is this that we can almost consider Sicily during these years as economically part of the Islamic world rather than of Western Europe. The same is true, incidentally, of Syria and Palestine, which, despite their Latin rulers and the Italians who thronged their ports, remained a preserve of Moslem merchants and made use of gold dinars, some coined by their own rulers, as their major medium of exchange.

That does not mean that the Genoese, Pisans, Venetians, and Christians from the kingdom of the Two Sicilies were not active in the east-west trade of the Islamic Mediterranean, for they were. The timber and arms which they brought to Islamic ports in the central and eastern Mediterranean, despite papal decrees against such traffic, were essential to the Moslem world's prosperity. And so, too, was the grain of Sicily and Calabria. But the point is that this growing traffic controlled by Italian mariners did not yet interfere with that carried on in Dar-es-Islam or compromise the prosperity enjoyed by its merchants. It fitted into a pattern of trade which for more than three hundred years had been basic to the Mediterranean world as a whole.

The same prosperity is noticeable when we consider agriculture and industry. There is no evidence that any major change took place in the industrial productivity of the Islamic world during these years—except perhaps for some increase in the industrial output of the Maghreb and Al-Andālūs. In agriculture, however, there was a significant increase or recovery of agricultural production in certain areas like Morocco, Valencia, Anatolia, Tunisia, and parts of eastern Islam where nomadic activities had been significantly reduced. In Egypt in Saladin's time we even find part of the Nile Delta, which had not been cultivated since late Roman times, again producing crops for peasantry which moved into this region and was protected by Saladin's soldiery. Through 1195, then, commerce, industry, and agriculture recovered sufficiently from the difficulties they had experienced during the eleventh century to make possible an overall level of population at least equal to that found during the tenth century and perhaps even slightly larger.

The prosperity which we have attempted to sketch here all too briefly had its financial side as well. In the west, thanks to an abundant supply of Sudanese gold available from trans-Saharan and Atlantic commerce, a large number of mints coined gold dinars called *maraboutins* which were in great demand throughout the Mediterranean. During this same period the Fatimids also coined dinars in large amounts until the time of Saladin—dinars which have been shown by chemical analysis to have contained a large amount of Sudanese gold and which circulated widely throughout the Near East. It is equally worth noting, however, that the Seljuks, the Gaznavids, and their successors had sufficient gold stocks—perhaps from supplies that reached them from India and East Africa—to coin dinars, too, though such money was not of the quality one finds in Fatimid or Almohad issues. In the east these years saw the silver mines of the Pamirs resume a production of dirhems which served as an important medium of exchange in Khorasan and Turkestan. As in earlier times, then, the Islamic world of this period was blessed by an abundant gold and silver coinage which facilitated its commerce and its economic productivity in general.

Along with this abundant coinage we also find a continual use of credit in centers like Cairo which were vital links in the international trade carried on by Moslem and non-Moslem merchants. Such merchants are also known to have continued to make use of a variety of partnerships and loan instruments to facilitate the business ventures in which they were involved on both the local and international scenes. And the resultant prosperity which they enjoyed explains why the culture of the Islamic world could continue to show so much vigor, and why an Averroes, an Idrisi, a Beda-al-Din, or an Al-Gazzali could flourish and find ready patronage. It also explains why we find Almohad Spain and Morocco, Fatimid Cairo, and Seljuk Konya and Isphahan able to produce architectural forms which were as remarkable as any built by their Islamic predecessors. By 1195, Islamic civilization as a whole seemed still vigorous, prosperous, adaptive, and able to defend itself against external and internal foes.

Equally remarkable was the revival which we find taking place in the Byzantine Empire—one which has frequently been underestimated or misunderstood by historians. This misunderstanding seems the result of a consensus among scholars that the Comneni should have concentrated their attention upon Asia Minor and the destruction of the Turks who controlled the Anatolian plateau—and that their failure to do so was a fundamental error which led directly to the Ottoman conquest three centuries later.

This view of the Comneni and their policies seems difficult to sustain in any serious way, for it ignores two basic facts. First, it fails to understand that during the twelfth century Byzantium's European provinces were *economically* more important to its rulers than those in Asia—a situation quite different from that which had prevailed earlier. Second, it ignores the fact that the basic threats to the empire during Comneni and Angeli times came from the west and not from the East—which made it necessary for these rulers to concentrate their attention in this direction and relegate Asia Minor as a whole to a very secondary place in their calculations.

The Normans of the kingdom of Two Sicilies were the Westerners whom the Byzantines feared most and with good reason. In 1147–48 they attacked the empire and were driven out of Corfu and central Greece only with difficulty. Again it was a Norman fleet which seized Saloniki, the second city of the empire, in 1185 in a kind of preview of the Fourth Crusade. Byzantium thought it wise to maintain a powerful fleet during this period to keep the Normans in check, but it used other methods as well, like its alliance with German emperors and elements in Italy down to the time when Frederic Barbarossa changed the policy of supporting Byzantium. In general, until 1180 Comneni emperors were relatively successful in this respect and even attempted briefly in 1154–56 during Manuel's reign to invade southern Italy and recover it for the empire.

A second persistent enemy in the West was the papacy which never ceased to desire an end to the schism between Greek and Latin churches on terms of subordination of the former which were completely unacceptable to Constantinople. The papacy represented a special danger to Byzantium because

it showed itself able to organize crusading armies which on their way to the
Holy Land threatened the empire's security. It took considerable diplomatic
skill for Manuel Comnenus to deal with such armies during the Second
Crusade and for his Angeli successors to do the same during the Third. But
at least down to 1195 Byzantium was able to do so and in the process maintain
her political and religious independence.

The third serious Western threat was represented by the Italian maritime
republics of Venice, Pisa, and Genoa—a threat which was both economic
and naval in character. Of the three, Venice seemed the most dangerous—
even though twice, in 1082–85 and 1147–48, its fleet proved a useful ally
against the Normans. But the Golden Bull which Alexius granted the Venetians and which John and Manuel renewed, sometimes, as in 1126, only
after considerable Venetian pressure, was dangerous to the empire both
because it gave Venice too much naval power in Byzantine waters and because it limited imperial revenues and made it difficult for native merchants
to compete with traders from the City of the Lagoons.

The Comneni were very much aware of this danger and attempted to deal
with it by maintaining a powerful fleet of their own and by favoring at times
Venice's rivals, the Genoese and Pisans. To them they gave special commercial privileges in 1113 and in the 1160s when the Venetians seemed
especially hostile. Finally, Manuel decided to use even stronger measures
against Venice. He annexed the Dalmatian coastal cities which the Venetians
coveted for themselves, for almost two decades allied himself to an Ancona
which was Venice's rival in the upper Adriatic, and finally in 1171 crippled
the Venetians by seizing more than a thousand of their ships in imperial
ports.

This destruction of Venice's power, however, only meant that Genoa and
Pisa replaced Venice as exploiters of the Byzantine Empire and as naval
powers who controlled routes leading to Constantinople. Hence the massacre
of these Italians in 1182 and the return thereafter of the Venetians to some
importance in the foreign trade of the empire. By Angeli times then, when
the imperial fleet was allowed to all but disappear, Byzantium found itself
facing dangerous Italian maritime cities whose ships it could not control and
whose economic skills were necessary to its very existence.

In the fourth place, Byzantium faced a Hungary in the Danube valley
whose monarchs claimed Dalmatia and were constantly eager to expand
Hungarian borders along the middle Danube and take over Serb and Croat
principalities which Byzantine emperors regarded as their own. In dealing
with Hungary, the Comneni used a combination of diplomacy and force.
They married into the Arpad House and kept ties with German emperors,
which checked Hungarian ambitions. And not infrequently, as in Manuel's
time, they used armed force as well. The result was that they were often
able to maintain a protectorate over Hungary which assured them of control

over Slavic Serbia and Croatia, a subservient Dalmatia, a Wallachia which was in their sphere of influence, and routes through the Carpathians to Kievan Russia, which had accepted some measure of overlordship down to the time of the Angeli in 1185.

Despite this concern with the West, it is worth noting that the Comneni did not ignore their eastern neighbors. The cornerstone of their eastern policy was a firm alliance with the powerful kingdom of Georgia, which, under three powerful monarchs—David III, Demetrius I, and George III— between 1082 and 1184, had expanded its borders to take in most of Armenia and Azerbaijan. These kings were able to control their powerful feudal lords, many of whom were of Armenian origin, and to make their realm a center of trade reaching Byzantine Trebizond or crossing the Caucasus on its way to Khazaria and Kievan Russia. Not only did Georgian monarchs marry into the Comneni families but their church was in full communion with Constantinople's Orthodox patriarch. Most important of all was the fact that Greater Georgia's position on the flanks of the Seljuks of Rum served to restrain the latter.

In general, these Seljuks, however, represented little threat to Byzantium and, once their borders had been stabilized in Alexius's time, ghazi raids almost ceased. This was because the Comneni through the 1170s regularly played the Seljuks of Konya against the Danishmends of Sivas, and because good relations with Constantinople were necessary if the Seljuks wished to dispose of their agricultural surpluses—a trade upon which the prosperity of their realm depended. Except on certain occasions, then, as at the time of the Second Crusade, the Seljuks of Rum sought Byzantine friendship and represented no serious problem to Constantinople. This remained true until 1176 when Manuel rashly attempted to invade their domains in force—an invasion which resulted in the disaster of Myrocephalae, which some historians have, with little justification, compared to Manzikert. Until this time, however, we must regard the Seljuk menace as much more in the minds of modern historians than in the reality of twelfth-century Byzantium.

The principal problem in the east, then, was not the Seljuks but rather the Armenians of Lesser Armenia and the Crusader-controlled principality of Antioch. The leaders of the First Crusade had failed to honor their promise to return these areas to Byzantine control. Instead the Rupenid princes of Lesser Armenia resisted the Comneni, and their Armenian subjects clung to their independent church, and the Latin princes of Antioch were equally unwilling to accept Byzantine rule. Alexius's efforts to change this achieved nothing, and John was only able to assert his authority there briefly between 1139 and 1142. Manuel, however, was much more successful and, until his expedition against the Seljuks, not only controlled Lesser Armenia but was able to compel both the prince of Antioch and the Latin king of Jerusalem to accept him as overlord. In the east as in the west, then, until the end of

Manuel's reign we can trace a story of success, with Georgia allied to the empire, the Seljuks friendly, and Lesser Armenia and the Crusader states finally coming under Byzantine influence.

The success achieved by these first three Comneni emperors in the west, the north, and the east was due to a number of things. First, it was the result of the effective central administrative system which they reorganized and placed under the control of a kind of grand vizier, known as the Grand Logothete. This administration supervised an efficient and somewhat ruthless collection of heavy taxes, made sure that the new gold coinage kept its value, and supervised effectively both the empire's foreign trade and its internal economy.

This civil administration provided the funds necessary to maintain a strong army commanded by a Grand Domesticus which was composed of a mixture of foreign mercenaries and native troops—many of whom were scattered in small garrisons throughout the provinces. These provinces tended to be smaller than the earlier themes and were commanded by military governors known as dukes or *catapans*. The Comneni also maintained a large navy under a Megas Dux—one which they rebuilt six times in the course of the twelfth century. Most of this navy, which was partly manned by Italians and partly by native seamen, was normally stationed near Constantinople, but some of its squadrons were based on Crete, Cyprus, and Dhyrrachium to watch potential foreign foes. And if there was one feature of this armed system which is striking, it is the way a balance was maintained between native element and foreign mercenary contingents—at least down to Manuel's reign when the foreign element steadily became more important.

During these years the empire seems to have been generally prosperous and to have been able to feed itself and to provide its population with necessary industrial goods and luxury wares. Constantinople, a metropolis where Venetians, Genoese, and Pisans were allowed to live in special quarters, was still the most important city with a population at least as large as that which it had had in the tenth century. There were two other important towns, however. One was Saloniki whose annual Fair of St. Demetrius attracted merchants from all parts of the Mediterranean, and Trebizond which was an important international Black Sea port. Though there was a tendency for much of the empire's trade from Aegean and Mediterranean ports to be in Italian hands, these traders were not allowed to participate in commerce which reached the empire via the Danube or the Black Sea. Thus, we find the same balance reflected in the empire's foreign trade during these years that we have noted in the composition of its military and naval forces. The fact that the empire's gold and silver coinage remained abundant and unchanged in value suggests that its economic balance of payments remained generally favorable.

In the third place, Byzantium remained religiously united. Though the

Comneni were unable to suppress all traces of Balkan Bogomilism or to come to terms with the independent Armenian church of Cilicia or papal Rome, they kept religious peace within their realm by good relations with the Orthodox hierarchy and the patriarch of Constantinople. They were also able to maintain close connections with the Russian church for which they generally supplied Greek metropolitans, with the Georgian church, and with the Slavic Serbian church and hierarchy. Generally speaking, then, under these monarchs Orthodoxy continued to represent a buttress to Byzantine civilization in general, both within the empire and beyond it.

Culture also benefited during this prosperous period. Twelfth century Byzantium enjoyed what historians have referred to as a silver age. Scholars like John Italus and historians like Anna Comnena kept alive traditions of classical Greek learning with a special emphasis upon Plato and the culture of fifth-century Athens. Equally interesting is evidence of a continued development of Byzantine art and architecture as reflected in the mosaics of Haghia Sophia and the frescoes of its Balkan churches. This art and architecture proved vital enough to affect that of Venice and Norman Sicily in the west and that of Kievan Russia and Georgia to the north and east.

Nevertheless, Comneni Byzantium was not without its weaknesses. Its rulers carried on a most expensive series of wars and relied upon a costly diplomacy which made it necessary for them to levy taxes, including some in kind, which were much too heavy for its population to bear patiently. Their intense militarization of society, especially under Manuel, changed the nature of the empire, not always for the better, by penalizing the more productive elements of the population. Also, the large number of Latin mercenaries and merchants increased the natural xenophobia of a native population which for centuries had regarded the outside world with considerable suspicion. Manuel was able to handle this attitude and even attempted to naturalize some of the Latins who lived in Constantinople and so assimilate them into the Byzantine body politic, but he was perhaps unusual in this respect. Certainly his views were not shared by the mass of the Greek population.

As a result, when Manuel died and left an underage son as his imperial successor with a Latin mother as regent and a Latin-French princess as his wife, things came apart. Manuel's anti-Western cousin, Andronicus, was able to seize power by inciting a riot in Constantinople in 1182 in which most of the Latins were massacred. This was followed by the murder of his rivals and a short reign during which he attempted to follow a thoroughgoing anti-Western and anti-aristocratic policy—thus paralyzing the armed forces, especially the navy which relied upon foreign mercenary elements in considerable measure. A Norman seizure of Saloniki in 1185 helped to bring Andronicus's downfall and the appearance of a new family of emperors, the Angeli. But the damage had been done. Since the fleet had disappeared during Andronicus's reign, the Venetians recovered some privileges in the capital, and the Aegean came under the control of three large pirate flotillas which were partly Greek and partly Pisan and Genoese in composition.

These fleets, which, along with Venetian flotillas, now controlled the seaways, made it impossible for the new emperor, Isaac Angelus, to influence events in distant Anatolian provinces which could only be reached by sea. So the Armenians of Cilicia threw off the Byzantine yoke and the island of Cyprus came under control of a Comneni pretender until in 1189 it was seized by Richard the Lionhearted in the course of the Third Crusade. Much the same thing happened around the Black Sea where Queen Tamar of Georgia, who had married a Kievan prince, intervened in Trebizond which she detached from Constantinople and gave to her nephews, who were Comneni too. At about the same time, in Bulgaria and across the Danube in Wallachia the members of a Bogomil family known as the Asens raised the standard of revolt and began to create a second Bulgarian-Vlach empire on both sides of the lower Danube. By 1195 the Byzantine world, having lost control of the narrow seas which were necessary to its survival, was beginning to disintegrate into its component parts and to face a darker future than any it had known since Manzikert.

While the Byzantine Empire was enjoying eight decades of vigor under the Comneni and then fifteen years of disaster under their successors, what was happening in that part of the Byzantine commonwealth—Russia—which lay north of the Black Sea? Here these years saw considerable change. As the twelfth century opened, at first the Rūs were fortunate in recovering considerable strength and unity, thanks to a series of able rulers of whom Vladimir Monomach (1113–25) was the most important. These rulers defeated the Cumans, reopened contact with Constantinople, and under their aegis a Kievan silver age emerged in which the *Primary Chronicle*, that history of early Kievan times, was composed and an important code of Russian laws came into general use. By 1136, however, things began to change. The northern trading center of Novgorod declared its independence, and princes of the House of Rurik who ruled other cities ceased to accept Kievan over-lordship. And, as the Cumans again used their power to isolate Kiev from the Black Sea, a general change in the orientation of Russia took place. Gradually, population and power moved northeast where the princes of Vladimir-Suzdal began to replace those of Kiev as influential leaders. Here on land newly won from the forest, a surplus of grain and other foodstuffs was now produced which could be sent to provision a Novgorod which had attracted a considerable colony of Western merchants from Gotland and northern Germany. From this part of Russia trade again began to flow south along the Volga to Turkestan and the Caspian. A new Russia had appeared as Kiev was sacked first by the prince of Vladimir in 1169 and then by the Cumans in 1184.

This new Russia was, we must hasten to add, rather prosperous, with a population which had grown to more than seven-and-a-half million or almost double what it had been in the tenth century—and this means that the entire Byzantine-Russian complex had a population at least equal to what it had at the time of Basil II and Yaroslav the Wise. Also Russia now had developed considerable industrial potential in its growing urban centers and a rather complex pattern of economic and social life as reflected in a revised set of laws codified in 1172. Its religious life, centered in powerful monasteries, was a vigorous one, while its literature, its art, and its architecture as reflected in Kiev, Novgorod, and Vladimir-Suzdal were already beginning to display certain distinctive Russian traits which were modifying the Byzantine elements on which they were based. By 1195 a Russia had been born which, if we can believe the *Lay of Prince Igor*, already felt itself unique in the world of the twelfth century.

To the east, the Indic and East Asian civilizations had flourished in a remarkable way during the eleventh century and continued to develop along similar lines during the twelfth. There were some important changes, however, which also took place in this part of the world, especially in China where about 1120 the Kitan Liao realm was taken over by a group of Jurched Manchurian tribesmen whom we know as the Chins. The Chins not only drove the Kitans westward, where the latter, also known as the Kara Khitai, established an empire in Turkestan, but they also moved south and by 1127 had driven the Sungs out of northern China. The Sungs were able to rally sufficiently to keep the Chins from advancing south of the Huai river—the rice-millet line—and, from a new capital located at Hangchow, were able to reconstitute a viable and prosperous state which was to endure another century and a half. But this meant that millions of Chinese south of the Great Wall, including the great city of Kaifeng, were now ruled by a non-Chinese dynasty of nomadic origin—which, incidentally, made Peking, in the north Chinese plain, its new capital.

The southern Sungs were successful for a number of reasons. First, they continued to maintain an efficient and effective centralized administration using the same commercially minded gentry who for more than a century had staffed China's government bureaus. Second, they kept their agriculture, their industry, and their external and internal commerce prosperous and supplied with ample money and credit. In the third place, they fortified the great cities of the Yangtze valley so that they barred any attack from the north. But most important of all, they developed a new and effective navy which could be used to defend both their coasts and the Yangtze River against the Chins and so neutralize their adversaries' advantage of having well-trained cavalry forces.

The Chins attempted to counter this by building a navy of their own in the 1150s and 1160s and using it to attack the Sungs. But their efforts ended in failure when the latter, using large warships equipped with incendiary bombs and rockets and commanded by a Lord High Admiral, destroyed their ships off Shantung. From this time until the end of the century, thanks to their maritime strength, the Sungs were able to persuade the Chins to accept a peaceful coexistence which allowed both realms to develop undisturbed.

The loss of northern China, however, resulted in more than a fortified heartland and a navy which, as a contemporary said, formed a new "great wall" between the Sungs and their enemies. It made foreign trade especially important, since only through increased commerce was there a hope to make up for revenues lost from provinces which now owed obedience to the Chins. Consequently, every effort was made to encourage trading ventures overseas, especially with Southeast Asia. These efforts were enormously successful. Customs dues levied upon this commerce grew to some 2,000,000 strings of cash a year or about five percent of total tax receipts, and the Sung capital, Hangchow, increased in size until its population came to over a million souls.

If the China of the southern Sungs showed itself able to continue along a path set earlier and to develop in addition a special naval and maritime emphasis of its own, the realm of the Chins proved equally remarkable. Its rulers found it was wise to follow the patterns of government which their Kitan predecessors had set up with tribal elements and Chinese administration coexisting successfully. Their civil administration was essentially Chinese in character and personnel. Their army, however, like that of the Kitans before them, was organized as an "ordo" system of tribally-based non-Chinese cavalry stiffened with well-trained Chinese infantry units. Chinese elements also were used to defend well-fortified cities and to serve as technical experts who could employ rockets and other missiles used in both attack and defense. In short, the Chins seem to have organized in northern China a highly militarized state, mixing Chinese and non-Chinese nomadic elements into a viable alternative to that of the southern Sungs. It was to profoundly influence the later Mongols and Manchus.

There seems little doubt also that the empire of the Chins was prosperous and was able to continue eleventh-century patterns of economic activity. For instance, its peasantry continued to produce abundant crops—much of which came from irrigated fields—and the iron complex centering in Kaifeng continued to pour out finished arms and other metal products until it was disrupted by the floods along the Yellow River which in 1194 caused this river to change its course and empty its waters south of the Shantung Peninsula instead of north of it. There is also evidence that the Chins were able to increase the volume of their internal and external trade, especially with the Tanguts and central Asia in one direction and Korea and Japan in the other. Indeed, it is this trade which, according to some historians, in part enabled the Chin empire to support a population of about 40,000,000, which, although it did not match the 65,000,000 who lived in the empire of the southern Sungs, was still a substantial total indeed.

The appearance of this powerful, prosperous, and highly militarized empire in northern China just to the west of warlike Hsi Hsia coincided with the development of an equally militarized Korea and Japan nearby. In Korea, which found it wise to acknowledge both the Chins and the Sungs as overlords, these years saw a noble family of aristocrats, known as the Ch'oe, establish themselves at Kaesong as hereditary military rulers who still preserved the theoretical primacy of their monarchs. In Japan much the same thing happened as two provincial warrior clans, the Taira and the Minimoto, fought for control of Kyōtō and the country as a whole—a struggle which ended in 1185 in a Minimoto triumph. What emerged out of this struggle was a unique system of military government known as the shōgunate which Yoritimo, the Minimoto leader, had organized by 1195 and which made it possible for him to set up a permanent headquarters or *bakufu* at Kamakura and control both the imperial court at Kyōtō and the provinces through a network of feudalized alliances. In East Asia, north of the Yangtze, then, what we now find appearing everywhere are more militarized forms of government which place authority in the hands of a new military elite. This elite, however, it is worth noting, takes over authority here as in the world of Islam or Byzantium without completely destroying the older governing upper classes which manage somehow to coexist with such warriors and maintain necessary traditions of government, economic life, and culture in the process. As for the other two East Asian realms which we have mentioned earlier, Nan-Chao and Annam, we can add little more concerning them— except that Annam continued to exert pressure upon Champa and at least some of the Thais advanced south in sufficient numbers to be able to set up small warrior states along the headwaters of the Mekong and Menan rivers— principalities which were to have a rather brilliant future in the next period with which we will be concerned.

As most of East Asian civilization developed toward a more militarized pattern of society—and one area in South China managed, for the first time, to develop a navy as highly organized and structured as those found in the Mediterranean or the northern seas of Western Europe, the Indic world changed in a number of ways, too. Unfortunately, however, we know very little about what happened in Greater India during these years because we lack the kind of records which are available elsewhere. For instance, we cannot be sure even whether this part of the world was prosperous or not, or whether its population remained stationary or grew in numbers.

Yet we can make a few observations which probably have a measure of validity. These years clearly saw the Chola empire of southern India decline, for reasons which are obscure to us, allowing Ceylon to recover its independence and helping to make possible the appearance of a number of new kingdoms in the Deccan—all of whom had considerable political and economic importance. Chola weakness also freed the waters of the Bay of Bengal, for its flotillas could no longer keep Arab merchants from sailing their ships to Srivijaya and Java or from proceeding to South China in pursuit of profit. As for northern India we only know that the small Rajput principalities into which it was divided became increasingly militarized and feudalized and here, as in southern India, there was a considerable revival in Hindu art and literature.

Beyond the subcontinent perhaps the most important event which took place was the rise of Cambodia, which reached its greatest extent and influence during the reigns of Suvajaravan II and Jayvarajarim VII who built Ankor Vat and Ankor Thom. These monarchs were powerful enough at times to establish control over the Mons of lower Burma at the expense of the rulers of Pagan, and during the last years of the twelfth century they conquered Champa. They were great builders of temples and irrigation works, and it was under their aegis that a new and vital Thervada Buddhism originating in Ceylon reached this part of the world and began to become the dominant faith of its population. However, the Khmer realm's conquest of lower Burma and Champa was to be only temporary, and probably owed a great deal to the Thai mercenaries who were used in their armies and which made their kingdom the strongest power in Southeast Asia during these years.

A third change was a steady growth in the importance of Kederi Java and a decline in power of Srivijaya. By now the Kederi realm had become a vital way station along trade routes which linked the Indian Ocean area with East Asia, even more important than Srivijaya itself, according to a Chinese author in 1168. Its ports were full of Chinese merchants attracted to its markets by the trade it controlled with the Spice Islands and the Celebes to the east, as well as its trade with Madagascar and East African shores. A new Javan commercial and maritime vitality had emerged as Srivijaya declined, the Cholas had lost their maritime empire, and Chinese merchants in increasing numbers sailed south to exploit the wealth of Southeast Asia.

Western Europe too, was making headway in the twelfth century—but not in the acquisition of territory. We have already pointed out that its attempts to expand into Spain, North Africa, Syria, and the Byzantine Empire on the whole had only a limited degree of success, for by 1159 it had only gained a band of territory in Iberia and the island of Cyprus while losing Jerusalem and the interior of Palestine and Syria. We cannot, then, regard Western European territorial gains during these years as in any way comparable to what had been accomplished during the preceding century.

On the other hand, there is a general consensus that this was a period of great accomplishment for Western European civilization as a whole—one which narrowed the gap between its level of culture and that of the other great civilizations. Let us first examine the political sphere, where the power of the papacy deserves our careful attention. During the twelfth century popes increased their power in the Latin West by continuing to insist on church reform, by backing new monastic movements like the Cistercians, by improving the administrative efficiency of their Curia in Rome, and by encouraging crusading in the Baltic, Spain, and the Near East. This made them so influential that they were at times able to humble German emperors like Henry V and Frederick Barbarossa and English kings like Henry II, while serving as almost the overlords of Iberian monarchs and central European rulers. By 1195 the papacy as an institution was unique in the world in its ability to exert leadership over an *entire* civilization. It was ready for the years of Innocent III and Innocent IV.

The popes, however, were not alone in being able to exert political leadership in the Latin West, for so too did some secular monarchs—especially Henry I and Henry II of England and Roger II of Sicily—all of whom managed combine feudal elements in their realms with a variety of nonfeudal legal, administrative, military, and financial institutions. What they accomplished was copied elsewhere—in Iberia, in the Denmark of the Waldemars, in royal and local governments in northern France, and in the Germany of the Hohenstaufens and of Henry the Lion. The trend toward more effective, nonfeudal centralized government, then, can be regarded as a European-wide phenomenon.

So too was the political growth of towns which during these years spread over the entire continent. Such towns, which tended to be ruled by a board of burghers, proved able to provide their inhabitants with personal freedom, special laws, and a measure of fiscal autonomy as well as walls for security against outside enemies. There was, however, little uniformity in the degree of independence they were able to achieve, for this ranged from the total freedom of northern Italian communes and the relative autonomy of those of northern France, the Midi, and Germany, to the more controlled urban centers of Britain, Castile, and Scandinavia. By 1195, though, militarized and autonomous towns joined the papacy and royal government as one element of that triad of political power which was found nowhere else and tended to give Western European society a special flavor of its own.

The Latin West also continued, during the twelfth century, to improve the efficiency of its agriculture. In part, this came from the way its peasants continued to clear new land for their crops, as the primeval forest was cut down, marshes were drained, and wastes were made productive in various ways. Sometimes this resulted in the establishment of new villages whose inhabitants were given special privileges and freedoms. Sometimes it was the work of ecclesiastical proprietors, like the Cistercians who established granges in the countryside for their lay brethren and kept large flocks of sheep on their estates. And everywhere such changes and a growing demand for foodstuffs in the new towns helped to destroy the serfdom of the older manors and to raise the level of the peasants toward tenant status, as well as making possible a considerable increase in the food supply.

Economic growth in the countryside was matched by a similar growth of urban population in areas in which towns were appearing for the first time. Some existing towns, too, were becoming larger and more economically complex. Such growth was especially marked in northern Italy, in the French Midi, and in that part of Europe which faced the English Channel and the North Sea and centered in a London-Paris-Cologne triangle. And this growth of population was so significant that by 1195 Western Europe could boast 70,000,000 to 80,000,000 inhabitants—which was double that of the Byzantine-Russian nexus and about equal to that found in the Islamic world or in Greater India.

Western Europeans during these years also continued to display considerable technological virtuosity not only in their agriculture but also in their industry, where innovations in textile processes and in metallurgy were very much the order of the day, and where ships were constructed with a mastery of materials which only the Chinese could match. Equally interesting is the way the Latin West found it possible to mine ores, smelt metals, and fabricate arms on a scale which provided for both a home market and overseas customers. By the last years of the twelfth century, Western Europe, which had been essentially agrarian, began to take the first steps toward an industrially and technologically advanced destiny.

Western Europe now began also to develop financial resources and skills to match the advances we have noted in her fields, workshops, and mines. One aspect of this was an ability to provide abundant silver money from mines located in the Mendips in England, Melle in Poitou, Goslar in Saxony, and a number of other places. Such money was supplemented by the development, for the first time in centuries, of an effective system of credit which spread from Italian and Provençal centers to the Fairs of Champagne as moneylenders followed in the wake of merchants. They helped facilitate the exchange of Belgian and northern woolens for Mediterranean goods and in so doing began to catch up with the financial acumen of their Byzantine, Moslem, Indic, and East Asian counterparts.

Western European merchants thus began to carry more goods than ever before along international and local trade routes. Some, like German merchants from Lübeck and other northern German towns, reached Novgorod and the eastern Baltic in larger numbers than ever before and carried their wares to London and Bergen. Still others, organized into merchant guilds in England, trafficked along Atlantic shores from Lisbon all the way to Norway and Denmark, while occasionally finding it possible to carry their cloth to Genoa or the Fair of Saint Gilles in southern France. Equally international was the commerce, already alluded to, which drew Italians, Flemish, and northern French merchants to the Fairs of Champagne or caused the Cahorsins, who were moneylenders from southern France, to establish trading contacts with Britain.

Most important, however, Western Europe's economy now became much more integrated with that of its Islamic and Byzantine neighbors. In part, this was the result of traffic along the Danube to the Byzantine Empire in which German, Jewish, and Hungarian merchants were engaged, or along the path northern Spanish traders followed to the marts of Andalusia. But mainly this integration was the result of the growing volume of commerce carried in Venetian, Pisan, Genoese, and Sicilian bottoms to Byzantine and Moslem Mediterranean shores. In fact, colonies of these merchants settled in Constantinople, Syria, Alexandria, and in the Mediterranean from Sicily and North Africa to the mouth of the Rhone. So profitable was this commerce that merchants eagerly extorted from their neighbors special trading privileges of various sorts which lowered the dues they paid and made their goods and persons secure overseas. By 1195 they were well on the way to establishing a control of the commerce of the Mediterranean world which up to then had eluded them.

While Western Europe made great gains politically and economically, what truly stands out during these years is the militarization that continued unabated and was even accentuated as castles spread into areas like Ireland, Scotland, Scandinavia, and Germany where they had been relatively rare. And as they spread, they were accompanied by an increasing number of mounted knights and castellans.

If the upper-class noble knight now became the norm in a countryside dotted with fortresses to a degree unmatched anywhere else in the world, it is worth noting that the towns which appeared everywhere were fortresses too and their inhabitants were also warriors, as the name "burgher" implies. Again and again they proved that they could fight as valiantly as their rural noble neighbors, whether we are talking about the *caballeros villanos* of Spain, the English militia of Stephen, the Flemish townsmen, the Milanese who defeated Frederic Barbarossa's knights, or the Genoese and Pisans who terrorized the Mediterranean. Nor were peasants without military skills either, especially those who served the Angevins and Capetians as mercenaries or who, as *ministeriales*, formed a knightly class in Germany. This pervasive militarization explains why Western Europeans could rally to the Crusades on such a grand scale. Their society was organized for war in a way which even the relatively militarized Byzantine, Islamic, Indic, or East Asian worlds could not hope to emulate.

Finally, in this period Western Europe perfected a culture which tended to unite the peoples who lived there. There was a revival of interest in intellectual learning, especially in law, medicine, and theology, which were beginning to be studied in institutions we know as universities. A romantic literary tradition of poetry and prose developed in northern and southern France, soon spread into Germany, and became international as the nobles who prized it spread their interest in chivalry and courtesy from Antioch to Dublin and from Palermo to Lund. We also now find a special Romanesque and Gothic architecture developing in this same French heartland and spreading widely, too—helping to distinguish Western European civilization from that of its neighbors.

Turning at last to maritime matters, we should note that Western Europeans during the twelfth century were not unchallenged in the Mediterranean. Until 1185, powerful Byzantine and Islamic fleets could on a local basis at times deny them access to areas which they coveted. They also had not yet surpassed the technical virtuosity displayed by the Chinese in East Asian and Southeast Asian waters, where various kinds of junks, navigated by seamen who used the compass, were superior to any vessel that Western Europe could muster.

Nevertheless, the Latin West did not fail to make progress in the maritime sphere during these years. In the Mediterranean, where Italians and Sicilians used the same kind of galleys and lateen-rigged and oared ships employed by their Islamic and Byzantine rivals, progress was more tactical than technical. They learned to use their ships much more effectively in war. The flotillas of the kingdom of the Two Sicilies which fought Byzantium to a standstill and captured North African ports between 1135 and 1150, like those Genoese and Pisan squadrons which seized Almería and Tortosa and the ports of Syria, showed they had developed a remarkable naval expertise—especially in the use of Greek fire, catapults, crossbows, and amphibious operations in general. Consequently, by the time of the Third Crusade they could transport entire armies to the Holy Land, instead of having Crusaders make use of land routes almost exclusively.

In northern waters, on the other hand, all our evidence seems to show a lack of most such tactical expertise, though this was balanced by considerable new technical advances which were to be important later on. One of these was the development of a system of stern rudders to replace steering oars on the cogs and hulks used more and more in Atlantic waters and in the North and Baltic seas. Still another was the practice of building fore and aft castles which made such ships more defensible when attacked at sea. Still a third was the use of a compass, first mentioned by an Englishman, Alexander Neckham in 1185, and which was so different from that used in China that it must have been developed independently. Also during these years northern Europeans began to make use of more elaborate sets of sailing directions, some of which described the shores and ports of the distant Mediterranean. Armed with such maritime skills, they periodically sailed their ships through the Straits of Gibraltar into the Middle Sea—particularly during the years of the Third Crusade. And in so doing, these flotillas, especially the great fleet of Richard the Lionhearted, helped spread northern European maritime skills to a Mediterranean world which in exchange offered Atlantic Europe the tactical skills and warlike abilities its seamen had developed by the last years of the twelfth century.

In summing up the developments which took place between 1100 and 1195 in the world of civilized Eurasia, we must emphasize that each of these five civilizations proved able to continue an independent and distinct life of its own despite continued pressure from Western Europe and the occasional, if intermittent, danger from nomadic groups who had played such an important role earlier. Increased militarization and internal fortification enabled them to survive even though it is true that few of them developed an upper class as militaristic as in Western Europe or Japan. In most, instead, what we find is a new military class, often feudalized, which seems to coexist with older elites which did not share either its values, its loyalties, or its expertise.

But we need also to emphasize another point which has a real overall significance—the extent to which these civilizations, though distinct, now began to mingle with each other. It is no accident, for instance, that the Genoese and Venetian merchants of the twelfth century made use of contracts and partnerships similar to those used by their Moslem and Greek rivals and lived in overseas colonies of *fonduks* whose very name reveals their Near Eastern origin.

Furthermore, it is clear that the Christian bodyguards maintained by the Almoravids and Almohads in North Africa had their counterparts in the Moslem and Greek military and naval contingents and administrators used by Roger II, the Turcopoles found in Crusader-controlled Syria, or the Latin mercenaries who manned the fleets and served in the armies of Emperor Manuel Comnenus. Nor was this confined to administration and warfare. Romantic literature prized by troubadours and trouvères was shared by Andalusians and seems to have animated the ethos of Saladin and his warriors, just as it did a Comneni court where tourneys took place and where Provençal poetry was prized. Nor is it an accident that one of Chrétien de Troyes's tales is set in Byzantium, and that the *Lay of Prince Igor* seems to be a kind of Russian *Chanson de Geste*. In the intellectual sphere we know how vital was the Western European borrowing of Aristotelian science and philosophy as well as medicine from Arab sources in Spain and Sicily. Even in northern China we see an increasing mingling of nomadic and Chinese elements— no doubt as significant as the feudalization of northern Indian Hindu society and not too different from that of the Seljuks. As each civilization reasserted itself, then, it also borrowed from its neighbors more directly than it realized and so laid the foundations of a quite different era which was soon to emerge.

Western European and Mongol Aggression, 1195–1270

The years between 1195 and 1270 represent a period of great historical changes which affected all five civilizations which we have been examining in this study. These changes were brought about by aggressiveness displayed by Western Europeans and by a new nomadic central Asian people, the Mongols, who expanded in all directions at the expense of their civilized neighbors and in doing so repeated in many ways what had happened in the eleventh century. Now, however, the effect of such aggression was much more extensive in character, for these two groups were able to overwhelm both the Byzantine-Russian and East Asian complexes during these years and to severely challenge in a number of ways the peoples who made up the worlds of Islam and of Greater India. Indeed, so successful were these nomads and Latin Westerners that a detached observer might well have concluded that Eurasia in 1270 had come to be divided between the Western European world headed by a pope living in Rome and the Mongol empire under the hegemony of a great khan whose capital was in Peking, each of whom was attempting in various ways to reach a measure of accommodation with the other. In other words, it was a far cry from the situation which had existed throughout the twelfth century.

Expansion by Western Europeans, which was such a feature of this period, began rather slowly and at first only affected two areas of the world—the eastern Mediterranean and the eastern Baltic. In 1195 the leader of the forces of expansion was the Hohenstaufen emperor Henry VI. Henry was not only preparing a large fleet in his Sicilian and Italian domains for use against the Byzantine Empire, whose ruler, Alexius III, was paying him large sums in the hope of buying him off. He was also playing a role in the eastern regions dominated by the Crusaders by giving a royal crown to the Hetumid prince of Lesser Armenia and encouraging his German subjects to form a new crusading order, the Teutonic Knights, for use in this part of the world. Interestingly enough, it was Henry's same northern German subjects who were taking the lead in expansion into the eastern Baltic area by securing from the pope in 1193 authorization for a crusade against pagan elements there—an authorization which resulted in a large army of crusaders landing in Livonia in 1198.

Neither of these movements, however, was destined to continue under imperial auspices, for when the able emperor died in 1197, it was the papal enemy of the Hohenstaufens, Pope Innocent III, who took over their direction and indeed became the guiding force behind Western European expansion for the next two decades. Innocent began by recognizing the Teutonic Knights as a religious order similar to the Knights Templars and Hospitalers and followed this up in 1202–1203 by giving his blessing to a second German order known as the Knights of the Sword, which had the conquest and Christianization of Livonia as its reason for existence. At the same time, he indicated a special papal concern for Iberian affairs by inviting the young king of Aragon, Peter II, to come to Rome and do homage to him for his lands. And finally he began to make an effort to launch a new crusade which he hoped would regain Jerusalem from the Ayyubid sultans who controlled it.

The resulting expedition, which we know as the Fourth Crusade, was, as is well known, diverted in large measure by the Venetians from its original objectives. Instead the Crusaders who took part in it first attacked Zara along the Dalmatian coast and then sailed to Constantinople which they conquered without much difficulty in 1204. This conquest was followed by the proclamation of a Latin Empire, an agreement reached between Crusaders and Venetians to partition the Byzantine world, and a forced union of the Greek and Latin churches with a Venetian prelate being chosen as Latin patriarch of Constantinople. Though Pope Innocent was at first intensely disturbed by the diversion of the Fourth Crusade and its attack on fellow Christians, he soon came to accept it as a providential event, since it seemed to promise an end to the schism between Latin and Greek churches on papal terms. This was what he was already pursuing in offering crowns to Balkan Slavic princes and to the new Asen ruler of Bulgaria, as well as encouraging the king of Hungary, who was a papal protégé, to advance into Galicia, which owed religious allegiance to the Orthodox metropolitan of Kiev.

The success of the Fourth Crusade, which dealt Byzantium a blow from which it was never able to recover, was due to a number of things. First of all, the Angeli emperors were unable to hold together an empire where Comneni in Trebizond, Bulgars in the Balkans, Armenians in Cicilia, and some others as well, had ceased to obey the imperial bureaucracy in Constantinople. Second, Emperor Alexius III was incompetent and lacked money to pay his troops. But most important of all, the Byzantine fleet had disappeared, leaving its capital on the Golden Horn open to the attack of a relatively small Venetian naval force, which in the days of Alexius I and Manuel could not even have reached the Sea of Marmora without being intercepted by superior Byzantine flotillas.

This undisputed control of the sea by Latin Westerners also explains both the successes and the failures which attended attempts to partition the empire. The Venetians were wise enough to take only areas which their fleet could defend, such as the ports of Conon and Modon, the islands of Crete, Euboea, and some of the Cyclades, and a special quarter in Constantinople. Soon the crusading Franks, too, revealed that they were dependent upon sea power. They were able to occupy Morea and Thebes and Athens in what came to be known as Frankish Greece, to take over Constantinople and its environs around the Sea of Marmora, and for a time to occupy Saloniki and some territory nearby. But they failed in their attempts to advance into the interior. Both Boniface of Montferrat and the Latin emperor were badly beaten by the Bulgarians, and other Franks were frustrated when they tried to absorb Lascarid Nicaea. What emerged, then, was not a Byzantine Empire under Latin control, but one divided into two parts. One half was ruled by Franks and Venetians. The other was divided between Greek pretenders to the imperial title in Trebizond, Epirus, and Nicaea; a Bulgarian tsar; a king of Lesser Armenia; and a Seljuk sultan who was at last able to break out of his uplands to reach the Black Sea and the Mediterranean in a number of places. This fragmentation of the Byzantine world was to continue long after 1270.

A second point that needs to be made about this Latin conquest is that its religious results never came to justify the hopes of Innocent III. The forced union of Greek and Latin churches remained a dead letter as far as Greek and Slavic populations were concerned, and within a few years all of them, whether they lived in Latin-occupied areas or not, looked to the Greek patriarch of Nicaea as the legitimate head of their church. Indeed, it seems fair to say that the Fourth Crusade caused such hatred in Orthodox monastic and secular priestly circles that it helped to create a special barrier between the two communions which was to endure for centuries.

The destruction of an effective Byzantine Empire, with all that that entailed, was one important event which took place during Innocent III's pontificate. But there were others, as well, which had a bearing upon Western European expansion in general. In the Baltic, for instance, these years saw

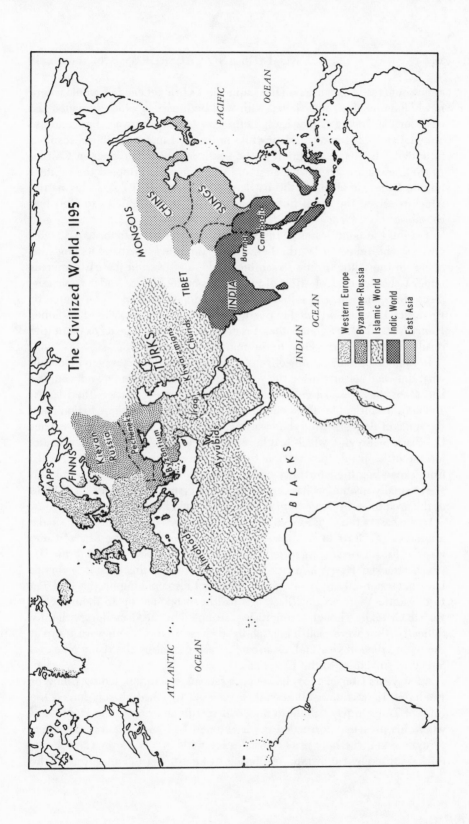

The Civilized World, 1195

ATLANTIC
OCEAN

LAPPS

FINNS

Kievan
Russia

Pechenegs

Spain

Byzantium

Maghrib

B L A C K S

Ayyubid

INDIAN
OCEAN

TURKS

Khwarzmians

Ghurids

Iraq

TIBET

INDIA

Burma

Cambodia

MONGOLS

CHINS

SUNGS

SUNGS

PACIFIC

OCEAN

Western Europe

Byzantine-Russia

Islamic World

Indic World

East Asia

a slow but steady expansion of the Latin West's bridgehead in Livonia where newly founded Riga was ringed with well-built castles which provided the basis for controlling native Livs, Letts, and Cours who were beginning to accept Latin Christianity. Meanwhile in Spain, Innocent's efforts resulted in a joint Christian expedition to the south in which the kings of Castile, Aragon, and Portugal participated and which in 1212 crippled the military might of the Almohads at the battle of Las Novas de Tolosa. This battle, which reversed the verdict of Alarcos, opened up Al-Andālūs to Christian conquest.

During the pontificates of Innocent III's successors, Honorius III, Gregory IX, and Innocent IV, the Latin West continued to expand its power in Spain, in the Baltic, in the Byzantine world, and even in the eastern areas under Crusader control. Most of this expansion took place under papal auspices, but some of it resulted from the independent efforts of Emperor Frederick II, who continued to pursue the goals and the policies of his father Henry VI and of his grandfather Frederic Barbarossa. Let us examine the results of these efforts down to the middle of the century.

In Romania the major objective of the Latin Westerners was to hold onto what they had seized during the years immediately after 1204, and until the late 1250s they were successful in doing so in Frankish Greece, the islands, and in Constantinople. The Venetians were also able to continue to dominate the trade of Romania from the bases they had seized and to begin to exploit the Black Sea region which had heretofore been closed to their merchants. On the other hand, they were not able to prevent the emperors of Nicaea from expanding their territory on the European side of the Bosphorus and were equally unable, as has been noted, to persuade the Greeks and Slavs of the area to accept communion with the Latin church.

In the east of the Crusaders these years also saw Western Europeans make a number of efforts to expand—not always successfully. The first of these was the Fifth Crusade organized by Innocent III's successor, Honorius III, which attacked Egypt in 1217–19. The objective of this assault seems to have been not only recovering Jerusalem but also opening up the Red Sea to the Latin West, as the Black Sea had been opened up to them by the Fourth Crusade. Though Damietta was occupied by the Crusaders with little difficulty, they were foolish enough to advance up the Nile toward Cairo at the wrong time of year and, as a result, were caught by the rising Nile and forced to surrender to the Egyptians.

A few years later in 1227, however, a second expedition, led by Emperor Frederick II, was more successful. Frederick, who had already forced the ruler of Tunis to pay tribute to him, sailed with an army to the Holy Land where his presence persuaded the frightened Egyptian sultan to cede him Jerusalem and the holy places of Palestine without a battle in 1229. Frederick's subsequent crowning of himself as king of Jerusalem outraged the pope, and imperial viceroys in the Orient were never able to exercise authority in the face of strong opposition from Syrian Frankish families like the Ibelins. Yet for some fifteen years a viable kingdom of Jerusalem existed, which controlled most of the interior of Palestine proper. This lasted until 1244 when a severe defeat at the hands of the Ayyubids, another Hattin, made the interior indefensible and allowed Jerusalem to fall again into Moslem hands.

Even then another crusade, led by Louis IX of France in 1248, might have remedied this loss. Unfortunately, however, Louis repeated the mistakes made by his predecessors during the Fifth Crusade. He insisted on advancing up the Nile from Damietta, which he had occupied, only to have his whole force trapped by the Nile and forced to surrender ignominiously to the Ayyubid sultan. Nevertheless, it is worth noting that even after 1250, although these efforts in the Near East failed to open up the Red Sea to the Latins or hold Jerusalem permanently, they did help to maintain a strong Western European presence in Cyprus and along the shores of Palestine and Syria and a control of the sea which made it possible to occupy an important port like Damietta without much opposition from Moslem opponents.

In the third area we have mentioned, the Baltic, the Knights of the Sword, who were encouraged by both emperor and popes, continued to expand their Livonian holdings, aided by frequent crusades and a Danish expedition sent to seize Estonia by a king who exercised considerable control over Lübeck and other northern German lands. In 1228–29 they were joined in their Baltic expansion by the other German crusading order, the Teutonic Knights, who began the conquest of Prussia. Soon thereafter the Knights of the Sword were unfortunate enough to suffer a serious defeat at the hands of the pagan Lithuanians, leading them to unite with the Teutonic Knights. This union allowed them to regroup and advance again successfully into the interior, but it did not give them sufficient strength to defeat the Russians of Novgorod and Pskov, who, after crushing the Swedes along the borders of Finland, checked the knights in 1241 in a famous battle fought on the ice of Lake Peipus. By midcentury, then, Germans and Danes had expanded Western European frontiers into eastern Baltic lands whose native population they were able to control through castles and a monopoly of commerce. But they were unable to advance deeper into the interior of Russia or Lithuania in the face of the the native population's hostility to the religious and political domination which these Latin Westerners were attempting to impose on them.

The fourth and last theater of Latin expansionism, Spain and the Maghreb, also saw considerable activity during these decades. Though, as we have noted, it was the Christian victory of Las Novas de Tolosa which made possible further Christian progress in Iberia, advances did not follow immediately on the heels of this battle. Instead, it was not until after the death of the Almohad ruler Al-Mustansir (1213–1224), when the Hafsids of Tunis made themselves independent, the nomadic Berber Merinids began to dispute control of Morocco with the Almohads, and great revolts took place in Al-Andālūs, that the Christian Spanish resumed the Reconquista.

They were uniformly successful almost at once. Between 1229 and 1232, Jaime of Aragon was able to capture the Balearics and went on to take Valencia which was entirely his by 1245. Meanwhile, the Castilians advanced south as well, taking Cordoba in 1236, Seville in 1248, and by 1250 with the help of Aragon forced Murcia to accept their rule and the king of Granada to become their vassal. At the same time, the Portuguese were moving south, too, and captured the Algarve. By the middle of the thirteenth century, the Moors had lost all of Spain except Granada. The Straits of Gibraltar, which in Moslem hands had so long separated Christian Atlantic flotillas from those which operated in the Mediterranean, were now controlled by the Latin West and patrolled by a new Castilian fleet built in the dockyards of conquered Seville. Western Europeans had opened up two barriers to further expansion—the Bosphorus and the Straits of Gibraltar—as well as establishing themselves firmly on the shores of Syria and Lesser Armenia which led to the interior of Asia and along Baltic coasts which controlled access to northern Russia. And in the course of this expansion, they had destroyed the Byzantine and Moslem flotillas and eastern Baltic pirate ships which had so long barred their way. From the Neva and the Gulf of Finland to the Crimea and the mouth of the Nile, the seas belonged to Western Europe, and its ships could sail freely, undisturbed by the possibility of hostile attack by any non-Latin power.

While all this was going on in the West, in the East a remarkable man, Genghis Khan, was laying the foundations of a great Mongol empire. Genghis Khan began his life as a minor chieftain in the Gobi Desert area, where, after many vicissitudes, he managed to unite the tribesmen who lived in the steppes between the Great Wall of China and the empire of the Kara Khitai into a single great confederacy. He did so by conquering the tribes of this region one after another and incorporating them into a larger political structure through the absorption of their chieftains into his extended family and the organization of their warriors into an army composed of *ordos* of ten, a hundred, and a thousand men each—a system which he no doubt copied from the Kitans and Chins. He also established a special set of laws known as the *Yasa* which insured justice and ended blood feuds. These years also produced an army which could maneuver effectively over immense distances and which was led by a number of brilliant generals who were completely loyal to Genghis Khan and his family.

Not until he had reached the age of forty did this great Mongol leader begin to attack more settled realms nearby. Then between 1205 and 1209 he began with an assault upon his least powerful neighbors, the Tanguts of Hsi Hsia—an assault which led them to accept his overlordship. Then he turned his attention to the much more formidable empire of the Chins. By 1215 he had defeated their armies, taken their capital of Peking, and driven them out of northern China. They managed to hold out in a number of southern provinces which they ruled from Kaifeng, the old capital of the northern Sung. Genghis Khan's victory over the Chins was of vital importance to him because he gained two things from it. First of all, thanks to his victory, he was able to add to his army a number of Chinese contingents who were skilled in siege warfare and able to use rockets and gunpowder. From this time on, the Mongols were able to take walled cities, which otherwise they would have been unable to conquer. Second, after the fall of Peking he was joined by a number of Chinese administrators who were experienced in organizing and governing settled populations. They were especially useful for their ability to set up an efficient taxation system and encourage commerce, both of which assured the Mongols the maximum possible benefits from their conquests.

Now that most of northern China was in his hands, Genghis Khan turned westward and sent one of his ablest generals, Noyon, to attack the Kara Khitai. By 1218 the latter had submitted and it was the turn of the realm of the Khwarazmian shah to feel the full fury of the Mongols. Large armies were sent to attack Persia and Khorasan, terrorizing cities that failed to submit promptly. They were able to converge on specific objectives after long marches which covered hundreds of miles. The Mongols also disorganized their opponents by pursuing the defeated Persian shah and his heir so relentlessly that they were never able to rally their forces effectively. As a result, during a two-year campaign between 1219 and 1221 they broke the back of Persian resistance to their conquest and followed this up in 1222 with a great reconnaissance raid led by their noted general Subotai who fought his way all around the Caspian Sea, shattering the forces of the Georgians and of the Cumans and Kievan Rūs who attempted to bar his way. Finally, in 1227, just before he died, the great Mongol khan completed his conquest of Hsi Hsia and incorporated it into his empire.

There was a brief lull in Mongol expansion when Genghis Khan died. But soon afterward, in 1229, Ogatai, his son, succeeded him as great khan, and parts of his western conquests were allotted as appanage fiefs to Chagatai and Batu. Chagatai received what had been the empire of the Kara Khitai, and Batu got more westerly areas which were to become the lands of the Golden Horde. Once this had been worked out, the Mongols resumed their conquests in Persia, which finally submitted to them unequivocally in 1231. They then turned their attention to Russia.

In many ways the 1236–37 Mongol campaign in Russia was a carbon copy of what they had waged in Khorasan and Persia, except that they fought, on this occasion, during the winter when rivers and swamps were frozen and thus unable to act as obstacles to their swift advances. We find them again sending their armies over vast distances to converge upon special objectives and using terror tactics and siege strategies to break the resistance of their opponents in the towns and cities of Russia. As a result, in little more than a year they had completed the conquest of the entire land—Cuman and Kievan alike. Even northern Novgorod, although it was never attacked directly and was protected by dense swamps and forests, preferred to submit to the Mongols rather than seek help from a Latin West which it felt was especially dangerous to its religious and political independence. Once Russia had been conquered, the Mongols then established a new capital for their Golden Horde at Serai on the lower Volga, and from here they began to exercise an authority which was to continue for several centuries.

Interestingly enough, the westward momentum of the Mongols did not end with the conquest of Russia. Instead, they decided to press on with Hungary as their next objective, perhaps because the Hungarians had long had a special interest in Galicia and because their king, Bela IV, had welcomed into his realm a number of Cumans who fled west after being defeated in the southern Russian steppes. Between 1241 and 1243 they attacked the Magyars in force, using two great armies which converged on the Hungarian plain. One of these armies attacked directly from the east, shattering Bulgar levies which attempted to bar its advance. The other made a great sweep north of the Carpathians destroying first a Polish army near Cracow and then a German one in Saxony before turning south and reaching the middle Danube. There they met the other Mongol force. The Hungarians were totally unable to defend themselves against these armies which sacked their cities, laid waste to the countryside, and pursued King Bela to the Adriatic where he barely managed to escape by boat from Mongol cavalry forces who followed him relentlessly. And then, hearing that the great khan Ogatai had died in Karakorun, the Mongols retreated back to Russia as swiftly as they had advanced, leaving behind them a band of devastated territory some five hundred miles wide.

These twin attacks upon Russia and Hungary were the most important ones launched by the Mongols during these years—and they thoroughly frightened Europe, which had no idea how to deal with their tactics. They were not, however, the only attacks they made during these years. In 1234, for example, they attacked the Chins again and forced the remnant of their once great empire to submit to them. Then in 1243 they advanced west from Persia into Georgia which, having been battered by Turkoman tribes and earlier attacks which took place in 1236, finally accepted them as overlords. Soon afterward in this same year they utterly destroyed the power of the Seljuks of Rum and forced them to accept their overlordship, too. Now as a third great khan, Mangu, took over in Mongolia, we find a Mongolian realm had come into existence which extended from the Pacific to the Carpathians and which had shown itself able to defeat the armies of northern China, Islam, Russia, and Western Europe to create an empire which included people from three great civilizations within its borders.

Now let us turn to the West where between the middle of the thirteenth century and the year 1270, when the death of St. Louis in Tunis ended the age of the Great Crusades, few important changes took place. In the eastern Baltic, for instance, a pause ensued as the united Teutonic Knights and Knights of the Sword held what they had but found it difficult to establish a land bridge in Samland which would form a link between their Livonian and their East Prussian holdings. And considerable friction also began to develop between the order and the archbishop of Riga—a friction which hampered their warlike proclivities.

In the western Mediterranean a similar lull occurred as the Aragonese, Castilians, and Portuguese attempted to digest their conquests and assimilate the considerable number of Moslems who now acknowledged their authority in southern and eastern Spain. In the central Mediterranean these years also saw a papacy preoccupied with the Hohenstaufen menace until in 1268 it was able to use Charles of Anjou and Tuscan bankers to destroy this house root and branch and turn over Sicily to the French Angevins. Nevertheless, a few events of importance did take place during these two decades. The Almohads finally were destroyed in 1269 as their capital of Marrakesh and Morocco itself fell to the Merinids, and the rest of their North African empire was divided between the rulers of Tlemcen and the Hafsids of Tunis. And as this happened all the successors of the Almohads found themselves forced to pay tribute, of a direct or indirect sort, to Latin Westerners—Granada and Morocco to Castile, Tlemcen to Aragon, and Tunis to Aragonese Sicily—thus creating a kind of Western European protectorate over what remained Islamic in this part of the world.

Somewhat less decisive was the Latin edge in the eastern Mediterranean where a kind of stalemate seems to have prevailed until 1270, even after the Ayyubids were replaced as rulers of Syria and Palestine by a new Mamluk dynasty. This stalemate existed because these latter hesitated to eliminate the last Crusader holdings along the coasts of Syria as long as the Mongols remained a serious menace to them, and because they lacked the sea power to confront the Franks of Cyprus or the Armenians of Cilicia successfully. In short, the Western European presence in this part of the Mediterranean, while not decisive, was still palpable enough to give pause to their Moslem opponents.

It would seem at first glance that the Latins were unsuccessful in the Byzantine world during these decades, being badly defeated in 1259 at Pellagonia in Greece by Emperor Michael Paleologus and losing the city of Constantinople in 1261—after which this great city again became the capital

of a revived Byzantine Empire and the seat of the Greek patriarch who
returned there from Nicaea. This revived empire, however, was much less
powerful than it appeared since the successes which Michael gained were
more the result of diplomacy and luck than they were of any inherent
strength. For instance, he was never able to persuade the Greek rulers of
Trebizond and Epirus or the Bulgarian tsar to accept his overlordship, and
he failed to build a powerful fleet capable of defending his capital and the
vital sea lanes that passed through the Sea of Marmora and linked the Black
Sea with the Aegean. So he was not only forced to grant the Genoese privileges at Galata and elsewhere, which made them almost independent of
Byzantine control, but in 1266 he even found it necessary to allow the hated
Venetians to return to their quarter in the city of the Golden Horn. By 1270
the Latins, despite apparent setbacks, were still the masters of Frankish
Greece and the islands and controlled the waters of the Black Sea and the
Aegean which led to Constantinople.

In contrast to what happened to Latin expansion the Mongols still continued to advance their frontiers, though some of their expansion followed
a different pattern and led them into parts of the world where they had not
been active before. One of these areas was the Fertile Crescent south of the
Persian plateau and Armenian and Anatolian uplands where the Mongols
were always most at home. Soon after 1250, however, the new great khan,
Mangu, gave to his kinsman, Hulagu, an appanage fief of former Islamic
territory in the west which centered in Persia and Khorasan. Almost at once
Hulagu decided, as the Seljuks had done two centuries before, to add Iraq
to his realm and led a large army into the low-lying Mesopotamian plains.
In a swift campaign marked by extreme brutality, Hulagu in 1258 took Baghdad and massacred a large portion of its population, including the Abbassid
caliph himself.

He then proceeded to absorb the rest of the Iraqi plain and advanced west
into Syria, after dealing with Mosul as brutally as he had with Baghdad. The
force which the Mongols used in Syria included a considerable number of
Christian auxiliaries from Georgia, Lesser Armenia, and Antioch and was
commanded by a Mongol general, Ketbogha, who was himself a Nestorian
Christian. It was also not as large as those used in the campaign against
Baghdad. Perhaps that is why, when it advanced south of Aleppo and met
a Mamluk army at Ain Jaluit in 1260, it was badly defeated and driven out
of Syria. For the first time, a Mongol force had met an Islamic army in battle
and lost.

During the same years when Hulagu was taking over Iraq and advancing
into northern Syria, other Mongol armies, mainly those under Chagatai,
were crossing the mountain passes which led from Persia and Afghanistan
into northern India and attacking the sultanate of Delhi. For reasons that
we will be discussing at some length later on, their attacks here were also

beaten off, and they were as unable to advance their frontiers into India as they were in Syria. In northern India by 1270 an Islamic state, relying upon the same kind of Mamluks as Egypt, successfully kept the Mongols at bay.

In the other theater in which the Mongols were active, the Far East, these years brought much more success. Their first victory was the conquest of Nan-Chao in 1253. Four years later a Mongol expedition attacked Annam and sacked Hanoi, and though ultimately unsuccessful, it showed that Mongol armies were capable of operating freely to the south as well as to the north and west of the Sung empire. In the next year, 1258, another great Mongol host invaded Korea and forced it to submit. All of East Asia except Sung China and Japan was now in Mongol hands.

Then in 1260, following the death of Mangu, the brother of Hulagu, Kublai Khan, became great khan in his turn. Kublai did not make Karakorum in Mongolia his capital but rather decided to settle in the Chinese city of Peking. He also proceeded to devote the first half of his reign to the conquest of the Sung empire. The Sungs resisted the Mongol attack with courage and tenacity, but by 1270 much of their navy had gone over to their foes, to be followed in 1276 by the loss of their capital of Hangchow. Three years later in 1279 the last Sung-held province had surrendered and the Mongols were supreme in China as they were in Korea, Nan-Chao, and distant Iraq.

As the Mongols rounded out their conquests in the Near East and the Far East, it was inevitable that they and the equally aggressive Western Europeans should come in contact with each other in ways which were different from the violent clashes which took place in central Europe during the years from 1241 to 1243. Indeed, it soon became apparent to both parties that they had much more to gain from cooperation than conflict. As the Ilkans, as Hulagu and his heirs were called, advanced in northern Syria, after taking Iraq, for instance, they had every reason to hope that they could persuade the Latin West, which controlled the sea and Syrian ports, to attack the Mamluks from the rear and so render their task easier. They and their brethren who ruled Russia, as the Golden Horde, also were interested in commercial contacts with Italian merchants who controlled the trade of the Black Sea and the Mediterranean.

If the Mongols by 1250 were beginning to see the political and commercial advantages to be gained from friendship with the Latin West, the latter was even more interested in some form of accommodation with these nomadic conquerors. The Westerners not only saw the Mongols as potential allies against their Moslem enemies in the Near East, but they also had the hope that they could convert them to Latin Christianity and so spread their faith deep into central Asia—a hope that rested on the knowledge that a number of the great khans had wives who were Nestorian Christians and that the khans themselves were hostile to the Islamic faith per se. Finally, Western European merchants, who were so active in northern Syria, Anatolia, and the Black Sea area, saw a special advantage to be derived from good relations with rulers who could allow them to trade directly with China and India over routes which were under their control.

Because of this, both the pope and King Louis IX of France sent a number of embassies to the courts of Mongol rulers before 1270 to explore the possibility of religious and military cooperation and to establish commercial contacts as well. These embassies were not very successful, it is true. But by the end of the seventh decade of the thirteenth century, they and commercial colonies like those established by Genoese and Venetian merchants in Mongol Russia and the Ilkan realm had laid the basis for a world in which a Marco Polo or a John of Marignola could wander freely all the way to Peking and Canton and link China and India to Western Europe in the late thirteenth and early fourteenth century.

Western Europe, which was able to expand its borders so successfully during these years, made great internal progress as well. In the political sphere the papacy continued to play a dynamic role as the leader of Western European society—even though at times it found itself challenged by Frederick II and his son Manfred of Sicily. Nevertheless, such popes as Innocent III, Gregory IX, and Innocent IV gave the Latin West a sense of direction as their centralized machinery of government in Rome, their power of taxation, their church courts and canon law made them the masters of the continent. John of England and Philip Augustus of France found it wise to submit to them. Philip of Austria and Otto of Brunswick found they had to accept the papal right to name an emperor. And the Hohenstaufen family learned that the popes had the power to confiscate their Sicilian realm and send them to the scaffold.

If political leadership in some ways ultimately rested in a remarkable papal monarchy, it is worth noting, however, that secular royal governments were able to play an important role in Europe at this time also, as had been the case in the previous century. It was precisely during these years, as a matter of fact, that the modern state began to take on form and substance in England under Henry III and Lord Edward, France under St. Louis, Spain under Jaime of Aragon and Alfonso El Sabio, Sicily under Frederick II, and Scandinavia under the Waldemars and Haakon the Old. All of these rulers were able in various ways to develop centralized administrations making use of nonfeudal law, more efficient systems of taxation to tap the wealth of their subjects, and a control over their nobility and middle class which changed the bases of their authority. Even in those areas where royal government was ineffectual, such as northern Italy and Germany, local princes and towns followed the same pattern of development, which made for a more effective control of those who lived under their rule.

It is impossible in the short space available to us to deal in any satisfactory way with the tactical and technical military expertise which so much of

Western Europe was able to develop on land and sea and which only Mongol and Mamluk armies and Sung naval flotillas were able to match. Suffice it to say that during these years we find castles built in a more sophisticated way, a general use of catapults and other engines in siege operations, and an ability to make use of combined arms in battle on a scale which was unknown earlier. On the sea this period saw northern Europeans, such as the Scandinavians and the English, begin to copy both the superior tactical formations and the technical expertise of their Mediterranean brethren, especially the use of catapults, Greek fire, the crossbow, and the convoy. These advances brought Latin Westerners success in their attacks upon their Byzantine, Islamic, and Baltic neighbors. With them, Westerners could breach the walls of Damietta, Constantinople, and Seville in amphibious assaults; control large hostile populations in Valencia, Cyprus, and Frankish Greece using relatively small forces as permanent armies of occupation; and learn to fight winter war in a distant Livonia, where pagan villagers were defenseless once the rivers and marshes were frozen over.

During this same period Western Europeans were also able to maintain a large measure of religious unity and common purpose. In part this was because the church did not hesitate to root out religious dissent among the Albigensians in southern France, for example, by launching a crusade and an Inquisition—thereby helping to form a climate of opinion which resulted in the tragic persecution of Europe's Jewish minority. But this religious unity also was maintained because religious reformers like Saint Francis of Assisi and Saint Dominic were able to bring the monastic movement out of its cloisters, and, as friars, serve the needs of the secular world through a creative poverty and a life of service. It also was strengthened by the way Saint Thomas Aquinas and Saint Bonaventura were able to use an organized scholasticism to shape Western Europe's intellectual thought in a Christian way. The Latin church then was able to successfully lead its communicants to victory in Spain, the Baltic, and the Near East in no small measure because it was able to direct and sublimate their energies in Western Europe itself.

What seems especially impressive, however, is evidence of the economic and technological skills which Western Europeans were able to display during these years. In the countryside these ranged from the astute estate management and use of crop rotation which lay and ecclesiastical proprietors found profitable in England, the *bastides* devoted to viniculture which began to appear in the Garonne valley, and the new grain fields cultivated by villagers in Pomerania and Brandenburg to the sugar plantations introduced into Cyprus, Crete, and Sicily by Latins who learned about them in Syria. They also included sheep runs which became a way of life in parts of Sicily, the Alps, the Cevennes, and the *meseta* of Iberia, and a cattle kingdom in areas of Estremadura and Andalusia newly captured from the Moslems. Everywhere such activities significantly increased Europe's food supply and

raw materials needed to fuel its industries and made possible a growth in
its population until it was double what it had been in the mid-eleventh
century.

Western Europe during these years did not develop any great metropolitan centers on the order of Constantinople, Baghdad, Peking, or Hangchow,
but some of its main cities, especially in Italy, grew rapidly, and some like
Naples, Milan, and Venice may have reached a population of more than
50,000. In the north only London, Paris, or Bruges approached such a size.
But everywhere we find evidence of a tempo of industrialization, especially
as textile production increased in the towns of Catalonia, northern Italy, the
Midi, and Germany to match that found in the older cloth centers of Britain
and the Low Countries. Especially interesting is evidence of a growth of
towns in Scandinavia, the Baltic, and Germany east of the Elbe—where
heretofore urbanism had lagged behind that found in the rest of Europe.

Technological progress was even more striking in agriculture, industry,
and mining. As the three field system and heavy plow spread across northern
Europe, better farm implements like the flail came into use. Watermills
were now found everywhere and were used not only to grind grain but to
full cloth mechanically in England and process ore in Austria, Bohemia, and
Saxony. Nor was the power of the wind ignored, for by the end of the
thirteenth century windmills were built in the Low Countries and England
to grind grain and pump water out of polders. Having harnessed power so
well to its needs, Western Europe was now able to produce cloth, arms,
and metalware of various sorts so inexpensively that these wares could compete successfully in the Near East with the products of local artisans. And
its special inventiveness extended from the use of interchangeable parts
pioneered by Venice's arsenal, to a stocking knitting machine invented in
Florence, to eyeglasses, which Italians seem to have discovered in part
because of Roger Baron's interest in optics, to gunpowder, which may have
reached the West from China, as well as to spaghetti, which was clearly
Italian in origin.

Perhaps the best example of a new technology and its impact on Western
European society, however, is provided for us by the compass, which was
already known in northern waters but which only now began to be used by
Italian and Catalan mariners. Once introduced into the Mediterranean
world, it soon spread in a special boxed form and had a great impact upon
shipping by making possible *portolan* charts which ship captains could use
to navigate directly from one port to another. This made it possible for them
to abandon their older practice of following coastal routes and also allowed
them to navigate when skies were overcast and sun and stars were not
available to fix their position accurately. Thus it was now practicable for
skippers to sail their ships for longer periods in Mediterranean waters than
had previously been the case and make two round trips a year instead of

one to distant ports. This in turn doubled the profits which Italians and Catalans could expect from the same vessels and further increased the advantages which they had over potential Byzantine and Moslem rivals. The use of the compass, then, with all that went with it, along with an increase in the size of galleys and round ships, helped the Western Europeans to dominate the Mediterranean by 1270 and for the next two centuries.

By now Western Europe had come of age financially as well. By the first years of the thirteenth century that rather simple system of partnerships, represented by *commenda* contracts, had developed in Italy into *societas* arrangements in which a number of investors could pool their capital for use in the building of ships and in various trading and business ventures. Such partnerships were not confined to southern Europe either, for we find them employed in the England of Henry III and, according to *The King's Mirror*, in the Norway of Haakon the Old.

These business arrangements explain why money lending now became so widespread and sophisticated and was carried on by the Templars or a great noble like Richard of Cornwall. But it was the Italians who took the lead in organized money lending which now had progressed to the point where we can think of it as banking. This was perhaps in part because of close connections which the Italians had with a papacy which needed to arrange the transfer of large sums of money from northern Europe to its papal court in Rome. At any rate, soon after 1200, we find bankers from Milan and Asti, Plaisence, Florence, and Siena active in much of Western Europe, with only the Cahorsins of southern France as rivals. They were loaning money to English kings, financing businessmen at Bruges and at the Fairs of Champagne, anticipating papal revenues, and providing Charles of Anjou with the resources he needed to conquer the kingdom of the Two Sicilies. The Latin West now at last had the financial expertise needed to match her economy, her technology, and her political and military establishments.

Under the circumstances, it is not surprising that these years saw Western Europe come of age intellectually and culturally, too, with Dominican and Franciscan friars producing great *summas* which organized all knowledge, with Romantic literature finding wider audiences as its vogue spread across all of Europe, and with Matthew Paris and Snorri Sturluson able to write histories with a range and a sweep that was truly remarkable. Equally striking is the way the Gothic cathedrals of the period married technical skills and artistic elements to produce magnificent *summas* in stone which reflect their age perfectly. Fortunately we possess in the building accounts of Henry III's agents and in the notebook of Villart de Honnecourt the proof that these buildings were not accidental affairs but rather the product of trained intelligence of the highest order.

These varied developments explain the marked increase in the scope and the range of Western merchants in the Mediterranean-Black Sea area. For

instance, now, for the first time, we find large numbers of Provençal merchants from Narbonne, Montpellier, and Marseilles joining their Italian
neighbors and trading with Sicily, Egypt, Syria, Lesser Armenia, Romania,
Andalusia, and the Maghreb and traveling with their Cahorsin brethren to
the Fairs of Champagne. And to them were added, by midcentury, Catalan
traders, who, after participating in the conquest of the Balearics, Valencia,
and Andalusia, began to traffic with Tunis and Oran and establish ties with
Alexandria and Seville.

A similar increase in the tempo of merchant activity is noticeable in northern Europe, too, where Norwegian kings knit together distant Scandinavian
settlements in the Faroes and Iceland and agreed to send an annual ship to
Greenland. Large German colonies appeared in Novgorod and other northern Russian towns, while merchants from southern Germany reached Venice
in large enough numbers to found a Fondaco di Tedesco in 1229. Still another
international center of commerce was provided by the Fair of Scania which
attracted merchants from England and the Low Countries. These years also
saw Gascon sailors carrying wine to northern ports and seamen from northern
Spain shipping iron to Britain, helping to take Seville from the Moors, and
joining the Portuguese in venturing out into the Atlantic to rediscover islands
like Madeira and the Canaries which had long been forgotten by Western
Europeans.

Even before the arrival of the Mongols Italian merchants, who had previously confined their activities to seaport towns, began to reach interior
cities like Aleppo and Damascus and trade with commercial centers in Lesser
Armenia and the Seljuk realm where they had been unknown earlier. Some
of them even reached Russia prior to 1250 where their presence was noted
by William of Rubuck—probably arriving there by way of Constantinople
and the Black Sea. Long before 1270, adventurous Genoese and Venetians
were beginning to penetrate the interior of Asia and move eastward toward
China and India. In Genoa, a city which was especially involved with this
expansion of European commerce toward the East and the West, the first
gold coins were issued in 1252, soon to be followed by the more famous
florins of Florence and ducats of Venice. By 1270, then, Western Europe's
symbol of commercial expansion was a new gold coinage in Italy, which soon
was to become the medium par excellence of international commerce.

The Islamic world and the Byzantine-Russian nexus were both very much
affected by the expansion of Western Europe and the Mongols during this
period. Indeed, the world of Byzantium and Russia, in particular, almost
ceased to exist as a viable, self-sufficient civilization. Not only did Venetians
and Franks between 1204 and 1261 control Constantinople and the waters
of the Black Sea and the Aegean which led to it, but they also held considerable island and mainland territory as well. This all but completely destroyed Byzantium's older merchant and financial class, except perhaps in

Trebizond or Nicaea where a few of them were able to carry on a precarious existence. Latin conquest also doomed the *hyperion* or gold byzant, which now became a coin which had only local importance—even though in Lascarid domains gold coins of good weight and value continued to be issued.

All of this meant that, when Michael Paleologus recovered Constantinople and reconstituted the empire again in 1261, it was a very different Byzantine world which emerged from his victory. It had lost twenty to thirty percent of its population; Constantinople itself had only 50,000 people within its walls. Its merchant class had lost out to alien Italians who were to dominate its commerce until Ottoman times, even though it retained enough industrial expertise to allow some of its city folk to maintain themselves as a prosperous part of the population. Its upper-class aristocrats controlled estates which were rapidly becoming hereditary and which they were using to make themselves independent of Constantinople and dominant over their servile peasants. Increasingly Byzantium was turning to its church for the leadership and unity it could find nowhere else, and it began to prize a mystic monasticism over the intellectual life which a few of its scholars still followed. And it now hated, above all else, the Latin church and the papacy which it saw as the symbol of a Western imperialism which had destroyed its peace and its prosperity.

The rest of the Byzantine-Russian world was also, by 1270, at a very low ebb—thanks to the Mongols, however, rather than the Latin West. By 1243, for example, as has been noted, the kingdom of Georgia had lost both its independence and the prosperity it had enjoyed under Queen Tamar the Great (1184–1222) and had been forced to accept Mongol suzerainty. The same fate had befallen the Seljuk sultanate of Konya which had also flourished mightily before Mongol armies ended its independence in the same year.

As for Russia, both that area where the Cumans held sway and that ruled by princes of the House of Rurik, the arrival of the Mongols in 1236–37 changed things significantly also. What emerged was a land ruled by the Golden Horde from their capital on the lower Volga, which in many ways had returned to the age of the Khazars. Serai was located near Khazar Itil, and the Golden Horde soon became so acculturated that they used Turkish instead of Mongol as the language of their court. Even the taxes which were levied upon the Kievan Rūs seem identical to those which tradition tells us the Khazars had imposed four centuries earlier.

The ruling khans of the Golden Horde allowed Russian princes to continue to rule their principalities provided they paid heavy taxes and appeared with a full complement when summoned for war. But they claimed the right to decide between heirs to Russian principalities and to invest them with their authority. They also went out of their way to conciliate the Orthodox church by exempting it from taxation and giving it extensive privileges which enabled it to dramatically increase both its landed holdings and its influence

during the next several centuries. This accommodation helps to explain why
the Kievan Rūs accepted Mongol overlordship with so little opposition and
seem to have preferred it to the kind of religious and political subservience
that they had learned to expect from the Hungarians and the Teutonic
Knights.

It may even be asserted that once the shock of conquest had worn off,
and the Russians had begun to recover from the destruction, deportations,
and depopulation which had attended it, they began to derive some benefits
from Mongol rule. For the first time in more than a century, northern Russia
was able to trade freely with the Black Sea area where by 1270 Italian
merchants had established colonies in towns like Kaffa and Tana—and at
the same time make use of safe routes leading to Turkestan and central Asia.
And in the north a general prosperity also prevailed in cities like Novgorod
which began to extend its boundaries eastward to include a vast hinterland.
Beneath the surface of the Tartar deep freeze, then, Russia continued to
live a relatively vigorous life of its own in preparation for a new destiny.

For the Islamic world, too, these years were filled with changes. Each
area of the Islamic West—Moslem Spain, Tunisia, Algeria, and Morocco—
emerged by 1270 in quite a different way. Moslem Spain, of course, suffered
most severely of all from the Reconquista, especially in Andalusia and the
Algarve where many Moslems refused to follow the example of their coreligionists in Murcia and Valencia and went into exile. This resulted in a
thoroughly disorganized society which only slowly was able to recover its
prosperity. Even Granada, which served as a refuge for Moslems and which
was spared invasion, presented its Nasarid rulers with serious economic
problems which were not easily overcome.

Morocco found itself equally troubled during this period since the Merinids, who gradually took it over, were a nomadic people who displayed little
sympathy for the problems of the settled peasantry and town folk. It is no
accident, then, that these years saw the end of the flourishing culture of the
Almoravid period and a debased gold coinage which formed a striking contrast to the fine maraboutins of the preceding century.

Further to the east in Algeria, a more prosperous realm had emerged by
midcentury—that of Tlemcen ruled by a Berber dynasty which was hostile
to the Merinids. These Aloualids owed their effectiveness to a prosperity
which came from trade with the Sudan by way of Sigilmasa and which reached
the Mediterranean at Oran. Over this route came considerable supplies of
gold which during this period made the rulers of Mali, who controlled its
source, the wealthiest monarchs of Africa and enriched a large number of
Jewish merchants who served as intermediaries.

We find Tunis, ruled by a Hafsid dynasty, was now independent and in
some ways was the most successful western Moslem principality of all. Tunis
was not very powerful militarily, and its rulers thought it prudent to purchase

peace from Christian neighbors by paying tribute to Sicily and by using a Catalan bodyguard to help maintain order. It also found that it had to allow Catalan and Italian merchants control of most of its foreign trade. But despite all of this, it was able to maintain internal peace and considerable rural prosperity and to keep nomadic tribes from interfering with its peasantry or with the trans-Saharan commerce which reached its oases cities. It also benefited from the attraction of its seaports to many refugees from Andalusia who brought with them considerable skills and talents which helped make Tunis, for the first time, a center of Islamic culture in general.

The middle part of the Moslem world had quite a different history during this period, for it enjoyed considerable political unity under the Ayyubid successors of Saladin and the Mamluk sultans who took over from them in 1250. These rulers were able to destroy two crusading armies which invaded Egypt, to recover Jerusalem and the interior of Syria from the Franks, and, in 1260, to defeat Ketbogha and his Mongol army at Ain Jaluit—a battle which saved Syria from the Ilkans.

Such successes, however, were probably less decisive than they seemed, for Egypt and Syria under the Ayyubids and early Mamluks were not very prosperous. It seems worth noting, for instance, that the rulers of Egypt were not able to protect their seaports and keep them from falling into Latin hands and that they lacked the naval strength in the Red Sea area to keep the Rassulids of Aden from taking the Yemen in 1240 and a little later encroaching on Hejaz. During this period we also find evidence of a serious decline in the textile industry, a failure to rebuild Damietta as a port, and an inability of Egypt's merchant class to maintain contact with their counterparts in the Maghreb and the rest of the Islamic west. It is almost as if that great trade route which for several centuries had stretched west from Egypt to the Straits of Gibraltar had at last come apart and been broken up into fragments. Perhaps the same thing was happening on the Indian Ocean side where, despite the activities of the *Karimi* or spice merchants, Rassulid control over the entrance to the Red Sea signals a similar weakening of commercial contacts with India. This may explain why no Geniza documentation exists for a period after 1250 and why, for the first time in centuries, Egypt and Syria abandoned gold dinars and used silver dirhems as their principal medium of exchange. For if the world of the Ayyubids and early Mamluks was militarily successful, it was also one which no longer played the vital economic role which for four centuries had seemed to represent its destiny.

The remaining area of the Islamic world was that conquered by the Mongols which by 1270 was almost completely controlled by the Ilkans of Persia. This area of western Asia, just prior to the arrival of these nomadic conquerors and their formidable armies, was enjoying a considerable economic revival. This revival seems to have been based on the restoration of the Persian Gulf

as the principal terminus of trade from India in place of the Red Sea which
had for several centuries been dominant. Such commerce was carried on in
large ships which made Ormuz their terminus and which are depicted for
us in a manuscript which dates from 1237. These ships seem to have been
equipped for the first time with stern rudders and, according to a Persian
source which dates from 1232, used compasses as well. Perhaps in part
because of Persian Gulf trade, Baghdad and Iraq, under Caliph An-Nasir,
recovered their importance, and Seljuk Konya and Georgia became so prosperous in the early thirteenth century that Italian merchants began to move
into the interior of this part of the Near East in search of profit.

Mongol attacks subsequently did considerable damage to Khorasan and
other areas where cities were destroyed and the population was massacred.
Abbasid Baghdad and Mosul also suffered the fate of Bokhara, Ray, and
Nishapur. There is evidence that both Mongol armies and the Turkoman
tribesmen whom these invasions set in motion did considerable damage to
the countryside in Anatolia, Iraq, Georgia, and northern Persia. Sometimes
the Mongols even destroyed whole communities like the Alamut of the
Assassins in northern Persia. But not every part of the Moslem east felt the
fury of their assaults, which tended to be confined to certain specific areas
of Iraq, Syria, and parts of Iran. So even though news of Mongol savagery
thoroughly alarmed the Islamic world and caused a whole range of intellectuals to seek refuge in Konya, Cairo, Shiraz, and Delhi, by 1270 the worst
was over and a new age could begin.

It is clear that the years between 1195 and 1270 were not easy for those
who shared in Moslem civilization. They saw a Latin Western conquest of
most of Spain, pressure on North Africa, and two assaults upon Egypt as
well as a frightening Mongol seizure of eastern provinces which ended the
Abbasid caliphate. It seems likely that this caused a considerable decline in
the population of the Islamic world as a whole, perhaps by as much as ten
percent. And as Western European merchants and shipping came to dominate the trade of the Mediterranean and kept Islamic businessmen from
communicating with one another except through Christian intermediaries,
there was a considerable decline in the prosperity of Morocco, Granada,
Egypt, and Syria. Whether the same is true of the Indian Ocean side is more
problematical as far as the Persian Gulf region is concerned, but it would
appear that these years were difficult ones for the Red Sea areas, as we have
noted. They were also, in the short run, disastrous for those parts of Persia,
Iraq, and Armenia which felt the full fury of Mongol attacks between 1220
and 1270.

On the other hand, the Moslem world somehow managed to endure these
disasters, and in Egypt under the Mamluks and in the sultanate of Delhi it
was beginning to create a new political and military system. This was a
mixture of the slave-mercenary organization of the tenth century and the

feudalized warrior system of the eleventh and twelfth. By 1270 this system had shown itself able to halt the Mongols and keep Latin Westerners from gaining any more territory, while it secured the support of the older upper-class merchant-administrative group who were still strongly entrenched in Moslem cities and business life. In addition to this, the Moslem world was able to minimize religious conflicts during these three-quarters of a century. Despite the end of the Abbasid caliphate, most of the population clung to Sunni orthodoxy strengthened by a growing Sufi movement and refused to turn aside from Islam and accept the religion of their Christian or Mongol conquerors. Despite their fragmented economies and different currencies, the Moslems preserved enough also of their old business organization, especially in the Indian Ocean area and the Sahara, so that they could build upon it when the opportunity presented itself to them. By 1270 Islamic civilization had suffered hard blows, but it was already displaying a remarkable vitality which was to lead it to a brighter future.

The peoples who made up Indic and East Asian civilizations, unlike those who lived in the Islamic and Byzantine-Russian worlds, were affected only by Mongol expansion during these seven-and-a-half decades and not by that of the Latin West. In conquering East Asia the Mongols experienced difficulties despite their formidable array of military skills. The empire of the Chins, for example, proved to be no pushover, taking twenty years to conquer, probably because its Chinese population, who had been integrated into its government and its army and were relatively prosperous, supported their Jurched rulers. Even the initial Mongol attack, which gained them Peking and North China, might not have succeeded had their armies not been aided by Sung naval contingents which raided coastal regions between 1204 and 1217. And afterward the Chins were able to reestablish themselves at Kaifeng and hold onto their southern provinces for almost two decades before they were finally liquidated.

Once the Chins had been destroyed, the Mongols paused in their advance, perhaps because they feared to tangle with the powerful Sung fleet which in 1237 contained some twenty squadrons amounting to 52,000 men and by 1243 was engaged in a building program to increase its strength. Instead of attacking the Sungs head on, then, they moved to isolate them by taking Nan-Chao in 1253, attacking Annam in 1257 and absorbing Korea in 1258, the latter providing them with much-needed naval contingents as well as serving as a springboard for an eventual attack on Japan.

It was not until after 1260, when Kublai Khan became the fourth great khan, with his residence in Peking, that the Mongols finally began to attack the Sung empire directly. And even then, it is interesting to note, they relied as much on diplomacy as force. First of all, Kublai Khan managed to enlist on the Mongol side a number of great merchants who resented the Sung authorities' practice of commandeering their ships without adequate compensation. Second, in 1270 he managed to persuade the Sung naval commander, who was of Persian birth, to desert and go over to the Mongols with a number of his warships. By 1276 Hangchow had fallen and the Yangtze valley had surrendered to Kublai's forces. Finally in 1279 the last remnants of the Sung fleet, which had taken refuge along the Fukien coast, followed suit. All of China was now in the hands of a Mongol or Yuan dynasty which was to control it for the next century.

To examine just how East Asia was affected by these years of Mongol conquest, we need to distinguish between the northern area which the Mongols conquered first and the southern area which remained in Sung hands until the 1270s. The north, consisting as it did of the Chin empire, Hsi Hsia, and Korea, suffered serious damage as Genghis Khan and his successors broke the resistance of its population to their rule. We learn from contemporary accounts that its cities were sacked, its townsmen massacred, and its countryside laid to waste. Some authorities have suggested that, as a result of this, northern China's population during these years declined by twenty percent, or about 10,000,000 in all—an estimate that may be rather high.

There is, however, another side of the picture. Even before the death of Genghis Khan in 1227, the Mongols began to show an interest in exploiting the resources of their newly conquered empire in a rational way. So they began to make use of a number of Moslem central Asian merchants and moneylenders for this purpose. These men, organized into guilds known as *ortaqs* and financed in part by the Mongol upper class, were interested in farming the taxes, disposing of booty, and investing in caravan trading ventures. Thus, by 1250, we find that North China began to benefit considerably from the commerce which these ortaqs encouraged—especially that which went west along caravan routes which the "Pax Mongolica" made more secure than they had been for centuries—routes which Western European merchants were to follow in the years to come.

Only one part of the civilized world of northern East Asia managed to escape Mongol control during these years—Japan. The Kamakura shōgunate which Yoritimo had established continued to rule the land, but soon after 1200 it was taken over by a new family of Hōjō regents. The Hōjōs, if anything, made the military control of the land exercised by their *Bakufu*, or governing headquarters, more effective by confiscating considerable land in the south and east from its proprietors, after a futile revolt by landowners opposed to their policies, and distributing it to their feudal supporters. Their *jitōs* and *shugōs*, who were feudal officials and fief holders who owed allegiance to Kamakura rather than to Kyōtō, represented a force for a more thoroughgoing militarization of Japanese society in general, as did a new feudal code, the Joei Formulary, which was introduced in 1232. By 1270 Japanese society was profoundly militarized and prepared to face the danger of a Mongol attack.

It is difficult to imagine a greater contrast between the world of the Mongols north of the Yangtze and the world of the Sungs south of this river during this period. Where Mongol society was essentially warlike, the Sungs were oriented toward peace and business. Even more important perhaps, while the Mongols' commercial interests—such as they were—caused them to be concerned with trade which followed overland routes to the west, the Sungs were oriented toward the sea and a maritime commerce which linked them with the Indic world of Southeast Asia. Indeed, never before or since in Chinese history were we to see a more maritime, commercially oriented government than that of the southern Sung between 1195 and 1279.

The maritime orientation of the Sungs had a number of interesting consequences. First of all, it caused their government to rely heavily on dues levied on external commerce to run their administration—such levies rising from five percent of total revenues in the twelfth century to twenty percent in the mid-thirteenth, or ten times in value over what they had amounted to in the year 1000.

Second, the southern Sungs increased commerce with Southeast Asia and much of the Indian Ocean area by encouraging their merchants to establish themselves in foreign ports and negotiating trade treaties with these parts of the world. As a result of all this, Chinese merchants in large numbers sailed south in search of profit. Thanks to a remarkable survey of the commerce their activities engendered, written in 1225 by a governmental official, we know that they did so in large, three- or four-masted junks, equipped with compasses and stern rudders, many of which could carry as many as 400 passengers. Such vessels now also began to pass through the Straits of Malacca or Sunda Strait and sail directly to ports in Ceylon and southern India, where they exchanged the porcelains, teas, silks, tin, and other wares which they carried for spices, Indian cottons, and Islamic wares available in this part of the world.

It is even possible that some of their ships sailed even further west to Ormuz and East Africa in pursuit of gain. A considerable amount of Chinese money, dating from this period, has been discovered in coin hoards unearthed along East African shores, always accompanied by fragments of thirteenth-century Chinese porcelains. It is also significant that precisely during this period so much Chinese *celadon* ware reached the Persian Gulf area that it caused a change in the pottery made by Islamic artisans, who now copied its designs and its glazes. And it was probably because of this contact with China that a Hariji ship of 1237 had a stern rudder and a contemporary Persian writer mentions the compass. By the early thirteenth century, then, we can see that the Chinese merchants and ships of the Sungs had begun to link East Asia with the Indic world on a scale previously unknown, bringing profit to both civilizations.

It must not be supposed, however, that the trade between China and

Greater India during this period was entirely in the hands of Chinese merchants and ship captains, for nothing could be further from the truth. Much
of it, as a matter of fact, was carried on by native merchants from Indonesia,
Champa, India, or the Islamic world who sailed their ships to Canton, Fukien, and Ningpo and who were so numerous that they formed large foreign
colonies in seaport cities and in Hangchow. It was no accident, it would
seem, that the Lord High Admiral of the Sung navy in 1270 was born in
Persia, for he was just one of the many foreigners who were welcomed in a
Sung world in which Quilon and Palembang were as real as Peking or Kaesong. And it was this overseas interest and tradition which Kublai Khan was
to inherit when he took over southern China in 1279.

The Indic peoples of Southeast Asia remained relatively unaware of the
potential menace of the eastern Mongols until Nan-Chao fell to this warlike
people in 1253. For them China was the peaceful empire of the Sungs to
which they sent embassies and with which they traded to the enrichment
of both their government and their merchant class. During the years of the
early thirteenth century, though a Burmese ruler held sway in Pagan and
though Champa still clung to a separate identity, it was Cambodia that was
the most important mainland realm. Its kings tended to dominate their
Burmese neighbors and to exercise a measure of control over the delta of
the Mekong River and to display their royal glory by constructing great
irrigation works and building great temple complexes at Ankor Vat and Ankor
Thom.

This period of Khmer greatness, however, began to come to an end soon
after the death of their last powerful king, Jayavarman VII, when two Thai
chiefs, in control of Thai tribesmen who had infiltrated the upper Menam
valley, defeated a Cambodian general and established themselves at Suk-
hot'ai near modern Bangkok. These Thais were soon joined by others who
seem to have been driven south by the Mongol seizure of Nan-Chao. As a
result, the Cambodians found themselves forced to evacuate Champa and,
although they refused to accept Mongol overlordship, they saw their northwestern provinces overrun by the Thais and their realm begin a slow decline
which was to continue during the next century. A similar decline, it is worth
noting, began to affect the kings of Pagan who also had their realm overrun
by Shans, cousins of the Thais, and found themselves subject to Mongol
demands that they accept the Mongols as their suzerains as well.

Mongol pressures on Burma and Cambodia between 1253 and 1270 were
indirect in nature. As far as Annam and Champa were concerned, however,
the reverse was true, for here the Mongols in 1257 substituted direct action
for indirect pressures. Interestingly enough, though, their attempt to use
force proved to be a failure. Though their armies seized and sacked Hanoi,
they were soon driven out by the Viets, and the only effect of this expedition
was to cause the Annamese to make peace with Champa, since the former

recognized that they and the inhabitants of what is today South Vietnam needed to cooperate if they were not to fall into Mongol hands at some future date. By 1279, then, as Sung China fell, it was an apprehensive Southeast Asian mainland that awaited the results of this Mongol victory.

Turning to the island realms that lay south of Cambodia and Champa, these years brought very few changes indeed. It is true that in 1221 the Kediri dynasty was overthrown in Java and its place taken by a new Singosari line of kings. But according to the information which reaches us from Chinese sources, this made little difference. Java continued to gain on Srivijaya as a commercial center and to dominate the eastern Spice Islands, while Srivijaya, which now consisted of some fifteen vassal states loosely controlled from Palembang, more and more showed itself unable to develop a coherent economic and political policy of its own. But this trend was one which had begun long before this time, as we have already noted in an earlier chapter.

Much more important were certain events which now began to take place in northern India—events which were not unconnected with Mongol expansion. I refer, of course, to the sudden appearance of the sultanate of Delhi—which represented a milestone in Indian history as the beginning of a really extensive Islamic penetration of this whole subcontinent and the appearance of a distinct Islamic element among its native population. The sultanate of Delhi began when a Gurid ruler of Lahore, Muizz al-Din Mohammed, (1173–1206) in 1193 advanced east and captured Delhi, thus breaching a line Hindu rulers had been able to maintain for almost two centuries. By the time of his death he had pressed on to capture the entire Ganges valley and transferred his capital to Delhi which was more centrally located than Lahore.

Muizz al-Din's heirs proved to be so incompetent that by 1216 they had lost all Gurid territory in Persia and Afghanistan to the Khwarazmian shah and failed to control their armed forces in India as well, which consisted of a mixture of Ghurr and Afghan tribesmen and Turkish slave contingents known as *gulams*. As a result, they were set aside and a new sultan was elected by the army—one who was of slave or Mamluk origin. Thus began a new Mamluk sultanate in Delhi which was to last to the time of the Moghuls and which was quite similar to that which, as we have noted already, appeared in Cairo a few years later.

It is difficult to ascertain exactly why the Delhi sultanate was able to survive until 1270 and even to prosper, because we lack the information upon which to base any accurate appraisal. We can, however, hazard guesses which have some degree of validity. First of all, we know that this sultanate benefited from the many warriors that fled there from Persia when the Mongols invaded the latter and that these warriors, when incorporated into Delhi's armed forces, increased its military potential. Second, the loss of Persian territory forced the rulers of Delhi after 1216 to Indianize themselves. This resulted in their modifying their Islamic type of iqtàs, or grants of land in return for military service, to conform to the prevailing northern Indian feudal system, which was somewhat different. Even more important, they found it wise to encourage the proselytization of Hindus who accepted their rule; this proselytizing was carried on by Moslem Sufis, or mystics, and was especially successful in Bengal. Also, they welcomed into their realm a considerable number of Moslem Persian intellectuals who, like the soldiers we have mentioned, sought refuge from the havoc the Mongols were wreaking in Iran and Khorasan and helped to give a scholarly lustre to their dominion. Last of all, they were successful in defeating all Mongol armies who attacked them—which made them the saviors of northern Indian society, Moslem and Hindu alike. Thus, during these years there emerged in northern India a new Moslem empire—which was a special blend of Islamic and Indian elements, belonging to both and neither of them at the same time. It can be considered, and often is, a simple extension of Islam. But it might be better to view it as a special new variety of Indic civilization formed in the crucible of a northern India under attack by Chagatai's Mongol hordes and discovering in the warriors of the sultanate of Delhi not so much foreign conquerors as protectors of its distinctive way of life.

In southern India during these years perhaps the most important event which took place was the final destruction of the Chola realm by feudalized Pandya and Hosala warriors. Thus, in the Deccan as in the northern plains of the Indian subcontinent, we find a triumph of militarized, feudalized society over more peaceful elements which had characterized the preceding century, though the results here were to lead to a divided southern India composed of a number of warring states and not a single empire like that which owed obedience to Delhi.

Ceylon, however, presents us with a mystery. Until the middle of the century Ceylon was ruled by a powerful line of kings who built a great capital in the interior of the island and relied upon an intricate system of reservoirs to hold monsoon rains for use during the dry season. These kings seem to have exploited their geographical location and the cinnamon, gems, and elephants which were valued export commodities to accumulate considerable wealth. Their kingdom also served as a center from which Hinayana Buddhist doctrines reached the mainland areas of Southeast Asia. Then suddenly in the late thirteenth century all of this ended. The old capital was abandoned, the reservoirs began to fall into ruins, and Ceylon itself ceased to be of more than minor importance to the world of Greater India for the next few centuries—a mystery which a new generation of historians and archaeologists will be called upon to solve.

There remains the question of how the Indic world fared economically during this period. Unfortunately, we are much less informed about this than we would like to be. As we have already made abundantly clear, during these years Greater India enjoyed a period in which peaceful maritime commerce flourished and began to link it even more closely with China and East Asia in general until we can almost think of the Indian Ocean and the South China Sea as one body of water. As this happened, there can be little doubt that certain regions like the Persian Gulf area, East Africa, the Malabar Coast, and Java enjoyed an unusual prosperity based upon the spices, tropical wares, gold, and gems which they produced and the trade that reached them from the worlds of China and of Islam. The Indic world also during these years seems to have improved both its ships and its maritime skills considerably and to have begun to approximate those found in the Mediterranean world of Europe and the East Asian world of the Sungs.

On the other hand, we know that parts of Greater India were anything but prosperous. The fury of the Mongol assault must have adversely affected the Indus and Ganges valleys, just as the Coromandel Coast was not immediately able to adjust itself to a warrior dominion which was not in tune with the more enlightened economic practices of the Cholas. As for Ceylon, we have already pointed out that disaster befell it. Even in the mainland of Southeast Asia by 1270 the situation had deteriorated as Thai and Shan warriors and Mongol armies began to undermine the older order of things. So we must conclude that Indic civilization during these years, while not affected as much as its Byzantine, East Asian, and Islamic neighbors, did suffer problems which seem to have stopped growth of its population and its economy until more favorable conditions presented themselves to its people.

Western European and Mongol World Domination, 1270–1368

The century which began in 1270 and ended in 1368 when the Mongol empire ceased to exist represents, in many ways, the culmination of the expansion of Western Europe and of Mongol power and influence which we have examined in such detail in the last chapter. During most of this century the Mongols continued to rule vast areas of the Byzantine-Russian, the Islamic, and the East Asian worlds and to send armies, navies, and embassies south in an attempt to dominate Greater India as well. It was a period which also saw Western Europeans, who were the masters of the North Atlantic, the Mediterranean, and the Black Sea, move east to learn something about China and India and venture into South Atlantic waters as well. It was an age, then, which served as a prelude for the later expansion of Western Europeans throughout the entire world.

Nevertheless, by 1368 we can also discern a contrary trend, especially after 1330, when the Mongol empire began to crumble and the Latin West, which was suddenly afflicted by serious internal crises, faltered. As this happened, the Islamic, Indic, and East Asian peoples and those of Russia as well began to reassert their own individuality in a special way. What had begun as a Mongol–Western European codominion over civilized Eurasia ended in a very different world which was to continue into early modern times when Western Europe finally achieved the dominion which had seemed within its grasp in the early fourteenth century.

In the late thirteenth century the Mongol empire was actually a loose collection of states which were theoretically controlled by a great khan, who lived in Peking. Kublai Khan, who held this office until his death in 1294, ruled China and the Mongolian heartland directly. The rest of the empire consisted of appanages controlled by other members of his extended family, the Golden Horde in Russia, the Ilkans in Persia, and the House of Chagatai in central Asia. By this time, it is also worth noting that there was considerable friction among these realms. The Golden Horde and the Mongols of Turkestan, for instance, were frequently at war with the Ilkans and did considerable damage to Khorasan in the process. Later, Chagatai's heirs were so hostile to Peking that Kublai Khan found it difficult to communicate directly with Persia via central Asian routes.

Except in the Far East, the Mongols allowed those who submitted to them to enjoy a large measure of autonomy. Thus, as long as they did the bidding of their overlords in Serai, Russian princes, as has been noted, could govern their own subjects without much interference. A similar autonomy was extended by the Ilkans to the rulers of Lesser Armenia, Georgia, Seljuk Anatolia, and southern Persia and by the House of Chagatai to the tribes and cities of central Asia, as far as day-to-day government was concerned.

Nevertheless, a certain common pattern or thread of overall control was imposed upon all parts of the empire beyond the Great Wall and even in China itself. Everywhere the Mongol people formed a privileged group, especially those who belonged to the family of Genghis Khan or were descended from his close associates—not all of whom were of nomadic origin. These people formed a special Mongol imperial elite or aristocracy who commanded armies, served as administrators and tax collectors, and were members of the powerful ortaqs who were so influential in commerce and economic life in general. This elite constantly recruited new members, but it is interesting to note that it was heavily dependent upon the skills of a body of central Asian Turkish and Uighur merchants and moneylenders, some of whom were Moslems and some Nestorian Christians, as well as a number of northern Chinese who had early shown a willingness to collaborate with their nomadic conquerors. We need to stress that while this elite had no special religious character, tending to run the gamut of religious beliefs found in central Asia—from animism, Buddhism, and Nestorian Christianity to Islam—it was hostile to both Orthodox Islam and Confucianism, probably because its two most persistent enemies, the Mamluks of Egypt and the Sungs of South China, respectively, held to these beliefs. Despite this hostility, however, there was a general tendency for western Mongol ruling houses to slowly but surely opt for Islam and those in China to turn to Buddhism. Even then, however, until almost the end of their empire one of the most distinguishing features which the Mongols displayed was the tolerance which they were willing to extend to all religious beliefs.

Everywhere Mongol government was characterized by heavy taxation and burdensome requisitions, generally controlled by ortaq tax-farmers, and by the requirement that subject princes and tribal leaders appear with well-equipped contingents when summoned for war. There was also a policy of requisitioning skilled craftsmen and moving them about the empire to suit the needs of the ruling class. And throughout, one is struck by an interest in commerce which explains Mongol authorities' determination to keep routes open and peaceful, maintaining a police and caravansary system for this purpose. Along such routes they also set up an efficient courier service so news could easily reach Peking from western subcapitals like Tabriz and Serai.

Despite the tendency for the entire empire to follow the same general rules, as time went on each area increasingly began to differ from the others as local personnel staffed governmental bureaus and local traditions began to prevail over Mongol imperial practices. By the early fourteenth century, for instance, the Golden Horde was more Turkish than Mongol and its subject Russian princes, despite the obedience they displayed to Serai, were governing their cities in a manner not too different from that of their earlier Kievan forebears. In the realm of the Ilkans the system of administration and taxation at the disposal of Rashid al-Din, the grand vizier, seems remarkably like that used by the Khwarazmian shahs or Nizam-al-Mulk—even though a few innovations like paper money had been introduced, which were not always successful.

Even in China, where the Mongols tended to use non-Chinese foreigners extensively as commanders of their army of occupation, as governors of their sixty provincial divisions, or to staff the censorial boards which supervised all aspects of their administration, a strong Chinese flavor is apparent. Their taxation system was Chinese; they issued paper money and copper cash, as of yore, to serve as their currency; and the lower ranks of their bureaucracy were Chinese as well. It is not surprising that in 1315 they even reintroduced the examination system which they had abolished when they captured northern China in 1237 and when they conquered southern China in 1279.

Down to the end of Kublai Khan's reign, and for a decade or so thereafter, the Mongols continued an effort to expand their boundaries in Japan and in Greater India. They did so partly by land and partly by sea. In 1274, even before the final collapse of the southern Sungs, they sent a large expedition, composed mainly of Korean ships, to attack Japan. This sea force landed in Kyushu and was finally driven out by Japanese warriors who rallied to the defense of their shōgunate. Seven years later an even greater force attacked Japan again—one which included a number of Chinese-built vessels. It proved equally unsuccessful, in part because the fleet which supported it was largely destroyed by a typhoon. Though a number of later plans were

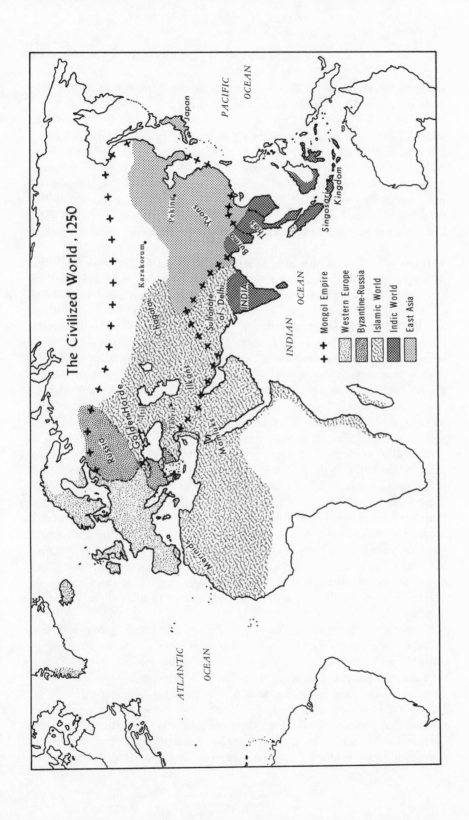

The Civilized World, 1250

+ Mongol Empire

Western Europe

Byzantine-Russia

Islamic World

Indic World

East Asia

PACIFIC OCEAN

Japan

Pekin

Yuan

Burma

Tibet

Karakorum

Chagatai

Sultanate of Delhi

INDIA

INDIAN OCEAN

Singosari Kingdom

Golden Horde

RUSSIA

Ilkans

Tabriz

Mamluks

Merinid

ATLANTIC OCEAN

made to invade Japan again and large fleets were built for this purpose, none ever sailed and the Japanese remained outside the Mongol orbit.

Southeast Asia was less fortunate. The Burmese had to face a series of attacks, beginning in 1273, mainly by Yunnan viceroys of the Yuan emperor. By 1299 these had forced Burmese submission to Peking and caused the collapse of their kingdom and the destruction of their capital city of Pagan. Almost as unfortunate were the Cambodians who found themselves subjected to intense pressure from the Thais who, as Mongol vassals, were now firmly established in the lower Menam valley. By 1350 they had lost control of all their western provinces and had seen their Khmer capital of Ankor Vat sacked by a Thai army.

The warlike Viets of Annam and their neighbors in Champa were subjected to similar pressures. Twice during Kublai Khan's reign large armies were sent into Vietnam. These were, however, unable to break the resistance of either the Annamese or the Champans and by 1287 had been driven out and their commanding general killed—an omen perhaps for the twentieth century. So complete was their victory, as a matter of fact, that, when a large Mongol fleet was sent south to attack Java a few years later, Champa's fleet kept it under surveillance to make sure it did not land on their shores. The Viets, then, were able to escape Mongol conquest even though in 1312, after Kublai's death, Peking had sufficient influence in this area to force the Annamese to evacuate the Champan kingdom which they had just conquered and allow it to regain its independence.

Mongol expansion, however, was not restricted to the Asian mainland. In 1281 we are told that the rulers of Srivijaya sent an embassy to Peking. And in 1293 it was the arrival of a large Mongol fleet which was responsible for the overthrow of the Singosari dynasty in Java and its replacement by a Majapahit house more friendly to Peking. Even the large fleet in which Marco Polo sailed to Ormuz in 1293 to deliver a princess to the Ilkan court must be regarded as a form of pressure upon Indian Ocean realms—a showing of the flag in distant waters. This seems especially true since we know that at about this time, in 1291, the Ilkans were employing the Genoese to build galleys in the Persian Gulf for use against the flotillas of the Rassulids of Aden.

If diplomatic pressure was one of the reasons for sending Marco Polo's squadron into the Indian Ocean, it had considerable success in this regard, for we know that at about this time the sultans of Bengal, who were striving to maintain their independence from Delhi, sent several embassies to Peking, while the king of Ceylon sent Kublai presents. Even the sultans of Delhi, the most powerful rulers in Greater India, felt Peking was so important that some three decades later one of them, Ibn Tugluk, made a special effort to send the Moslem traveler Ibn Battuta there as an envoy. Though it was the Mongol Yuan dynasty that attempted most persistently to expand into Greater India, it is worth noting that Delhi had also to contend with continuing attacks launched against northern India by the Mongols of central Asia—attacks which powerful sultans like Balban and Ala-ud-din were able to repel only with great difficulty.

If Mongol pressures on Japan and the Indic world were continuous over several decades, so were their attacks directed against Mamluk Syria, which had not been forgiven for the defeat it had meted out to a Mongol army in 1260 at Ain Jaluit. Again and again and especially in 1281, 1300, and 1312, large Mongol armies attempted to conquer Syria and in the process did great damage to cities like Aleppo and Damascus and to the countryside in general. Despite the very considerable contingents which the kings of Lesser Armenia and Frankish princes of Cyprus and northern Syria furnished to these armies, they all failed to achieve their objectives, and after 1312 the Ilkans ceased their attacks altogether. But until that time the threat they represented to the Mamluks was very real indeed. We must then regard the Mongol empire as sufficiently powerful during these decades to be able to keep Japan, Vietnam, Delhi, and Mamluk Egypt on the defensive, to reduce much of Southeast Asia to vassalage, and to open up the East Indies and the Bay of Bengal to Mongol influence. From Canton to Ormuz, Mongol influence continued to be exerted, linking China with the West along these routes just as it did along terrestrial routes passing through central Asia.

During these same decades, until the deaths of Edward I of England and Philip the Fair of France, Western Europe presents a pattern of political power almost as intricate as that we have found in the Mongol empire. In general, between 1270 and 1300 the papacy continued to exercise much overall political leadership, as had been the case earlier—a leadership, however, in which Capetian France now participated as a kind of junior partner. The French monarchy, furthermore, could generally count on Castile, Genoa, Hungary, and the House of Luxembourg to support its policies and on England, Flanders, and Portugal in the Atlantic, Aragon and Venice in the Mediterranean, and the House of Hapsburg in Germany to oppose them. Despite the papacy's help, for instance, Philip the Fair was not able to force the powerful Edward I of England to give much ground in Gascony or Flanders, nor was France able to stop the House of Aragon from taking over Sicily and forming what some have thought of as a maritime empire in the western Mediterranean. While all this was going on in the cockpit of Western European politics, in the north another story was unfolding—the steady growth of the powerful Hanseatic League of North Sea and Baltic German trading cities, which was beginning to dominate this area and humble the rulers of Denmark, Norway, and Sweden in the process.

In some ways the humiliation of the papacy at the hands of French and English monarchs and its move to Avignon in 1303 did not change this basic situation very much, except to make the popes junior partners instead of senior partners in a Capetian-papal combination. But it did reduce papal prestige by making its subservience to Paris obvious to all. Thus, popes could no longer play the role of mediators between contending political forces like Genoa and Venice and France and England, as they had done earlier. This meant they could not exercise very effective leadership in the political sphere as a whole.

More than a loss of political prestige, however, was involved in the move to Avignon. It proved tremendously expensive for the popes to develop this city as a center of their administration and their Curia. As a result they had to increase their exactions which they levied on the church and on lay society in general. Such exactions made the papacy seem corrupt and alienated powerful reform elements within Latin Christendom like the Spiritual Franciscans, whom Pope John XXII declared heretical. At odds with reform monasticism, attacked by Marsilio of Padua in his treatise *Defensor Pacis,* and abandoned increasingly by mystics who found little spiritual meaning in its sacramental system, the Avignon papacy could no longer furnish Europe with religious leadership any more than it could exercise the kind of political leadership which had seemed so natural to an Urban II or an Innocent III.

At first, this increasingly divided and leaderless Western Europe was able to achieve considerable success in confronting its Moslem and Byzantine neighbors because it made effective use of its sea power. Starting in the Atlantic, Moroccan shores were neutralized by organized Castilian and Portuguese fleets, based at Seville and Lisbon, respectively, both of which contained large Genoese components. These fleets patrolled the Straits of Gibraltar and served to back up the predominantly Castilian and Portuguese Christian bodyguards of the Merinids. Though the Genoese were especially powerful in Atlantic Iberian waters, there was a Catalan colony at Seville, and Aragonese ships traded along Moroccan shores as far west as Safi. Other ships, mainly Portuguese, were sailing further southwest to rediscover the Canaries and Madeira in the Atlantic.

In the western Mediterranean, a different situation prevailed during this period. Here the Genoese had eliminated the Pisans as rivals in 1284, only to find themselves faced by a Catalan-Aragonese presence, which, having absorbed Majorca and Valencia, went on to add Sicily to the House of Aragon and, early in the fourteenth century, Sardinia as well. Despite strong French and papal efforts to regain Sicily, which weakened Aragonese unity, a new maritime power, centering in Barcelona and Majorca, had appeared in the western Mediterranean. Since the Aragonese had seized all the islands in the central Mediterranean like Malta, Pantelleria, Djerba, and Kerkenes, and controlled the Christian bodyguards of the Moslem sultans of Tunisia and Tlemcen, and had good relations with Egypt and Cyprus as well, they were unusually powerful. Indeed, we might consider that they had recreated that great east-west Moslem trade complex between Egypt and Al-Andālūs via Sicily—except now this trade route was under Aragonese Christian, not Moslem, control.

In the eastern Mediterranean the situation also favored the Latin West. Though Syrian seaports were lost by 1291, control of Cyprus and Lesser Armenian ports assured Western merchants access to the world of the Mongols. Cyprus also served as a naval bastion along Syrian shores—one which made it difficult for a Mamluk navy to operate effectively. Further to the north in Aegean and Black Sea waters, which had been Byzantine, a dual system of control existed—one Venetian and one Genoese. Venice still held Conon, Modon, Crete, some Aegean islands, a quarter in Constantinople, and had access to the Black Sea where her colony of Tana and treaty with Trebizond gave her a measure of control. Genoa held Lesbos, Chios, and Smyrna, a fortified Galata opposite Constantinople, and a powerful Black Sea outpost at Kaffa, as well as a large colony in Trebizond. Rhodes, which controlled the sea lanes along the southwestern shores of Anatolia, was occupied by neither the Genoese nor the Italians but by the Knights Hospitaler. All three major maritime powers had treaties with Egypt and maintained colonies of merchants in Alexandria, especially the Catalans and the Venetians.

There was considerable hostility and rivalry, as we have noted, between the Genoese, the Venetians, and the Aragonese during these years—which often took the form of naval engagements. But none of them was able as a result of such conflicts to eliminate the others from any particular trading area. Instead, what developed down to the middle of the fourteenth century was a curious pattern of trade in which there was a tendency for each to be predominant in a particular part of the Atlantic-Mediterranean-Black Sea area and subordinate in others. Genoese, for instance, were predominant in the Atlantic, with Catalans a poor second, and Venetians a very poor and late third. In the western Mediterranean, on the other hand, Catalans predominated from Montpellier to Messina and Genoese from Marseilles to Palermo. In the eastern Mediterranean, Venetians were dominant, with Genoese and Catalans coming second; while in the Adriatic and Aegean, the Venetians tended to be more important than the Genoese and the Catalans played no role whatsoever. Finally, we have Constantinople and the Black Sea where the Genoese definitely had the lead, with the Venetians in second place and the Catalans totally unimportant. But wherever we look at this time, we are impressed with the Latin West's overall maritime strength. A few Moslem pirate ships by 1330 were able to operate out of Maghrebi ports, a small Mamluk navy had been formed, and Turkish emirs preyed on commerce along southern Anatolian shores, but these were minor matters indeed. From the Canaries to Kaffa and Trebizond, the seas belonged to the Latin Westerners and their ships patrolled these waters and kept their Moslem and Byzantine neighbors on the defensive.

It is perhaps worth noting, also, that two of the most powerful political and economic units in the north—England under Edward I, II, and III and the Hanseatic League—were essentially maritime powers, making use of islands and enclaves too. This explains why Edward I expanded to take over Wales, Scotland, and Ireland and held onto Gascony and kept Flanders friendly in the face of the opposition of Capetian France. It also makes it clear how the Hansa cities could neutralize Scandinavian power, while their allies, the Teutonic Knights, kept a firm hold on Livonian and East Prussian Baltic enclaves, and their merchants established themselves in overseas colonies stretching from Novgorod, Stockholm, and Bergen to Bruges and London. The genius of Western Europe during these years, then, lay in its ability to control the sea and make use of this control to monopolize the commerce which followed maritime routes.

Under these circumstances, it should not surprise us that a maritime-minded Latin West was able to offer little assistance to the Mongols in battles with Islamic enemies which took place on land rather than on the sea. Nor would we expect this kind of Western Europe to be able to spread Latin Christianity into North Africa or central Asia, India, and China, despite the devotion of a Ramon Lull, who tried to bring Christianity to Moslem North Africa, or of friars who traveled hopefully to Karakorum, Peking, and Zayton over a period of several decades. Indeed, the Latin West was not even able to convert the pagan Lithuanians at this time.

What this kind of maritime, commercially minded society was able to produce was adventurers. Many of them were, as we all know, merchant adventurers like the elder Polos and the many Genoese and Venetians who established themselves in Kaffa, Trebizond, Tabriz, and Lazicco and journeyed by land to North China or by sea, via India, to Canton and Hangchow. Others just as numerous, perhaps more so, were the military adventurers, the overseas counterparts of the Italian *condottieri* or the mercenaries who served the French and English in the Hundred Years War. We find such adventurers enrolled in the Christian bodyguards of Maghrebi rulers. We find them as mercenary *Almogavers* from Aragon-Catalonia who left Sicily for Romania, served Byzantium briefly, and ended up in control of Athens and Thebes. We see them as the *Renegrado Frangi* who helped to organize the Mamluk navy and manned their artillery in battle and by 1360 were serving Bahmani sultans in the Deccan. Western Europe during this period, then, had begun already to produce a special type of adventurers who were to carry its civilization to every part of the world during the sixteenth and seventeenth centuries.

While all this was happening, the Latin West saw the tempo of its economic life quicken considerably—at least until the middle third of the four-teenth century. This was especially true of central European areas like Bohemia, Poland, Hungary, and the Balkans where new mines were opened to exploitation, towns grew to become cities, and agricultural productivity increased. Everywhere throughout the Latin West, however, these years at first seem to have been boom times for those who were able to exploit effectively fields, forests, mines, and workshops to produce foodstuffs and goods on a scale which was not to be matched again until the sixteenth century. Much of this production was moved from one part of Europe to another by water, since this was the cheapest form of transport—hence, the emphasis, which we have already noted, on maritime elements, both within and outside Europe.

This emphasis was true for both the Mediterranean–Black Sea complex and northern Europe as well. In the north, England's wealth came from a commerce in three great basic commodities—the wool and wheat of Britain and the wine of Gascony which was distributed to much of Atlantic Europe by sea. For the Hansa, it was timber and naval stores, grain, and fish. But a similar emphasis on bulk commodities is also noticeable in the Mediter-ranean complex where grain, timber, salt, wool, cotton, wine, alum, and various kinds of ores formed the cargoes upon which the prosperity of Bar-celona, Majorca, Genoa, and Venice was based. Textiles, weapons, and lux-ury goods were, of course, also shipped by water and, along with spices, formed the cargoes of the expensive galleys of the period; but ninety-five percent of all cargoes and seventy-five percent of the profits came from bulk commodities which more and more were carried in relatively large sailing vessels which plied the waters of the Baltic, the Atlantic, the Mediterranean, and the Black Sea.

This remarkable productivity was also reflected in a population which increased everywhere down to the middle of the fourteenth century until, according to our very imperfect statistics, the Latin West was the most populous civilization in Eurasia. Though it had a large number of cities, it still lacked any large metropolitan centers like Delhi, Cairo, or Peking and had to content itself with a number of cities in Spain, Italy, and northern Europe which were in the 50,000 to 120,000 class, as well as many more in the middle range between 20,000 and 50,000. But by now it found, for the first time, that its population had begun to reach a level that strained its resources. More and more, the internal frontier of unoccupied forest, marsh, and fen had ceased to exist, and poor soils were put to plough, decreasing agricultural production.

As this happened, we begin to find serious shortages and an increased competition for food. In the highly urbanized Mediterranean, the surplus grain of Sicily and the Black Sea were prizes worth fighting for, and it was its control of Baltic grain which gave the Hansa its stranglehold on Scandinavia. By 1315 the first of a series of bad harvests had begun to produce famine conditions in parts of the Latin West. An agricultural crisis had begun to make its appearance at a time when Europe seemed to be enjoying a period of great prosperity.

At this same time we also find Western Europe developing business skills to match its remarkable productivity. The business class of Italy, Catalonia, and southern France, which dominated the Mediterranean world, led in this regard and began to introduce these skills into northern France, Belgium, and England. A few figures which reflect the prosperity accompanying the exercise of such skills are worth noting. In 1293, an especially good year, it has been estimated that the value of the commerce which entered and left the port of Genoa amounted to over 4,000,000 pounds Genoese. Several decades later Florence is said to have produced cloth worth 1,500,000 gold florins annually. At about the same time, it has been estimated that the value of commerce reaching North Africa from Barcelona and Majorca amounted to between 400,000 and 500,000 gold dinars a year and that sent to Egypt about 300,000 dinars annually.

Such profits were not restricted to the Mediterranean. The new customs dues which Edward I introduced in 1275 resulted in revenues which were seven times those of King John's time, while estimates of the money which this great king spent on his wars are surprisingly high—amounting to several hundred million pounds on a modern basis. It is also interesting to note that early in the fourteenth century Bordeaux annually averaged an amazing total of over 1,000 ships a year carrying wine to Britain and other parts of northern Europe—more than double the vessels and tonnage which cleared Boston during the 1750s and 1760s.

This was a golden age for Italian bankers in Western Europe. Great banking firms like the Bardi and Peruzzi of Florence had capital at their disposal which was much more extensive than what the later Medici had, amounting to 1,266,755 florins or over 2,000,000 pounds in gold, according to Pegolotti's early fourteenth-century account. And the Ricciardi of Lucca and the Frescobaldi of Florence who served Edward I and II as bankers were almost as rich. So, too, were a number of English businessmen who had considerable capital at their disposal and who largely handled the Staple, England's monopolistic export of her wool clip, and a handful of German capitalists who traded as part of the Hansa or trafficked across the Alps with Venice. The late thirteenth and early fourteenth centuries were an age of great merchants and bankers, who had factors and partners spread all the way from Constantinople and Famagusta to London, Paris, and Bruges and who, according to Pegolotti, author of a manual of business practices, knew the current value of currencies and the price of goods as far away as the coasts of China.

Linked first by business and finance, northern and Mediterranean Europe also became linked by sea as the Genoese in the 1270s, then the Catalans, and finally the Venetians began to send out fleets of specially built galleys to sail through the Straits of Gibraltar past Seville and Lisbon to England and to Flanders. This, of course, ended the importance of the Fairs of Champagne, since there was no longer any need to maintain such a meeting place for northern and southern European merchants and bankers. And as galleys traveled north carrying compasses and portolan charts, other smaller Mediterranean vessels ventured out into the Atlantic, sailing along African shores as far as Senegal and marking out Atlantic islands like Madeira for future settlement. It is perhaps because of this closer contact with the Atlantic that we find Mediterranean sailors beginning to adopt the cog for commercial use in the Middle Sea since its stem rudder and single sail made it much more economical to operate than their old lateen-rigged round ships. Although it is true that few European vessels ventured beyond Seville and entered the Mediterranean—most of the traffic being carried in Mediterranean bottoms—these years did see a number of English fishermen begin to sail out into the Atlantic to catch cod off Iceland and so move toward Greenland and the North American continent, which was still an area only Scandinavians knew about.

As all this came about, we also find by the 1320s and 1330s a number of Western European adventurers beginning to explore the Indian Ocean area, which they could now reach from Ormuz, and to visit Ethiopian Axsum, which they believed to be the realm of Prester John, that mysterious fabled eastern Christian prince. Perhaps that is why in 1291 two Genoese, the Vivaldi brothers, sailed past the Straits of Gibraltar in an attempt to reach the Indies by sea and why the son of one of them, Sorleone Vivaldi, in the early fourteenth century visited East African shores in search of his Vivaldi kinsmen's whereabouts—thus anticipating the Portuguese by several centuries. The expansive prosperity of the Latin West in this period, then, seemed to spill over in all directions and impel its sons to seek their fame and fortune in areas which lay thousands of miles from their homes.

Was the Mongol empire as profitable for its inhabitants during this period as Western Europe was for most of those who shared in its civilization? Not exactly. It is true, of course, that the Mongol empire was extremely profitable for its favored elite and for those who controlled the ortaqs, which were associations very similar to the societas and banking partnerships of Italian, Catalan, and Provençal businessmen. But for others it was not—even after the shock of conquest had worn off. A recent scholar whose specialty is Russia, for instance, has written that the Mongol period was essentially regressive—even though he admits that Novgorod flourished after 1270 and that there was considerable clearing of land in the Vladimir-Suzdal area. Nor is he impressed by Russia's foreign trade, despite the fact that eastern Russian merchants in some numbers took advantage of the Pax Mongolica to trade with Serai, the Caucasus, and Black Sea ports—a trade fully substantiated by recent archaeological excavations at Novgorod.

In the same way, there is considerable evidence that after 1290 conditions improved for the peasantry of Iran and Iraq, especially during the years when Raschid al-Din functioned as the Ilkan grand vizier, and that commerce and industry recovered a measure of prosperity. But it has been shown that this recovery was limited, so limited that Ilkan revenues never amounted to more than twenty percent of what earlier rulers had derived from the same areas before Mongol conquest. Regions like Georgia or a capital like Tabriz might flourish, but the overall economic picture was not very bright.

The same is true of Yuan China. Despite a drop in its population to somewhere in the neighborhood of 80,000,000, things improved for this part of East Asia during the reign of Kublai Khan who seems to have insisted upon maintaining internal communication systems like the Grand Canal and to have run an effective, if oppressive, government. But the failure of the iron industry of North China to revive is probably symptomatic of a general failure of the Chinese economy. And, as a recent scholar has noted, although the Mongols from Kublai Khan on were keenly interested in maritime expansion and foreign trade, their confiscation of merchant ships, their costly maritime expeditions, and their penchant for regulating external commerce all contributed to a decline during the early fourteenth century. This meant that the Yuan period was never able to match that of the later Sungs in the value of its foreign trade—especially that which reached the Indian Ocean—although it did remain respectable. And Chinese merchants and financiers, both at home and abroad, failed to keep pace with their Western European counterparts.

This helps to explain why the Mongol empire declined so swiftly during the mid-fourteenth century. This decline was apparent, first of all, in the Ilkan realm which by 1335 had lost its last effective rulers and was racked by internal disorders, especially among a peasantry which resented being tied to the soil as serfs. These peasants rose in revolt against both their landlords and the military elite who had enslaved them. As they did so, the last Ilkan died in 1346, and power fell into the hands of minor princelings who were unable to restore order in the countryside or to restrain nomadic Turkoman tribesmen who roamed the land. The Ilkan realm had not only ended; it had collapsed in disaster.

In China the Yuan dynasty lasted two decades longer before it suffered the fate of the Ilkans, but here, too, after the 1330s it was all downhill. Incompetent rulers and bad finance characterized the last years of Mongol rule, which also saw an increase in the hostility which the mass of the Chinese felt for an alien set of conquerors. Great revolts swept through the empire and especially through southern provinces which had never accepted the rule of Peking with equanimity. By 1368 these revolts resulted in the appearance of a new native Chinese dynasty, the Mings, which drove the Mongols out of China and established a new capital at Nanking in the Yangtze valley. In doing so, the Mings, in reaction to their Yuan predecessors, also drove most foreigners out of China and curbed foreign trade—thus launching China on a new and somewhat xenophobic course which was to characterize much of its later history.

Mongol rule lasted longest of all in Russia, but here, too, by 1368 or soon thereafter, considerable changes had taken place. These began as early as 1299 when the Russian metropolitan left Kiev and established himself at Vladimir to the northeast. Soon thereafter, the Mongols elevated the prince of Moscow, Ivan Kalita, to the position of grand prince of Russia, which meant he was their chief collector of taxes from the other Russian princes. About the same time, the metropolitan moved to Moscow, which thus became the principal ecclesiastical as well as political center of Russian life. From this time on, slowly but surely, the princes of Moscovy consolidated their control over their neighbors north of the steppes, except for Novgorod and Lithuania which itself was expanding to take in White Russia and the Ukraine. Finally, in 1378, Dmitri, the Muscovite ruler, defeated a Mongol force, rebuilt the Kremlin by changing its wooden walls to stone ones, and advanced south to crush a great army of the Golden Horde at Kalikova in 1380. Though the Mongols were able to redeem themselves a little later and reestablish a measure of control over Moscow, their great days were over. What had been a great world empire had now been reduced to a network of quarreling tribes who lived between the Black Sea and the Great Wall of China.

While the Mongol empire was crumbling, Western Europe began to have troubles of its own as well, some of which were of a political character. The Latin West's political crisis came about because of a lack of leadership not only from the Avignon papacy but from its secular rulers as well. After 1330 the picture is one of a weak Holy Roman emperor, of Castile paralyzed by internal revolts, of Genoa soon to be overrun by Milan and in conflict with Venice and the House of Aragon, and of France and England drifting toward the Hundred Years War which was to break out in 1337.

It is certainly not surprising, in light of all this, that Moslems in Tunisia took advantage of the situation to recapture Djerba and the Kerkenes Islands from the Aragonese in 1335 and that the Merinid ruler of Morocco, Abu al-Hassan (1331–1350) should advance east to seize Tlemcen and Tunisia and then in 1340 cross the Straits of Gibraltar into Andalusia. It is true that the Merinids were badly defeated at the battle of Rio Salado and a joint Portuguese-Castilian-Genoese destroyed their fleet and regained control of the Straits of Gibraltar. But their attack had the effect of loosening the grip of the Aragonese and Castilians on the Maghreb. A new era was at hand.

On the heels of this challenge to the Latin West, in Italy came another crisis—a financial one—which was to have serious economic and political repercussions at home and abroad. This was the collapse of the Florentine banking houses of the Bardis, the Peruzzis, and others as a result of the default by Edward III of England on obligations he had incurred in preparing for the initial years of the war he was waging against the French. Interestingly enough, Edward did not abandon his French plans following this default. Instead, he followed his naval success at Sluys with a great victory over the French army at Crecy in 1346, and soon thereafter captured Calais which gave him a bridgehead on the other side of the Channel. Nevertheless, the failure of the great Florentine banking houses marks the end of an era of financial expansion that had been almost continuous since 1270.

Worse was to follow on the heels of Western Europe's first financial panic and collapse. In 1347 the dying Mongol world sent Europe as its parting gift a terrible plague we know as the Black Death. This disease, partly bubonic and partly pneumonic in nature, spread rapidly throughout the continent, which had not known such a disease since the eighth century and which had, therefore, not had an opportunity to build up any immunity to its ravages. Between a third and a half of the Latin West's population perished between 1347 and 1350, and after it became endemic to the European countryside and returned as an epidemic again in the 1360s, it killed many others who had escaped its first visitation.

The ravages of the Black Death were no more able to stop Edward III's militaristic fervor than the failure of Italy's banking system. Instead, he continued his continental campaigns which badly affected the prosperity of the French countryside. Soon after he had won a great victory at Poitiers in 1356 and forced the Capetians to accept the humiliating Peace of Bretigny in 1360, he extended the war into the Iberian Peninsula. There his son, the Black Prince, won a great victory over the French-backed Castilian faction at Najera, only to lose the war when the Spanish prince the English supported, Pedro the Cruel, was assassinated in 1369. But the main losers were the Castilian people, who had mercenary armies march across their land, destroying its prosperity as France's had been destroyed by three decades of conflict. By 1368 a lack of political leadership, which alone can explain this disastrous Hundred Years War, was added to the Latin West's spiritual crisis, its agricultural crisis, its financial failure, and the loss of life resulting from the Black Death to halt its prosperity in its tracks.

Even before the full effects of these crises had been felt, however, the Latin West began to find itself at some disadvantage in dealing with its Moslem neighbors. As the Ilkan realm weakened in the 1330s and commerce began to desert the Persian Gulf for the Red Sea, control over Cyprus and Lesser Armenia, as way stations leading to China and India, meant very little. It was no coincidence then that Venice negotiated a new trade treaty with Mamluk Egypt in 1346, just as the Ilkans disappeared, for now Alexandria was the only entrepot in the eastern Mediterranean where one could be sure of procuring oriental wares in abundance. This same new commercial importance of Alexandria and lack of importance of Lesser Armenia explains why there was so little Western European opposition to the Mamluks as they absorbed Lesser Armenia and reduced Cyprus to a tributary state by 1375. In fact, Western Europeans confined their activity to one raid on Alexandria in 1365, an attack which had no sequel.

It is probably for the same reason—the lack of Eastern wares reaching this part of the world after 1343—that we find so little Western European activity in the Black Sea area. The Genoese maintained their outpost at Kaffa; they and the Venetians still traded with Trebizond, and both of them kept their footholds in Constantinople and in the Aegean, but that was all. The great days when Black Sea ports and Cyprus led to China and India were over, not to return again for a long, long time.

Let us now examine how the other four civilizations of Eurasia fared during the middle third of the fourteenth century. In East Asia, of course, the principal power by 1368 was the Ming empire. Although the Mings formed it as part of a sustained and conscious reaction to their Yuan predecessors, they owed a considerable debt to the latter as well. For instance, while these new emperors deliberately attempted to set up a state which followed Confucian ideals and which employed mandarin bureaucrats chosen by examination, they thought it wise to continue to maintain military and naval establishments as powerful as those which the Mongols had established and not too dissimilar from them. Nor did they disband the censorial apparatus of their predecessors, which continued to operate under somewhat different rules. And like the Yuan and unlike the Sung, they continued a policy of pressing the peasantry into service for the good of the state. Soon after 1368 they even moved their capital north to Peking, which both the Chins and the Mongols had made the center of the China which they ruled.

It seems significant that the Mings retained Nan-Chao and Hsi Hsia as provinces and that Korea remained a dependency of the Son of Heaven. It is equally interesting that they tended to think of Southeast Asia as in their sphere of influence, demanding recognition of their superiority from the Burmese and the Thais and again sending armies into Annam. They were also sufficiently concerned with Mongolia as a potential threat that they constantly intervened in its affairs, as the Chins had done before them. And although in theory they forbade Chinese to venture abroad without express governmental permission, in fact at first they allowed their merchants considerable leeway in trading with Southeast Asia on their own, as well as encouraging many of those who lived along the coast to cross into Formosa and begin to transform this island into a Chinese province. The China of the Mings, then, though conservative and traditional in its culture and less interested than its predecessors in the wider world, was still the heartland of East Asian civilization and the political center of its existence.

There was only one realm in East Asia which did not accept Ming pretensions to overall control. That was Japan, which also had refused Mongol overlordship. Here by 1368, however, certain changes had taken place which deserve comment. These began when the Hōjō regents, who ran the Kamakura shōgunate, found themselves in trouble, largely because they lacked land to distribute to the warriors who had saved Japan when it was attacked by the Mongols in 1274 and 1281. Consequently, by 1334 the Hōjō lost control of the land and their power was assumed by a new Ashikaga family of shōguns. The Ashikaga, however, who lived in Kyōtō rather than in Kamakura, were much less powerful than their predecessors and had to contend with an imperial family attempting to recover authority. This led to a much more decentralized and feudalized Japan than that found in Kamakura times—and one which was to go its own way far removed from the world of the Mings on the Asian continent.

Important changes also took place in Greater India as the Mongol threat ended and a new era began to dawn. The most important event which occurred during these years was the expansion of the sultanate of Delhi south in the Deccan—an event which changed Indian history. This began when the forces of the sultan, having defeated the Mongols and broken the power of the feudal Rajputs of Rajistan, moved south and in 1297 forced Gujerat to accept their overlordship. A few years later Kafur, an able general, expanded the authority of his sultan still further south of the Vinya range. In 1327 Ibn Tugluk, who was now the ruler of Delhi, annexed the Telagu realm of the Kakatiyas and continued to send conquering armies north into Kashmir and south toward Cape Cormorin until the entire Indian peninsula except the extreme south and the island of Ceylon had submitted to him.

The Indian subcontinent, which was now virtually united into a single realm for the first time since Asoka's reign centuries earlier, developed in a number of ways. Politically, it seems fair to say that the sultanate was less successful and found itself unable to control governors in distant provinces who made themselves independent and founded local dynasties as in Bengal. One such subordinate was Ala-ud-din (1347–1358) who managed to set up an independent Bahmani sultanate in the western part of the newly conquered Deccan—and so ended Delhi's unified India almost before it began.

In the economic, religious, and cultural spheres, however, the story was quite different. Delhi's conquests resulted in the spread of Islam throughout much of the subcontinent. In part, this was due to a considerable immigration from Persia and other Moslem lands. In part, it was the result of proselytization in towns and cities carried on by Moslem Sufis, a proselytization which attracted Hindu merchants and artisans who found conversion to Islam made for social mobility and a freedom from caste restraints. This explains, of course, why whole groups of merchants, like those of Gujerat, found acceptance of the Moslem faith such an advantage. In some parts of India, however, such as Bengal and Mysore, peasants converted en masse to Islam, for reasons which are still obscure to the historian. At any rate, by 1368 the expansion of the sultanate of Delhi had resulted in a sizable group of Indians adopting the Moslem faith in the northern plains, in Bengal, in Gujerat, and in the south—especially in the towns and cities of the subcontinent.

The sultanate of Delhi profoundly affected India's economy as well. Its gold and silver coinage gave this subcontinent for the first time in its history an acceptable common medium of exchange which stimulated commerce and, despite an unfortunate experiment with paper money, made possible a network of credit which extended into other Indian Ocean areas. Commerce benefited, too, as all of the northern plains area and its two outlets, Gujerat and Bengal, came under the same laws and the same administrative controls. This made possible the large-scale export of Indian textiles and metalware throughout the Indian Ocean and the ability of such products to compete with industrial wares produced in Islamic and East Asian areas. There is evidence that both the sultans of Delhi and their successors in the Deccan, the Bahmani rulers, made efforts also to improve Indian irrigation systems so that monsoon rains could be utilized more efficiently. Even Ibn Tugluk's moving of his capital from Delhi to Dalautabad to the south was probably less the result of a foolish eccentricity than a desire to locate it near the economic center of his domains. The Delhi sultanate, then, ushered in a new economic era in India in which agriculture received needed attention, industry and trade flourished, a new financial system was made possible, and Delhi so increased in size that Ibn Battuta, that Moslem traveler who had ventured everywhere, could regard it as the largest metropolis in the entire Islamic world. In fact, it was probably during this period that India's population began to increase rapidly and catch up with that of Western Europe and East Asia which up to 1300 had far exceeded it in size.

These years also saw the development of a distinctive Indian Islamic culture which is too often ascribed completely to the later Moghuls of the sixteenth and seventeenth centuries. The wealth of the new Moslem masters of the subcontinent attracted intellectuals from all over the Islamic world—and especially from Persia which, by 1335, was in anarchy. Such intellectuals began to establish a written tradition in poetry, history, and literature in what had been an essentially oral society. We also find in Delhi and the Bahmani realm a remarkable blending of Hindu and Islamic Persian styles to produce a special architecture and style of decoration which foretold the Taj Mahal and the Red Fort of Delhi—and proclaimed in stone a culture not so much Islamic or Indian as a blend of both.

It is interesting to note that it was this new blend of culture and, specifically, the Islamic faith in Indian form, which now began to be exported overseas to areas of Greater India heretofore indifferent to the religious beliefs of merchants from Near Eastern lands. Now, however, during the last years of the thirteenth century we begin to find evidence of Islam's spread into parts of Malaya, Sumatra, and Java which were frequented by newly converted merchants from Bengal and Gujerat—thus beginning a shift to Islam which was to be completed in Indonesia in the period of the Dutch colonial empire. The Islamization of this part of the world, which altered the culture of its people, was the direct result of the Islamization of much of India and could not have taken place without it. The same may also be true of the spread of Islam along the shores of East Africa during these years, an area which was also as much frequented by Indian merchants as it was by those from the Red Sea and the Persian Gulf.

The appearance of a powerful Moslem state in India, with all its implications, was certainly the most important event which took place in the Indic world during this period, but it was not the only one. In India proper the spread of Islam was not without friction as far as the Hindu masses were concerned, since not all proselytization was peaceful by any means. Instead, it was marked by plundered temples, slaughtered priests, and frequent persecution of the Hindu population, especially in parts of southern India. All this explains why a Hindu reaction appeared in the Deccan about the middle of the fourteenth century which rallied the Dravidian population to new leaders who opposed militarily further Moslem expansion. By 1368 a militantly Hindu state known as Vijayanagar emerged, controlling a large part of southern India. It was to last until Moghul times.

Turning to Greater India overseas, the most important development was a new Thai kingdom which, by 1350, had relegated Cambodia and Champa to minor political roles and which periodically was able to dominate Malaya and the Mons of southern Burma as well. The Thais were able to combine a Hinayana Buddhism and legal system which they borrowed from the Mons with a political organization, a writing system, and an art and architecture of Khmer origin. They also continued to make use of a military feudalism to which their own warriors were accustomed. The combination of all these elements helped to create a realm which still exists and which has a distinct civilization of its own.

By 1300 a new Majapahit dynasty had come to power in Java which was much more powerful than its Kediri and Singosari predecessors and which not only controlled this entire island but tended to dominate an overseas empire to the east and a number of the rajas to the west who had heretofore owed allegiance to Srivijaya. This Majapahit realm, which was still not much affected by the spread of Islam, was to remain powerful until the rise of a new sultanate of Malacca in the next century. Balancing Moslem India, then, were Vijayanagar, Thai, and Majapahit realms which remained loyal to the older religious and cultural traditions of Indic civilization which had survived the Mongol assault.

Thanks to a relatively abundant documentation from Islamic, Western European, Chinese, and native sources, and especially the writings of Marco Polo and Ibn Battuta, we can speak with more authority about the commerce and shipping found in the Indic world between 1270 and 1368 than we could for any earlier period. What emerges from an examination of this evidence is an extremely active maritime world, which was stimulated by the prosperity of the Delhi sultanate and by China, which was displaying considerable interest in this part of Eurasia. What is also quite apparent is that Indian Ocean commerce, like that found in the Mediterranean and northern seas of Europe, was primarily concerned with bulk transport.

It is true, of course, that spices and aromatics from the Yemen, the East Indies, and southern India, gems from Burma, Ceylon, and the Deccan, pearls from the Persian Gulf and Coromandel Coast, gold from East Africa, Sumatra, and southern India, and ivory and ebony from Zanzibar and Pemba formed a valuable part of the cargoes carried in the vessels plying the Indian Ocean during these years. So did textiles from the Punjab, Bengal, and Madras, silks and porcelains from China, and glass and textiles from the workshops of Egypt and Iraq.

Nevertheless, what generally filled these ships were goods of quite a different character: copper from the Red Sea and Thailand, iron from Orissa, tin from Malaya and Sumatra, salt from the Persian Gulf and Java, rice from Burma and Cambodia, timber from the Malabar Coast, Burma, and Borneo, elephants from Ceylon and Burma, and horses from any number of Islamic ports on the other side of the Arabian Sea. The trade of the Indian Ocean, then, unlike that between Greater India and East Asia, consisted mainly of bulk commodities which could be handled cheaply by sea over long distances.

The passenger trade of this period was equally important—sometimes involuntary as with slaves, but more frequently involving large numbers of pilgrims. Not only do we now find an increasingly large number of Moslems, many newly converted, traveling by sea to visit Mecca and Medina from India and other parts of the Indian Ocean, but we also find a number of pilgrims of other faiths like Buddhism, Hinduism, and Christianity traveling to their own holy places, too. A number of important shrines in Ceylon, for instance, attracted Buddhist pilgrims from Southeast Asia and China, while Mailapur and Axsum in Ethiopia attracted a considerable number of Christian travelers eager to pay their respects to Saint Thomas. Even more important in stimulating travel were the great Hindu shrines, especially Benares and those of Gujerat and the Coromandel Coast.

The ships carrying such human and nonhuman cargoes during this period were often quite large, especially Chinese junks which were well built and were sailed by their masters as far west as Quilon and Ormuz. By now, however, we begin to have evidence that not all the junks sailing in Indic waters were Chinese. Some of them were built east of Cape Cormorin by Javanese and Burmese shipwrights who preferred to use teak for ship timber and sails made of cotton cloth or rattan rather than split bamboo. Even the more traditional vessels of the Arabian Sea were not all the ill-made *sambucks* mentioned by Marco Polo. Some of them were large ships with more than one mast, built with nails, and were quite similar to the *capels* which the Portuguese found in these waters a century and a half later. And most of these ships were handled by captains who navigated with compass and astrolabe and had charts which were as accurate as those used in the Mediterranean. In short, by this period, if not earlier, the Indic world possessed maritime skills which were the equal of those found in European or East Asian waters.

While Greater India had not yet developed a financial system as advanced as the banking organization of the societas arrangements found in the Latin West, or the ortàqs and special business partnerships that flourished in Mongol China, it now possessed a workable system of credit and international finance on a par with and similar to that found in the Islamic world. This meant that, while some Indic merchants operated on their own, most found it advisable to make use of *commenda* type business arrangements, many of which cut across religious lines.

Generally speaking, merchants who engaged in international trade in the Indian Ocean found it useful to belong to a merchant association which was more than local in scope—like the *Karimi* or spice merchants who had a head or *rais* in Cairo, another in Aden, and a third in Malabar ports, or those Jewish traders who did likewise, except that the heads of their association were known as *wakils*. And since a little later we find a similar system used for merchants trading across the Bay of Bengal with Malacca, it would probably be wise to consider that such a system dated back to this period also. Both Moslem and non-Moslem merchants in this part of the world, then, found it useful to belong to some kind of international grouping of traders similar to those used in the Mediterranean by the Genoese, Venetians, or Catalans and in northern Europe by the Hanseatic Germans. There were local associations of merchants as well in various ports or cities, generally based upon a common religious affiliation, each of which was headed by one of their number, generally known as a *rais*.

Important developments took place in the Islamic world also during this period. In the western provinces, as we have already noted, the most powerful state was Morocco under the Merinids, with Hafsid Tunis and Granada especially important in cultural and economic matters, and Aboualid Tlemcen bringing up the rear. Briefly between 1335 and 1351, the Merinids were able to unite North Africa and to intervene in southern Spain. But, as we have pointed out, this ended in failure and probably explains why by 1368 their empire was in full decline. Nevertheless, their efforts, abortive though they turned out to be, were of some value in helping to break the hold of the Latin West upon the Maghreb and to turn its inhabitants toward a defiance which was increasingly to take the form of piracy which made Christian shipping hazardous along North African shores.

Across the Sahara to the south of the Barbary Coast states, we also begin to find an interesting development taking place—the appearance of the powerful empire of Mali. Mali arose in the early thirteenth century as a successor to Ghana. It owed its importance to the control that its powerful black rulers exercised over both the gold of the Sudan and the salt of Taglassa. Their dominion stretched along the Niger with Timbuktu as their capital. In 1327 Mansa Musa, the Malian ruler, decided to make a pilgrimage to Mecca and did so with a huge entourage and a store of gold which much impressed the Cairenes and others in the Near East. By this time, then, although the Latin West closed the Mediterranean to them, the Moslems of North Africa were able to compensate by expanding trade and contacts along Saharan caravan routes that led from black Africa north to the Maghreb and east to Egypt.

The middle area of the Islamic world, controlled by the Mamluks, was quite different from the Maghreb. First of all, the Mamluks remained militarily powerful enough to destroy the last Crusader strongholds along the Syrian coast and by 1312 to end the menace of the Mongols. During this period also, despite considerable pressure from nomadic tribes, they successfully intervened in Nubia and kept the Rassulids from taking Mecca and Medina and dominating the Red Sea.

At first they were less successful in maintaining a respectable naval establishment and in eliminating a Lesser Armenian realm that gave Western European traders access to Indian Ocean commerce. A turning point, however, came in 1346, when trade began to desert the Persian Gulf and return to the Red Sea. Suddenly Egypt became more important as a terminus, and Venetians, Catalans, and other Western merchants now considered trade with Alexandria vital. Soon the Mamluks were able to rebuild their fleet, set up a new advanced base at Aleppo, and renew attacks on Armenian Cilicia. By 1375 they had ended Cilician independence, forced Cyprus to accept their overlordship, and become in some ways the masters of the eastern Mediterranean.

It might seem that during these years, as they slowly but inexorably took over the Mediterranean littoral and established their authority there, that the Mamluks would have fixed their eyes upon the sea. This, however, was not the case. Instead, they were chiefly concerned with the interior; it was Cairo in Egypt rather than Alexandria or Damietta, and Damascus and Aleppo instead of seaport cities along the coast which were important to them. This explains why they destroyed the fortifications of the Crusader strongholds after they captured them and settled Kurdish and Turkoman tribesmen in nearby coastal plains—leaving only Tripoli as a fortified advance naval base and Beirut as a commercial center which handled most of the cotton sold to Italian merchants. It is equally interesting, too, that they never thought it worthwhile to repair the damage done to Damietta by the Fifth and Sixth Crusades and made no effort to refortify Alexandria after it had been sacked by a Latin fleet in 1365. Cairo, Aleppo, and Damascus were considered important enough to be embellished with mosques and other public buildings during this century, but not towns which faced the Mediterranean. One can only conclude that this neglect reflected the Mamluks' lack of confidence that they could control a sea where Latin Europeans were still so powerful.

It is true, nevertheless, that foreign trade with Western European merchants was essential to the Mamluk state. Only from them could they procure an adequate supply of slaves from the Black Sea which they needed to man their armies and their administration. Only the Catalans and the Italians could supply them with the timber and the arms which they desperately needed to equip both their small fleet and their armies. It was also the Latin West which sent them the *renegrados* who brought with them military and naval expertise—especially in the use of firearms and cannon. But essential though such trade and contacts were for them, they kept them at a minimum and under a very strict state monopolistic control. They also maintained state control over the spice trade—both that with the West and that which the Karimi spice merchants handled by way of the Indian Ocean, though other commodities from Iraq and the Indic world seem to have been imported into Egypt and Syria without too much difficulty. In short, the Mamluk realm boasted a control over external commerce which was more extensive than any that had been found in this part of the world for several centuries.

When we examine Egypt's and Syria's internal economies, we find an interesting state of affairs. The Mamluk elite were compensated for their military and administrative duties in part with salaries and in part with large estates. Most of them proceeded to sell the grain and other produce from these estates in towns and cities like Cairo and so increase their cash revenues. This meant that the average powerful Mamluk official was also a landowner who engaged in business and developed close ties, including marriage alliances, with the older urban elite still serving as ulema, businessmen, and administrators. This group of notables, who were unarmed, also shared these foreign-born warriors' prejudices against native Christians and Jews and supported a policy of excluding them from public office and subjecting them to discrimination and outright persecution.

The Mamluks during most of this period were able to maintain a stable dinar and an abundant silver coinage, and by 1368 they had again made

Egypt the main entrepot of the spice trade. The elite could enjoy a luxurious life in great interior cities, but at the cost of a carefully controlled foreign trade, a largely lifeless littoral facing the Mediterranean, a listless class of fellaheen in the countryside, and a turbulent body of artisans in the towns who derived little profit from their labors. Under such a system, military strength could be maintained, Cairo could rewrite the Arabian Nights and think of itself as Abbasid Baghdad, and architecture could flourish in a way which only Granada and Delhi could match. A narrow elite could even patronize and support a number of historians and literary figures. But speculative or scientific thought no longer attracted intellectuals, and Cairo and Damascus ceased to participate in the wider world of which they once had been very much a part.

The situation was much worse by the middle of the century in Islamic areas which had been under Mongol rule. In Persia, Iraq, and Khorosan an anarchical situation prevailed with a decline of urban prosperity, peasant revolts in the countryside, and nomadic Turkoman tribes operating without any restraint from the weak authorities who succeeded the Ilkans. Conditions were almost as bad in the realm of the Golden Horde and the Mongol principality of Turkestan. Such disorders explain why so little trade reached Genoese Kaffa and Trebizond from either the Indian Ocean or China. Here as in Lesser Armenia the great days of the early fourteenth century were over.

There was one area of the Islamic world subjected to the Mongols, however, where something quite different was happening. That was Anatolia. Here, as the Seljuks disappeared to be followed several decades later by the Ilkans and Turkoman tribes moved west toward the Aegean, a special situation arose. We suddenly begin to find a number of frontier or ghazi emirates arising along the southern and southwestern coasts of Asia Minor. Most of these emirates, like Aydin and Attalia, attracted warriors who took to the sea and raided Greek shores and Christian shipping passing these shores—which was one reason why the Knights Hospitaler moved to Rhodes where they could defend Western commerce and attack Turkish-held coasts in retaliation.

One of these ghazi emirates, however, that which belonged to the Ottomans, was somewhat different. It arose in territory which had been the empire of Nicaea—an area whose border defenses had been neglected by the Paleologues and which had been devastated by the Catalan company before it moved back into Europe to establish itself over Thebes and Athens. In other words, the Ottoman emirate, unlike all the others, arose in territory which was essentially Greek and not Turkish in character. And second, this Ottoman emirate initially was not in any way connected with the sea and piracy, but a state based upon a land army of warriors. These warriors, by 1346, had taken over the entire countryside and established themselves under their leader, Sultan Orkan, in the city of Brusa. A few years later the last cities inhabited by the Greeks had been taken and the Ottomans ruled unopposed between Ankara and the Sea of Marmora.

Even before this time, however, they began to be involved intimately in the Byzantine world by serving as mercenaries in civil wars which claimants to the throne of the empire continued to wage with one another. In the course of these wars, in 1356 they were able to occupy their first holding in Europe, the city of Gallipoli on the other side of the Hellespont. Though a crusading expedition drove them out of this conquest, they soon recaptured it and a decade later had defeated the Bulgars, taken over most of Thrace, and under their second sultan, Murad, had moved their capital from Asiatic Brusa to European Adrianople. By 1368 they were driving into Macedonia and beginning to form an empire which was to be one of the brightest jewels in the crown of Islam—and one which had already breached the line separating Western Europe from the Islamic world in the fourteenth century.

At this point we need to assess the importance of what had happened to the Islamic world by 1368 after it had rallied from the disastrous years when it was on the defensive against the Mongols and the Latin West. It had regained the initiative in the Maghreb, so that it could reduce Western European control, attack across the Straits of Gibraltar, and send pirate craft out to sea to prey on European shipping. In the Middle East Mamluks had taken over all of coastal Syria and Lesser Armenia, denied Westerners easy access to the Indian Ocean and central Asia, and created an effective small fleet. In Anatolia, new ghazi emirates had formed, one of which, controlled by the Ottomans, had crossed the Hellespont and was beginning to expand into Europe. At the same time, Islam had managed to convert the Mongol ruling class in the West, so the Golden Horde was now Moslem, and Islam was in the saddle as well in the former realms of the Ilkans and in Turkestan. The Latin West now faced a hostile Islamic world which stood between it and the worlds of India and China.

Perhaps more significant, Islam had proved capable of penetrating other cultures. It had done so in India and Indonesia. It had done so in southern Russia and Byzantine Anatolia. It had done so in the black world south of the Sahara and along the shores of East Africa. Though Western Europe had begun this century as an incipient world civilization capable of dominating Byzantium and reaching the Chinese and Indic worlds in some force, it was Islam and its civilization which ended up with the victory. One can see this with special clarity if one examines the travels of that self-conscious apostle of Islam, Ibn Battuta, as he wends his way from his birthplace in Ceuta to Timbuktu, through the Middle East, to Moslem Russia and central Asia, to Delhi and East Africa, and to India and China—thereby delineating rather deliberately the Islamic imperium of the mid-fourteenth century.

Why was Islam so successful when it is clear that it had fallen far behind both Western Europe and China in the effectiveness of its political institutions, in its ability to provide a livelihood for the mass of its population, and in its technological inventiveness? Its population was declining, even in areas which were not affected by the Black Death, and by 1350 nomadism had emerged triumphant over the settled populations in many regions. How then was it possible for this civilization to hold its own and even to expand in all directions beyond its original heartland?

One reason was, of course, military. During this period the Islamic world was able to develop armies, especially those composed of Turks, which were remarkably successful in battle. Mamluk Egypt, the sultanate of Delhi, and the Ottomans are prime examples. Without such armies, the Moslem world could neither have held its own nor begun to expand so successfully. But there is another important and seldom analyzed reason why it did so well— its religious organization. This organization was not directed by any centralized force, since the Abbasid caliphate, which was destroyed by Hulagu in 1258, was not really reconstituted. Islamic religious and cultural strength was rather the result of a combination of a relatively simple totalitarian system of religious law, known as the Sharia, which was interpreted by an international ulema elite, and of a vision of life spread by mystics or Sufis in every corner of the Islamic world. Between them, the ulema and the Sufis touched the two basic chords of human existence, the head and the heart, the practical and the ideal, in a way that the average man or woman could understand. They, much more than warriors, kept Islam vigorous and compelling as a faith during those years and continued to do so in the years ahead, as African blacks, Balkan Greeks, and Slavs and Hindus left their older traditions behind them and opted for Moslem civilization.

Last of all, we need to consider Byzantine-Russian civilization, which in many ways by 1368 no longer existed in its older form at all. We have already pointed out that Russia had survived its time of troubles and by the late fourteenth century was gathering strength for a new life of its own under the leadership of Moscow, Lithuania, and Novgorod. The steppes area was now part of the Islamic world and was to remain so until the eighteenth century when Peter the Great and Catherine the Great changed its destiny.

What of the Byzantine world, however, that third and most vital part of the Byzantine-Russian nexus? As was pointed out in our last chapter, its revival under Michael Paleologue was more illusory than real. This talented emperor won a place for his revived Byzantium more by diplomacy than by force, did nothing basic to deny the Venetians and Genoese control of the empire's commerce and of the sea, and gave the aristocracy almost complete control over the peasantry. In 1274 he made the further error of alienating his church by proclaiming a union with Rome, in the hope of getting the pope to restrain Charles of Anjou who was planning an attack on Constantinople.

Under his immediate successors, the empire he and the Lascarids had put together began to unravel very swiftly. His heir, Andronicus II, was forced to break with Rome, and from this time on Byzantine emperors found they were unable to control their own church. Instead, leadership in this vital organization increasingly came from the patriarch of Constantinople and the great monastery complex of Mt. Athos, both of which were much respected in a Greco-Slavic Orthodox world which frequently had only contempt for the Paleologues.

Then, as the Turks began to absorb the last Byzantine holdings in Asia Minor and a powerful Serbia began to expand in the Balkans and Paleologue princes engaged in senseless civil wars which could only result in disruption and disunity, Byzantine society was torn apart by two movements. One of them was a social protest on the part of the peasantry and the lower classes in the cities, which we know as the Zealot movement. The Zealots, who seem to have resembled their counterparts in Persia or the rebellious fourteenth-century peasantry and urban lower class of Western Europe, desired, above all, to destroy the power of the aristocracy in town and countryside and to return to a system unknown since the time of the empire of Nicaea, when the government was the protector of the small landholder and the artisan. The second movement, that of the Hesychasts, which also had its counterparts elsewhere among the Sufis of Islam and the mystics of the Latin Western church, was a rejection of worldly intellectualism and culture and a withdrawal into a mystical world of the spirit—especially appealing to those who were attracted to monasticism. Such a movement made it difficult to use the church effectively as a rallying point for any political program and weakened the hold of its emperor and hierarchy over it.

These two movements sometimes worked together and sometimes were in opposite camps. But by 1368 it was apparent that one of them, the Zealot movement, was going to fail to achieve its goals, as the upper class, often assisted by foreign mercenaries and allies, suppressed its adherents in brutal fashion. The Hesychasts, on the other hand, triumphed over intellectualism and those in the Orthodox church who were oriented toward the Latin West and so prepared Byzantine society for a new role it was to play in an autocratic Russia and an equally arbitrary and autocratic Ottoman Empire. By then, however, any chance for a viable Byzantine society had ended. Its economy was in worse shape than it had been in 1270, as Italians continued to dominate the trade of the Black Sea and Aegean, slave raids depopulated their shores, and Byzantine authorities, almost without resources, found themselves restricted to enclaves about Constantinople, Saloniki, and in the Morea. Byzantine society seemed powerless to act vigorously in every sphere except the cultural one. It sat waiting for the barbarians.

The question in 1368, then, was not whether the Byzantine side of the Byzantine-Russian nexus could survive, for it was clear that it could not, nor whether it could be taken over by the Latin West, for the 150 years which had elapsed since the Fourth Crusade had shown the latter incapable of doing so. Rather, the question was, who was to be the heir to Byzantium— the Serbs or the Ottoman Turks? Until the death of Stephen Dushan in 1356, the odds seemed to favor the Serbs. Orthodox in their religious faith, rich from a mineral wealth pouring out of newly organized mines in the Balkans, warlike and aggressive, the Serbs advanced south and east deep into Byzantine territory. As they did so, they proclaimed their leaders tsars, adopted Greek law codes, and showed in the churches they built an appreciation of the best aspects of Byzantine art and architecture. They were even able to create in Dubrovnik a naval rival to the Venetians.

The death of Stephen Dushan ended all this. His heirs were incompetent and divided the Serbian empire amongst themselves and failed to get any real support from the Greek population in areas the Serbs had occupied. So it was the new Ottoman state that prevailed. This state offered complete tolerance to Christians who submitted to it, lightened the burden of taxes and dues upon the peasantry, and organized powerful armies based on tribal levies, a heavily armed cavalry (known as *timars*) which received land in return for military service, and a slave infantry, (the *janissaries*), drawn from the Christian population. By 1368 both the Ottoman armed forces and their system of government had proved their worth and they were advancing from their new capital in Thrace to take over the Balkans. An Ottoman empire was being formed in Byzantine territory in which the patriarch of Constantinople and the Greek church in general were to serve as junior partners— an empire which was to last until the twentieth century.

Epilogue, 1368–1500

The first section of this book has tried to analyze the five great civilizations of the Old World: the East Asian, the Indic, the Islamic, the Byzantine-Russian, and the Western European, as they appeared around the year 1000. In doing so an attempt has been made to identify their basic cultural patterns and the differences and peculiarities which at this time distinguished each from the other four.

The rest of the volume has been concerned with explaining how two great forces, nomadic peoples and Western European Crusaders, played a role in changing, modifying, and, at times, even weakening these civilizations during the nearly four hundred years of the High Middle Ages until 1368.

It has been shown that the first wave of nomadic assaults upon these civilizations took place during the eleventh century and was carried out by Berbers and Arabs whose original homes lay in the Sahara and the deserts of Arabia and by Turkish tribesmen who inhabited the wastes of central Asia. Then, after a century of calm, nomadic assaults again resumed during the thirteenth century, and this time the main nomadic protagonists were the Mongols of central Asia. The Mongols attacked all five Old World civilizations and managed to create, in the process, a large and powerful empire which stretched all the way across Eurasia. As for Western European civilization, its crusading efforts, which much increased its territory and its influence, were continuous during the entire period of the High Middle Ages. Crusades were most successful, however, when they coincided with the nomadic assaults on the rest of the civilized world.

In presenting this story in these pages we have also tried to show how these two great movements, or forces, nomadic and crusading, affected each of these Old World civilizations by the end of the fourteenth century. And why one of them, Western Europe, ended up the gainer, while the four others fell behind as decisive forces in the world which was to emerge in modern times.

We have concluded our story around the year 1368 for a number of reasons. First because by this year the Mongol empire, which represented nomad expansionism at its most successful, had completely disintegrated and by then too Western Europe's original crusading movement had also ended. This happened as the last North African Moorish intervention in Spain in 1340 was turned back at the Battle of Rio Salado, as a final crusading assault on Alexandria failed in 1365, as attempts to stop the Ottoman movement across the Hellespont into Europe were abandoned in this same year, and as the Teutonic Knights gave up efforts to expand into Lithuania and link together their Livonian and Prussian bridgeheads in the eastern Baltic.

The century or so which followed proved to be a lull for Western European civilization until in the late fifteenth century it resumed its efforts to expand, as first the Portuguese, then the Spaniards, and then other Western Europeans sailed forth and used the maritime and other skills which they had developed during the period covered by this book to achieve a new world destiny. In the course of the next four centuries, as we all know, they conquered the Americas and were able to establish dominion over the four other great civilizations of the Old World which had been their medieval contemporaries. They also seized control of black Africa, Australia, and Oceania, made themselves the masters of the seven seas, and produced the only civilization which in modern times has come to be worldwide in its scope and influence. And this time they did all this without the help of the nomadic forces which had assisted their efforts during the High Middle Ages.

What was just a lull for Western Europeans, however, proved to be something quite different for those who lived in the other great civilizations of medieval Eurasia. Rather, the centuries which followed 1368 proved to be not so much a pause as an epilogue or postscript. And it might be even more accurate to describe these years, except in the fields of art, architecture, and literature, as a kind of waning of their late medieval civilizations, a waning which continued into relatively modern times. To understand all of this, let us briefly survey each of them, the Byzantine-Russian, the Indic, the East Asian, and the Islamic, to see if we can discern a pattern or patterns of how this epilogue to their later medieval past was to affect them down to 1500, and even later.

Byzantine-Russian and Indic civilizations from the start emerged as the weakest and least successful of the Old World civilizations. By the late fourteenth century the Kievan portion of the former was still caught in a Mongol deepfreeze from which its princes of Moscow were painfully trying to escape. It was not until almost a century later that they finally gained complete independence during the reign of Ivan III. Yet the Third Rome proclaimed by Ivan III in 1462 still did not include most of the Ukraine and White Russia, which had been absorbed by an expanded Poland-Lithuania, and the Turkish-speaking people of the southern Russian steppes had decided to accept the Ottomans as their overlords, not the rulers of the Kremlin. Even a century later, when Ivan III had been succeeded by Vassily and Ivan the Terrible, Moscow was only partially successful in its efforts to expand its territory—especially toward the south and west.

After Ivan the Terrible died during the first decade of the seventeenth century, Moscovy again found itself very weak, so that Polish armies were able to briefly occupy Moscow itself. It was not until the reigns of Peter the Great and Catherine the Great in the late seventeenth and eighteenth centuries that all the lands which Yaroslav the Wise had ruled finally became part of a united Russian empire. Even then a large number of Ukrainians still refused to accept the Russian Orthodox metropolitan of Moscow as head of their church, insisting instead that the Uniat Church with which they were affiliated continued to come under the authority of the pope, as it had since 1438.

As for the Byzantine area by 1368, as we have noted, it had been reduced to Constantinople and two other enclaves ruled by the Paleologue family, while its Slavic neighbors were in the process of being absorbed by the victorious armies of Ottoman sultans. Despite some futile efforts by the Hungarians and other Latin Westerners to halt Turkish advances, the Osmanli rulers continued to expand their authority, until by 1462 they had absorbed the entire Balkan Peninsula and Constantinople itself, which fell to Mehmet the Conqueror in 1453. Soon thereafter, having taken over Trebizond from the Greek rulers and cleared the Black Sea and its littoral of foreign foes, the Ottomans began to build a fleet which was to challenge Venetian control of Crete, the Aegean Islands, and the eastern Mediterranean.

During these years and long afterward, most of the population of the Balkans and much of Asia Minor still enjoyed a common Orthodox Christian civilization under the religious leadership of the patriarch of Constantinople and the monks of Mount Athos. The Armenians, continued to follow the leadership of their Armenian catholicos or primate. But Byzantine civilization, though it prized accomplishment in art and architecture, was extremely narrow and anti-intellectual and was controlled by an other-worldly hesychast spirit which had triumphed in the Byzantine-Russian world back in the fourteenth century. Most Greeks, Romanians, and Slavs remained in the grip of this other-worldly "Great Church in Captivity," as Stephen Runceman has called it, until the time of the French Revolution, when they awakened and began to seek a new destiny for themselves.

Indic civilization found itself in similar straits by 1368. By this time in the Indian subcontinent large numbers of Moslems from Iran, Afghanistan, and

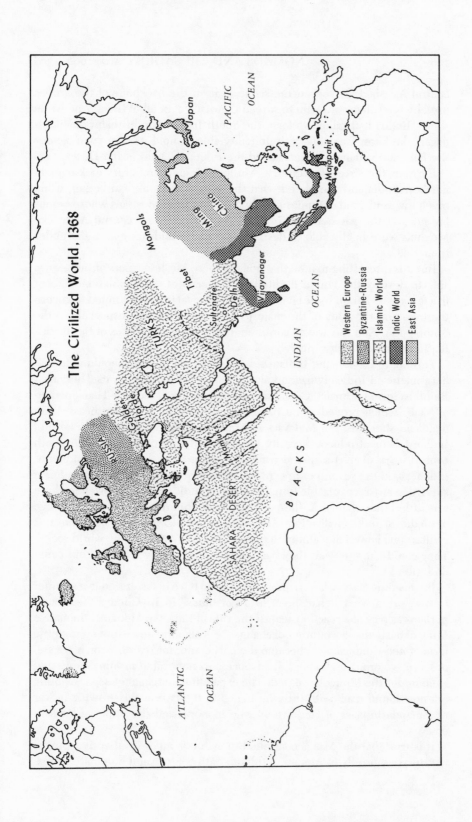

The Civilized World, 1368

Western Europe
Byzantine-Russia
Islamic World
Indic World
East Asia

PACIFIC OCEAN

Japan

Ming China

Mongols

Majapahit

Tibet

Sultanate of Delhi

Vijayanager

INDIAN OCEAN

TURKS

Golden Horde

RUSSIA

Mamluks

SAHARA DESERT

BLACKS

ATLANTIC OCEAN

central Asia had arrived on the scene to form the backbone of the armies used by the sultans of Delhi to spread their rule over all of India. And while some Hindus had rallied to form the South Indian Hindu realm of Vijaya-nagar, the latter was only with difficulty able to hold its own even against the Bahmani sultans who succeeded the rulers of Delhi in the Deccan.

Early in the sixteenth century, Moslem Moghul emperors took over in northern India and completed what the sultans of Delhi had begun, using much the same kind of armies largely recruited from Moslems whose homes lay beyond the Khyber Pass in Iran, Afghanistan, and central Asia. The Moghuls were finally able to destroy Vijayanagar and bring all India under their rule.

But it is interesting to note that none of these Moslem rulers of India were able to destroy the Hindu tradition of the mass of the population. Except in a few areas, Hindu Indic civilization of medieval times continued to govern the lives and thoughts of the majority of the population—especially in the countryside. And this was to continue until the modern times of the British Raj in the nineteenth century.

Turning to Ceylon and Indianized realms in the East we should note that here medieval Indic civilization also continued to flourish in its Thervadan Buddhist form in Burma, Cambodia, and especially in the new Thai kingdom of Siam, which proved to be the most powerful of these Southeast Asian mainland states. But in Malaysia and Indonesia slowly but surely a form of Indian Islam introduced here by Bengalis and Gujeratis in the fourteenth century took over. Its spread continued even after the Dutch conquered Indonesia in the seventeenth century until only in Bali did Indic Hinduism survive in any recognizable form. In Greater India overseas, however, there was little other change in the patterns of life inherited from an earlier age of medieval Indic civilization. And none of the peoples who shared in this civilization showed any ability to expand into new areas on the world scene. They could cling to what they had when conquered by outsiders but could do little else.

By this time East Asian civilization seems to have been altered in a number of ways from what it had been in Yuan times. In its Chinese heartland, perhaps as part of a reaction against the rule of the alien Mongols, the native Ming dynasty made a number of changes. Foreigners were expelled, a sterile form of neo-Confucianism became the norm, and, for reasons which are still obscure, vigorous technological advances, so noticeable in Sung times and even under the Mongols, ceased. The expanding merchant class of the Sung era now found itself with little influence in the face of the growing power of a mandarin class of landowners who monopolized the imperial bureau-cracy.

It is true that the Mings continued to maintain a powerful army, using it to intervene briefly in Annam in the fifteenth century and dominate Korea.

During their reign much immigration continued to take place from Kwang-
tung and Fukien to Formosa and areas of Southeast Asia. And early in the
fifteenth century the Mings even built a huge fleet which for some decades
sailed past a friendly Malacca into the Indian Ocean.

All this, however, proved of short duration. By 1460 the fleet had been
allowed to decay and its crews were transferred to duty on the Grand Canal.
Overseas, Chinese to the south found they had been abandoned by an imperial government that had lost interest in the external world. By 1500, or
even earlier, Japanese *wako* pirates and others of their ilk were able to raid
Pacific shores with impunity and bring in goods which they traded in coastal
areas in defiance of Ming regulations. The Ming empire continued to decay
and was soon to see the seas along its shores dominated by the Portuguese,
the Dutch, and other Western Europeans, while the Manchus to the north
prepared to invade across the Great Wall.

Though some Japanese in this same period were now beginning to show
a new vigor, especially on the sea, their Ashikaga shōguns, who ruled before
1500 in what is known as the Muromachi period, were so weak at home that
they could not control their feudal samurai and take any lead beyond their
borders. Only late in the sixteenth century were great warlords like Hide-
yoshi and Ieyasu at last able to force a unity upon Japan's warring factions.
They did not change Japan's medieval culture in the process but rather
refined it into forms it was to maintain down to modern times. And though
they briefly attempted to intervene in Korea and encouraged foreign trade,
that was all abandoned by the 1630s, and Japan deliberately secluded itself
until it was forcibly opened up by Perry in the mid-nineteenth century.
Japan, like China after 1368, had failed to either change its medieval society
or move to take a place in the wider world.

At first glance the Islamic world seemed much more successful, especially
after its Ottoman sultans, who by 1500 had come to dominate the old Byzantine Balkan, Anatolian, and Black Sea heartland, had expanded their
dominion under Selim the Grim and Sulieman the Magnificent to include
almost the entire Arab world as far west as Morocco. At the same time they
conquered Hungary and challenged the powerful Hapsburgs and their Italian
allies for control of the Mediterranean. During these years, still another
Islamic dynasty, the Safavids, built up a powerful empire in Iran, especially
at the time of Shah Abbas. And at about the same time, as we have noted,
the Moghuls completed what the sultans of Delhi had begun and conquered
all of the Indic world which they made into a powerful empire. But it is
worth noting that none of these gunpowder empires except that of the Safavids, drew its strength from the older Islamic heartland of the year 1000
or even 1200. Instead, in both the Ottoman realm and the empire of the
Moghuls, the center of their power lay in areas whose population had only
partly accepted Islamic civilization. For instance, though Islam had

triumphed by 1500 in central Anatolia and a little later became firmly established in Bosnia, Albania, and the Dobruja, the majority of the population who lived in the Balkans and much of Asia Minor remained Christian and attached to their medieval Christian civilization. The same thing is true of India where the mass conversion of Bengal, Kashmir, and Gujerat to Islam was not followed by a similar process elsewhere on the part of the Hindu population. Islamic civilization of the time of the Ottomans, Safavids and the Moghuls might seem to have been a formidable enemy and a rival to Western Europe, but it could not hope to compete with it successfully on the world scene over a long period.

In contrast, after 1368 Western European civilization at first seemed halting and unsure of itself. For a century it paused as its banking system collapsed, its internal frontier closed, and the Black Death decimated its population in town and countryside alike. The long Hundred Years War between France and England, which did not end until 1452, and the Great Schism showed the bankruptcy of both its political and spiritual leadership. But by the late fifteenth century those factors which this volume has shown had invigorated it during the High Middle Ages again came to the fore. It again made steady progress at home and overseas which was to eventually make it the master of the wider world—a story that will need to be followed at another time.

It would be wrong, however, to conclude that by 1368 the forces of either nomadism in Eurasia or the crusading spirit in Western Europe had completely disappeared, although they certainly no longer were as powerful as they had been earlier. For instance, in the late fourteenth century a self-conscious Tamerlane attempted to revive Mongol rule from his homeland in Turkestan. He had some success in doing so and was powerful enough to conquer Syria, which had escaped an Ilkan takeover, shatter the power of both the Golden Horde in Russia and the sultanate of Delhi in India, complete the ruin of the irrigation system of Iraq, and briefly stop the Ottomans in their tracks. He even encouraged a belief among Western Europeans that they could form an alliance with him and undermine Islam from within as they had hoped to do with the Mongols. It is often asserted that it was fear of his nomadic power that helped persuade the Mings that they should move their capital to Peking and send their fleet out into the Indian Ocean. But Tamerlane's empire proved ephemeral and unable to survive after his death, and the Black Death decimated the nomadic population of his part of central Asia. His quarreling Uzbek successors ceased to be a menace to anyone. The nomadic threat to the West and Near East ended once and for all. Only Manchu invaders of China kept alive a tradition which Turks and Mongols of central Asia had begun.

As for the crusading spirit in the West, its original impetus ended, as we have noted, with Peter of Cyprus's attack on Alexandria in 1365, the defeat of the last Moorish invasion of Spain at Rio Salado in 1340, and the late fourteenth-century *chevauchées* of Western knights along Prussian frontiers with Lithuania. Yet the Ottoman menace did revive in Europe something of a neo-crusading spirit again. The later crusades which resulted from all this were not very successful, as proved by the disasters at Nicopolis in 1396 and Varna in 1429 and the failure to save Constantinople from the Ottomans in 1453. But the crusading spirit was powerful enough in the West, and especially in Iberia, to help explain the Portuguese seizure of Ceuta and Moroccan shores and to aid Ferdinand and Isabella in their conquest of Granada. Later this same spirit seems to have helped inspire both Portuguese and Spanish expansion overseas. The Crusades in a real sense were over, but not only had they helped Western Europe triumph over its Byzantine and Islamic neighbors during the High Middle Ages, but they also played a forceful ideological role for those who later were to carry the banners and values of Western European civilization to the four corners of the world.

BIBLIOGRAPHY

WESTERN EUROPE TO 1368

General
Lewis, Archibald R. *Emerging Medieval Europe*. New York, 1967.
Lopez, Robert S. *The Birth of Europe*. Philadelphia, 1957.
McNeill, William H. *The Rise of the West*. Chicago, 1963.
Previte-Orton, C., ed. *The Shorter Cambridge Medieval History*. 2 vols. New York, 1975.

Economic, Social, and Technological
Bautier, R. H. *The Economic Development of Medieval Europe*. London, 1971.
Cambridge Economic History of Europe. Vols. 1–3. Cambridge, 1941–46.
Lopez, Robert S. *The Commercial Revolution of the Middle Ages, 950–1350*. New York, 1976.
McNeill, William H. *The Pursuit of Power, Technology, and Armed Force since A.D. 1000*. Chicago, 1982.
Postan, M. M. *Medieval Trade and Finance*. Cambridge, 1973.
Russell, Josiah C. *Late Ancient and Medieval Population*. Philadelphia, 1958.
White, Lynn T., Jr. *Medieval Technology and Social Change*. Oxford, 1962.
———. *Machina Ex Deo. Essays on the Dynamism of Western Culture*. Cambridge, 1968.
Ziegler, Philip. *The Black Death*. London, 1969.

Maritime and Naval
Lewis, Archibald R. *Naval Power and Trade in the Mediterranean, A.D. 500–1100*. Princeton, 1951.
———. *The Northern Seas: Shipping and Trade in Northern Europe, A.D. 300–1100*. Princeton, 1958.
Lewis, Archibald R., and Timothy J. Runyan. *European Maritime and Naval History, A.D. 300–1500*. Bloomington, Ind., 1985.
Unger, Richard W. *The Ship in the Medieval Economy, 600–1600*. London, 1980.

Special Areas and Subjects
Balducci Pegalotti, Francesco. *The Practica della Mercatura*. Edited by A. Evans. London, 1970.
Bishko, C. Julian. "The Castilian as Plainsman. The Medieval Ranching Frontier in La Mancha and Estramadura." In *The New World Looks at Its History*. Edited by A. Lewis and T. McGann. Austin, Tex., 1963.
———. *Studies in Medieval Spanish Frontier History*. London, 1978.
Cambridge History of Poland. Vol. 1. Cambridge, 1941.
Carus-Wilson, Edith, and Coleman, O. *England's Export Trade, 1275–1547*. Oxford, 1963.
Dollinger, Philippe. *The Hansa*. Berkeley, 1961.
Douglas, David C. *The Norman Achievement*. Berkeley, 1969.
———. *The Norman Fate*. Berkeley, 1976.

Dufourcq, Charles. *L'Espagne et le Maghrib aux XIIIe et XIVe siècles*. Paris, 1966.
Foote, Peter G., and Wilson, David W. *The Viking Achievement*. London, 1983.
Hillgarth, Jocelyn N. *The Spanish Kingdoms*. Vol. 1, *1250–1410*. Oxford, 1976.
Lane, Frederic, C. *Venice and History*. Baltimore, 1966.
————. *Venice, a Maritime Republic*. Baltimore, 1973.
Lewis, Archibald R. *The Development of Southern French and Catalan Society, 711–
    1050*. Austin, Tex., 1967.
————. *Medieval Society in Southern France and Catalonia*. London, 1984.
O'Callaghan, Joseph R. *A History of Medieval Spain*. Ithaca, N.Y., 1975.
Oliveira Marques, A. *History of Portugal*. Vol. 1. Cambridge, 1972.
Setton, Kenneth M. *The Papacy and the Levant*. Vol. 1, *The Thirteenth and Four-
    teenth Centuries*. Philadelphia, 1976.
————. *Europe and the Levant in the Middle Ages and Renaissance*. London, 1978.
Vicens-Vives, Jaime. *Approaches to the History of Spain*. Berkeley, 1970.

BYZANTIUM AND RUSSIA TO 1368

Overall
Bratianu, George. *La Mer Noire*. Monarchii, 1969.
Lopez, Robert S. *Byzantium and the World around It*. London, 1978.
Oblensky, Dmitri. *The Byzantine Commonwealth*. New York, 1973.

BYZANTINE EMPIRE AND ROMANIA

General
Bon, Antoine. *Byzantium*. Translated by D. Hogarth. London, 1973.
Ostrogorsky, George. *History of the Byzantine State*. Brunswick, 1969.
Runciman, Steven. *Byzantine Civilization*. London, 1956.
Vasiliev, Alexander A. *The Byzantine Empire*. 2 vols. Madison, 1958.

Maritime and Naval
Ahrweiler, Helène. *Byzance et la mer*. Paris, 1966.
Lewis, Archibald R. *Naval Power and Trade in the Mediterranean, A.D. 500–1100*.
    Princeton, 1951.
Lewis, Archibald R., and Runyan, Timothy J. *European Maritime and Naval History,
    300–1500*. Chap. 2. Bloomington, 1985.

Special Areas and Subjects
Ahrweiler, Helene. *Études sur les structures administratives et sociales de Byzance*.
    London, 1971.
Angold, Michael. *A Byzantine Government in Exile: Government and Society under
    the Lascarids of Nicaea*. London, 1978.
Brand, Charles N. *Byzantium Confronts the West, 1180–1204*. Cambridge, Mass.,
    1968.
Canard, Marius. *Byzance et les Mussulmans du Proche Orient*. London, 1973.
Der Neressian, Serapie, *Études Byzantines et Armeniennes*. Louvain, 1973.
Foss, Clive. *Byzantine and Turkish Sardis*. Cambridge, Mass., 1971.
Geanakoplos, Deno J. *Byzantine East and Latin West*. New York, 1966.
Jacoby, David. *La Féodalité en Grece mediévale*. The Hague, 1971.
————. *Société et demographie a Byzance et en Romanie*. London, 1979.

Lewis, Archibald R. "The Social and Economic History of the Balkans in Comneni Times." In *The Sea and Medieval Civilizations*. London, 1978.
———. "The Danube Route and Byzantium, A.D. 802–1185." In *The Sea and Medieval Civilizations*. London, 1978.
Luttrell, Anthony. *The Hospitalers in Cyprus, Rhodes, Greece and the West*. London, 1978.
Moravcsik, Gyula. *Byzantium and the Magyars*. Amsterdam, 1970.
Oblensky, Dmitri. *Byzantium and the Slavs*. London, 1971.
Setton, Kenneth M. *The Catalan Domination of Athens, 1311–1388*. Cambridge, Mass., 1948.
Vryonis, Speros. *Byzantium and Europe*. London, 1967.
———. *Studies on Byzantium, Seljuks and Ottomans*. Malibu, 1981.

RUSSIA

General
Riasonovsky, Nicholas. *A History of Russia*. New York, 1977.
Vernadsky, George. *A History of Russia*. Vols. 1–3. New Haven, 1943–55.
Vernadsky, George, and Karpovich, Michael. *A History of Russia*. New Haven, 1947.

Special Areas and Subjects
Curtin, Jeremiah. *The Mongols in Russia*. Boston, 1908.
Thompson, Michael W. *Novgorod the Great*. London, 1967.
Vernadsky, G. *Medieval Russian Laws*. New York, 1969.

THE ISLAMIC WORLD TO 1368

General
Cambridge History of Islam. Vols. 1–2. Cambridge, 1970–73.
Encyclopedia of Islam. Vols. 1–8. London, 1954–84.
Hodgson, Marshall E. *The Venture of Islam*. Vols. 1–2. Chicago, 1974–78.
Lewis, B., ed. *Islam*. 2 vols. London, 1976.

Economic, Social, and Technological
Ashtor, Eliyahu. *A Social and Economic History of the Near East in the Middle Ages*. London, 1971.
———. *Studies in the Levantine Trade in Middle Ages*. London, 1978.
Goitein, Solomon D. *A Mediterranean Society*. 3 vols. Berkeley, 1967–73.
Lombard, Maurice. *The Golden Age of Islam*. Translated by J. Spencer. New York, 1975.
Watson, Andrew M. "The Arab Agricultural Revolution and Its Diffusion." *Journal of Economic History* 34 (1974).
———. *Agricultural Innovation in the Early Islamic World*. New York, 1983.

Maritime and Naval
Lewis, Archibald R. *Naval Power and Trade in the Mediterranean, A.D. 500–1100*. Princeton, 1951.
———. "Northern European Seapower and the Straits of Gibraltar 1000–1350." In *The Sea and Medieval Civilizations*. London, 1978.
———. *European Naval and Maritime History, A.D. 300–1500*. Chap. 3. Bloomington, Ind., 1983.

Special Areas and Subjects
Arié, Rachel. *L'Espagne Musulmane au temps des Nasarides, 1232–1492*. Paris, 1973.
Ayalon, David. *Gunpowder, Firearms in the Mamluk Kingdom*. London, 1956.
———. *Studies on the Mamluks of Egypt*. London, 1977.
Bovill, Edward W. *The Golden Trade of the Moors*. 2nd ed. Oxford, 1968.
Brunschvig, Robert. *La Berbérie Orientale sous les Hafsids*. 2 vols. Paris, 1947.
Cambridge History of Africa. Vols. 2–3 Cambridge, 1975–80.
Cambridge History of Iran. Vols. 4–5. Cambridge, 1971–76.
Ehrenkreutz, Andrews S. *Saladin*. Albany, 1972.
Glick, Thomas F. *Irrigation and Society in Medieval Valencia*. Cambridge, Mass.,
        1970.
———. *Islamic and Christian Spain*. Princeton, 1979.
Ibn Khaldun. *The Muqaddimah*. 2 vols. Rev. ed. Translated by F. Rosenthal. Prince-
        ton, 1967.
Idris, Henri. *La Berbérie Orientale sous les Zirites Xᵉ-XIIIᵉ siècles*. Paris, 1962.
Kabir Mafizullah. *The Buwayid Dynasty of Bagdad*. Calcutta, 1964.
Lapidus, Ira. *Islamic Cities in the Later Middle Ages*. Cambridge, Mass., 1967.
———. *Middle Eastern Cities*. Berkeley, 1969.
Le Tourneau, Roger. *The Almohad Movement in North Africa in the Twelfth and
        Thirteenth Centuries*. Princeton, 1969.
Wittek, Paul. *The Rise of the Ottoman Turks*. London, 1965.

INDIC CIVILIZATION TO 1368

General
Cambridge History of India. Vols. 2–3. Cambridge, 1922.
Thapar, Romila. *A History of India*. Vol. 1. Baltimore, 1965–66.

Maritime and Naval
Gibson, W., ed. *Polynesian Navigation*. Wellington, 1963.
Hourani, George. *Arab Seafaring in the Indian Ocean*. Princeton, 1951.
Lewis, Archibald R. "Merchants in the Indian Ocean, 1000–1500." In *The Sea and
        Medieval Civilizations*. London, 1978.
Richards, D., ed. *Islam and the Trade of Asia*. Philadelphia, 1970.

Special Areas and Subjects
Nilakanta Shasti, K. *History of South India*. 2d ed. Oxford, 1958.
———. *The Colas*. Madras, 1959.
Quereshi, I. *The Muslim Community of the Indo-Pakistan Continent*. The Hague,
        1962.
Stein, Burton. "The Coromandel Trade in Medieval India," in *Merchants and Schol-
        ars*. Edited by J. Parker. Minneapolis, 1965.
———. *Peasant State and Society in South India*. New York, 1980.
———, ed. *Essays on South India*. Honolulu, 1975.
Strivastava, A. L. *The Sultanate of Delhi, 711–1526*. Agra, 1950.
Yule, H., ed. "Cathay and the Way Thither." In *Hakluyt Society*, 2d ser., vol. 41.
        London, 1916.

SOUTHEAST ASIA

Coedes, George. *The Making of South East Asia*. Berkeley, 1966.
———. *The Indianized States of Southeast Asia*. Honolulu, 1968.

206 Bibliography

Hall, Daniel E. *A History of Burma*. London, 1956.
————. *A History of South East Asia*, 4th ed. New York, 1967.
Maung Htin Aung. *A History of Burma*. New York, 1967.
Moreland, William H. "The Shabandar in the Eastern Seas." *Journal of the Royal Historical Society* 21 (1920).
Pigland, Theodore G. T. *Java in the Fourteenth Century*. The Hague, 1960.
Walters, Bart M. *Early Indonesian Commerce*. Ithaca, N.Y., 1967.
Wheatley, Paul. *The Golden Khersonese*. Kuala Lumpur, 1961.

EAST ASIAN CIVILIZATION TO 1368

Overall
Fairbank, John K., and Edwin C. Reischauer. *History of East Asian Civilization*. Boston, 1960.

CHINA

General
Grousset, René. *Histoire de la Chine*. Paris, 1942.
Needham, Joseph. *Science and Civilization in China*. Vols. 2–5, esp. vol. 4. Cambridge, 1954–81.
Rodzinski, Withold. *A History of China*. Vol. 1. New York, 1979.

Maritime and Naval
Lo, Jung-pang. "The Emergence of China as a Seapower during the Late Sung and Early Yuan Periods." *Far Eastern Quarterly* 14 (1954–55).
————. "Maritime Commerce and Its Relation to the Sung Navy." *Journal of Economic and Social History of the Orient* 126 (1962).

Special Areas and Subjects
Aubin, F., ed. *Études Sung: Sung Studies in Memory of Etienne Balacz*. Paris, 1970–71.
Komroff, M., ed. *The Travels of Marco Polo*. New York, 1953.
Kracke, Edward A. *Civil Service in Early Sung China, 960–1067*. Cambridge, Mass., 1953.
McKnight, Brian E. *Village and Bureaucracy in Southern Sung China*. Chicago, 1971.
Scherman, H. F. *The Economic Structure of the Yuan Dynasty*. Cambridge, Mass., 1956.
Shiba Yoshinabu. *Commerce and Society in Sung China*. Translated by M. Elvin. Ann Arbor, 1970.
Simkins, C. R. *The Traditional Trade of China*. Oxford, 1960.
Wang Gung-wu. *The Structure of Power in North China during the Five Dynasties*. Stanford, 1967.

JAPAN

Hall, John W. *Government and Local Power in Japan*. Princeton, 1966.
————, ed. *Japan in the Muromachi Age*. Berkeley, 1977.
Lewis, Archibald R. *Knights and Samurai: Feudalism in Northern France and Japan*. London, 1978.
Reischauer, Edwin O. *Japan, the Story of a Nation*. Rev. ed. New York, 1974.
Sansom, George. *A History of Japan to 1334*. Vol. 1. Stanford, 1958.

THE CRUSADES TO 1368

Atiya, Aziz S. *The Crusades in the Later Middle Ages*. London, 1938.
————. *Crusade, Commerce and Culture*. Bloomington, 1962.
Burns, Robert I. *The Crusader Kingdom of Valencia*. 2 vols. Cambridge, Mass., 1967.
————. *Medieval Colonialism*. Princeton, 1975.
————. *Muslims, Christians and Jews in the Crusader Kingdom of Valencia*. Cambridge, 1984.
Mayer, Hans E. *The Crusades*. London, 1977.
Prawer, Joshua. *The Crusaders Kingdom*. London, 1972.
Setton, K., ed. *A History of the Crusades*. Vols. 1–4. Madison, 1959–83.
Urban, William R. *The Baltic Crusade*. DeKalb, Ill., 1975.
————. *The Prussian Crusade*. Lantham, Md., 1980.
————. *The Livonian Crusade*. Washington, D.C., 1981.

NOMADS IN THE ARAB WORLD AND IN CENTRAL ASIA TO 1368

Boyle, J. A. *The Mongol World Empire, 1206–1370* London, 1977.
Grousset, René. *L'Empire des Steppes*. Paris, 1948.
————. *Conqueror of the World*. Translated by D. Simon. New York, 1966.
Hillgarth, Jocelyn N. *The Spanish Kingdoms*. Vol. 2, *1410–1516*. Oxford, 1976.
Ibn Khaldun. *The Muqaddimah*. Edited by N. Dawood. Princeton, 1967.
————. *Histoire des Berbères*. Translated by deSlane. 4 vols. Paris, 1978.
Philips, E. D. *The Mongols*. New York, 1965.
Whaley, Arthur, trans. *The Secret History of the Mongols*. London, 1963.
Xavier, de Planol. *Les Fondements géographiques de l'histoire de l'Islam*. Paris, 1968.

EPILOGUE, 1368–1500

Gad, Finn. *A History of Greenland*. Vol 1. Montreal, 1971.
Gray Ian. *Ivan III and the Unification of Russia*. New York, 1954.
Hess, Andrew C. "The Evolution of the Ottoman Seaborne Empire in the Age of Oceanic Discoveries." *American Historical Review* 75 (1970).
————. *The Forgotten Frontier: A History of the Sixteenth Century Ibero-African Frontier*. Chicago, 1978.
Hillgarth, Jocelyn N. *The Spanish Kingdoms*. Vol. 2, *1410–1516*. Oxford, 1976.
Hucker, Charles O. *The Censorial System of Ming China*. Stanford, 1966.
————. *The Ming Dynasty*. Ann Arbor, 1978.
Itzkowitz, Norman. *The Ottoman Empire and Islamic Traditions*. Chicago, 1980.
Lane, Frederic C. *Venetian Ships and Shipbuilders of the Renaissance*. Westford, Conn., 1975.
Lewis, Archibald R. "The Closing of the Medieval Frontier." *Speculum* 33 (1958).
————. "Maritime Skills in the Indian Ocean, 1368–1500." In *The Sea and Medieval Civilizations*. London, 1978.

Ma Huan, Ying-Yai Sheng Lan. *The Overall Survey of the Ocean's Shores 1433*.
       Translated by J. Mills. New York, 1970.
Parry, John H. *Europe and the Wider World*. New York, 1964.
———. *The Age of Reconnaissance*. Berkeley, 1981.
Pilenski, Jaroslav. *Russia and Kazan, 1438–1564*. The Hague, 1974.
Runciman, Steven. *The Great Church in Captivity: A Study of the Patriarchate of
       Constantinople*. London, 1968.
Ruy Gonsalez de Clavijo. *Life and Acts of the Great Tamerlane*. Translated by Mara-
       ton. In *Hakluyt Society*, 1st ser., 26. Reprint. London, 1959.
Sansom, George. *A History of Japan, 1334–1615* Vol. 2. Stanford, 1961.
Setton, Kenneth M. *The Papacy and the Levant II: The Fifteenth Century*. Phila-
       delphia, 1978.
Shaw, Stanford J. *History of the Ottoman Empire* Vol. 1. Cambridge, 1978.
Spear, Percival. *History of India*. Vol. 2. Baltimore, 1966.
Verlinden, Charles. *The Beginnings of Modern Colonization*. Ithaca, N.Y., 1970.
Vryonis, Speros. *The Decline of Hellenism in Asia Minor and the Process of Islam-
       ization*. Los Angeles, 1971.

INDEX

Aethelred the Redeless: Viking raids on England, 82–83

Agriculture: climate in East Asia, 4; irrigation in Indic world, 16–17; class in Islamic world, 31; Islamic world, 37, 122; Kievan Russia, 54; products of Byzantium, 56; technology in Byzantium, 58; Western Europe, 69–70, 73–76, 133–34, 151–52; agricultural revolution in China, 107; crisis in Western Europe, 175–76

Alexius Comnenus: reorganization of Byzantium, 101

Algeria: emergence of Tlemcen, 156

Almansor: control of Spain and Morocco, 41

Almohads: recovery of western region of Islamic world, 114–15, 117; administration, 117; decline, 147

Almoravids: advances in eleventh century, 96

Amalfi: trade with Byzantium, 59; sea power of Byzantium, 66; political system, 84–85; maritime strength, 85

Anatolia: ghazi emirates, 189

Annam: East Asian world, 9; Mongol expansion, 162–63, 170

Aragon: papacy, 172; influence in western Mediterranean, 172–73; hostility toward Genoa and Venice, 173

Armenia: religious unity of Byzantine-Russian world, 50–51; Byzantine conquest, 93; resistance to Byzantine rule, 125–26

Baghdad: commerce of Islamic world, 36; population, 40

Baltic: decline in commerce, 106; Western European expansion, 140, 142, 143, 147

Basil II: military and landed aristocracy in Byzantium, 63

Bedouins: advances in eleventh century, 95–96

Berbers: influence on Islamic world, 42. See also Almoravids

Black Death: impact on Western Europe, 180, 200

Bogomilism: religious unity of Byzantine-Russian world, 51

Buddhism: Cambodia, 132; Korea, 10; Tibet, 5

Burma: Indic world, 20; emergence, 111; Mongol expansion, 170

Buyids: eastern region of Islamic world, 44–45

Byzantine empire: frontier military zones of Islamic world, 34–35; trade with Islamic world, 39; military threat to Fatimids, 43–44; maritime threat to Islamic world, 47; as trade complex, 55–59; sea power, 65–66; isolation from Western Europe, 80; campaign against Sicily, 90; military decline, 93–94, 100; economics, 100–101, 126; reorganized by Alexius Comnenus, 101; recapture of Asia Minor, 101–102; Norman threat, 123; papacy as threat, 123–24; Venetian threat, 124; Hungary, 124–25; alliance with Georgia, 125; Armenia, 125–26; civil administration of Comneni, 126; religious unity, 126–27; silver age of culture, 127; disintegration of empire, 128; Fourth Crusade, 139–40; revival of empire, 147–48; effects of Western European and Mongol expansion, 154–55; end of revived empire, 191–93

Byzantine-Russian world: boundaries unclear, 48–49; geography, 49; religion and unity, 49–51, 53; economics, 53–55, 59–61; culture and unity, 61–62; population, 62; military, 62–65; Cumans, 102

Cambodia: Indic world, 20; rise of, 111, 132; decline, 162; Mongol expansion, 170

Canton: maritime commerce and foreign merchants, 13, 26

Ceylon: decline, 164

Champa: Indic world, 20; merchants in China, 23; Mongol expansion, 170

Chin empire: conquest of northern China, 129–30; administration, 130–31; Mongol conquest, 144–45, 159

China: resources, 4–5; culture and East Asian world, 5; population, 7, 107–108, 131, 160; Sung dynasty compared to Tang, 8–9; economic domination of East Asia, 12–14; maritime trade with Indic world, 23; foreign merchants, 23, 26; agricultural revolution, 107; iron and steel industries, 107; economics, 108–109; trade with Islamic world, 121; Chins and Sungs in twelfth century, 129–31; Mongol administration, 168; economy under Mongol empire, 178; Ming administration, 181. See also Chin empire; Ming empire; Sung empire